PIONEER LEGACY

VOLUME II

Skeena

River

Country

◆

PIONEER LEGACY

Chronicles of the Lower Skeena River

VOLUME II

Compiled by
Norma V. Bennett

◆

"To everything there is a season,
and a time to every purpose under the heaven."
Ecclesiastes 3:1

Dr. R.E.M. Lee Hospital Foundation
4720 Haugland Avenue
Terrace, British Columbia V8G 2W7

Copyright © 2000 the authors

All rights reserved. No part of this publication may be reproduced, stored in a retrieval system or transmitted, in any form or by any means, without prior permission of the publisher or, in the case of photocopying or other reprographic copying, a licence from CANCOPY (Canadian Reprography Collective), 214 King Street West, Toronto, Ontario, M5H 3S6

Edited by Helene McRae

Published by the Dr. R.E.M. Lee Hospital Foundation
c/o 4720 Haugland Avenue
Terrace, BC
V8G 2W7

Canadian Cataloguing in Publication Data

Main entry under title:

Pioneer legacy

Includes bibliographical references and index.
ISBN 0-9683026-0-2 (V. 1) —ISBN 0-9683026-1-0 (V.2, hard) — ISBN 0-9683026-2-9 (V. 2, pbk.)

1. Skeena River Region (B.C.)—History. 3. Frontier and pioneer life—British Columbia—Skeena River Region. I. Bennett, Norma V., 1912–2000. II. Dr. R.E.M. Lee Hospital Foundation.
FC3845.S59Z48 1997   971.1'85   C97-911003-3
F1089.S5P56 1997

Printed in Canada

Respectfully dedicated to the memory of Norma Bennett, whose dedication in collecting and recording the history of our pioneers and area made the publication of this book possible.

Contents

Norma Vletcha Bennett — 8
A Note on Volume II — 9
Foreword — 11
Skeena Country • *Norma V. Bennett* — 15
Riverboat Landings • *Norma V. Bennett* — 17

EARLY SETTLERS
REMO — 23
The Bateman Family • *Emma Lindstrom* — 23
The Lindstrom Family • *Emma and Charles Lindstrom* — 27
The Breckenridge Story • *Emma Lindstrom* — 29
Bill Lindstrom Reminisces • *Bill Lindstrom* — 30
EBY'S LANDING—KITSUMKALUM — 33
Edward Eby • *A.E. "Ted" Johnston* — 33
The Ebys • *Vina Eby* — 34
The Thomas Marsh Story • *Thomas Brown Marsh* — 36
Henry Frank • *Floyd Frank* — 38
The Giggeys • *Clair Giggey* — 40
"Dad" Weeks • *Terrace Omineca Herald* — 42
The Ross Story • *Robert Ross, Jr.* — 44
Kitsumkalum • *Belle Watt* — 48
COPPER CITY—COPPER RIVER — 49
Stuart's Landing—Dobbie's • *A.E "Ted" Johnston* — 49
A Lady Takes a Look Back into the Past • *Rita Rogerson,* — 50
Copper River—Skinner's Landing • *Material from Terrace Omineca Herald files* — 53
MEANSKINISHT—CEDARVALE — 54
The Holy City • *E.M. Whitlow* — 54

Life at Meanskinisht • *Robert Tomlinson, Jr.* — 56
Memories of Meanskinisht • *Annie Moberly* — 58
Philip Sutton • *Stan Rough* — 71
One of Three • *Edith M. Essex* — 72
Stolen • *Edith M. Essex* — 73

THE TALKING WIRE
THE COLLINS OVERLAND TELEGRAPH — 77
Date Capsule — 77
The Pioneer Telegraph Survey of British Columbia • *P.J. Leech, C.E.* — 78
Excerpt, "From Pack Trail to Radio and Then What?" • *S.A. Cunliffe* — 80
Telegraph Trail • *From The Shoulder Strap* — 82
An Enormous Task • *Willard Ireland* — 83
Success or Failure? — 84
Langevin's Report, 1872 • *Hon. H.L. Langevin* — 86
Hazelton — 86
THE YUKON TELEGRAPH — 87
A Short History • *Norma V. Bennett* — 87
Excerpt, "From Pack Trail to Radio and Then What?" • *S.A. Cunliffe* — 89
Excerpt from *The New Garden of Canada* • *F.A. Talbot* — 92
The Long Trail to Home Sweet Home • *J. Wellsford Mills* — 93
THE DOMINION GOVERNMENT TELEGRAPH SERVICE — 100
Branch Line—Port Simpson to Hazelton • *Norma V. Bennett* — 100
NORTH FROM KITSUMKALUM — 105
The Diary of Robert Ross — 105

A Pictorial Diary by Henry Percival
  Rutter • *Courtesy Margaret
  Bartlett* — 114
Christmas Day on the Government
  Telegraph Line • *Omineca Herald* — 122
Date Capsule — 127

ON HER MAJESTY'S SERVICE— THE MAIL SERVICE

Date Capsule — 127
Oldest Mail Carrier Blazed Trail in
  1900 • *Stan Rough* — 129
Sperry (Dutch) Cline • *Wiggs O'Neill* — 131
The Mail Went Through • *Sperry
  Cline* — 132
RMS Dog Team—Kitimat to
  Hazelton • *Northwest Digest* — 134
The *Omineca Herald* Reports — 137
Sam Kirkaldy as Postmaster — 140
The Mailman • *Sperry Cline* — 143

RAILS WEST

History of the Railway • *Courtesy
  CNR* — 147
Date Capsule — 151
The Construction of the Grand Trunk
  Pacific Railway in British
  Columbia • *J.A. Lower* — 152
The Building of the Grand Trunk
  Pacific • *Phylis Bowman* — 166
The Coming of the Steel • *Blaine
  Boyd* — 178
A Note on the Yellowhead Pass •
  F.A. Talbot — 181

The Resident Engineer's Camp •
  F.A. Talbot — 182
A Railway Construction Hospital •
  F.A. Talbot — 185
The Surveyor • *Sperry (Dutch) Cline* — 187
George Raymond • *Norma V. Bennett* — 188
Accidents • *Hubert Times and Bulkley
  Valley Advertiser* — 190
The Man from West Virginia • *Wiggs
  O'Neill* — 191
Skeena Trip is Described • *Big
  Canyon Weekly* — 192
Twelve Thousand Head North • *Wes
  Jasper* — 194
The First Big Snow Slide at Mile 44 •
  Wiggs O'Neill — 201
Winter on the Skeena . . . 1910 •
  Syd Cooper — 203
Local Newspapers Track the
  Railway's Progress — 204
First Passenger Train Left Rupert
  Today — 211
Life is Made Pleasant for Railroad
  Workers • *Omineca Herald* — 212
Toward Completion • *Norma V.
  Bennett* — 214
Townsite Tattle • *Compiled by
  Norma V. Bennett* — 219
Town Promotion . . . 1913 Style •
  Stan Rough — 225
A Link of Empire • *The London
  Times* — 234

Notes — 236
Photo sources — 237
Index — 238

Norma Vletcha Bennett

April 27, 1912–April 17, 2000

Norma Bennett, daughter of Fred and Emma Nelson, Alberta pioneers, was born April 27, 1912, in Wetaskiwin, Alberta.

She was for many years a teacher in the days of the one-room rural schools and chose always to apply in those districts where she could bring grades nine and ten to students who might otherwise have received no high school education.

On September 10, 1939, the day Canada declared war, she and Bill Bennett were married in Vancouver. Bill was already in uniform and on December 15, 1939, he left for overseas with the Seaforth Highlanders. Norma did not see him again for five-and-a-half years plus a day. She returned to Alberta, and to teaching.

In January 1943 she joined the RCAF (WD) in Edmonton. She graduated as a sergeant from the Code and Cypher School in Guelph, Ontario. She remained there as an instructor until the course closed down. Next she was posted to No. 9 Bombing and Gunner School in Mont Joli, Quebec, for three months and then was called to Ottawa, along with three other girls, to take charge of the Code and Cypher Office at Air Force Headquarters. She was commissioned in Toronto, then back to Ottawa for the duration.

Following the war, she and Bill lived in Vancouver, BC, and Bremerton, Washington, before arriving in Terrace in 1958. They owned and operated "The" Motel for twenty-nine-and-a-half years. Norma had said that was where she found the time to collect local area and pioneer histories. Doubtless her interest in early Canadian beginnings stems from her own background.

Norma is survived by her husband Bill, son Ric and wife Lynn, four grandchildren and one great grandchild.

A Note on Volume II

Norma Bennett passed away April 17, 2000, with the knowledge that her Volume 2 of *Pioneer Legacy* would be published. Many of Norma's days in the past year were filled with pain, but with her determination she was able to find time to oversee the putting together of this material.

She maintained her gracious manner and humour to the end. Our last conversation was discussing her accumulation of material on Terrace for Volume 3. With a little chuckle she said, "Maybe we can call it, 'A Town Called Terrace.'"

Yvonne Moen, Casey Braam and I have been privileged to have known Norma, and to know that we have helped to make one of her dreams come true. We have learned of her knowledge of history, her orderly manner of filing letters, photos and research material and of her dedication to this area.

I have been extra privileged to have been entrusted with the accumulation of the material that she gathered over the years and only hope that it can be used in a manner she would be proud of. Norma's Foreword and Introduction for Volume 1, which I believe capture the spirit of this work, are reproduced in this volume.

Helene McRae

TERRACE & AREA HEALTH COUNCIL

☐ EXECUTIVE OFFICES
4720 HAUGLAND AVENUE, TERRACE BC
V8G 2W7
TEL (250) 638-4045 • FAX (250) 635-7639

☐ MILLS MEMORIAL HOSPITAL
4720 HAUGLAND AVENUE, TERRACE BC
V8G 2W7
TEL (250) 635-2211 • FAX (250) 635-7639

☐ TERRACEVIEW LODGE
4103 SPARKS STREET, TERRACE BC
V8G 5G9
TEL (250) 638-0223 • FAX (250) 635-9775

☐ OSBORNE HOME
2812 HALL STREET, TERRACE BC
V8G 2R7
TEL (250) 635-7027 • FAX (250) 635-7639

March 1, 1999

Mrs. Norma Bennett
4704 Scott Avenue
Terrace, BC
V8G 4H6

Dear Mrs. Bennett

    We (the Dr. R.E.M. Lee Hospital Foundation, CHC Board, staff and physicians of Terrace and Area Health Council) very much want to acknowledge your tremendous contribution to the Dr. R.E.M. Lee Hospital Foundation through the funds raised by the sale of your book *Pioneer Legacy*.

    I would like to congratulate you on producing a most informative collection of stories. The book represents many years of compiling information and organizing the book and it provides an excellent history of the Skeena River.

    Thank you again for your wonderful work and congratulations on a great accomplishment. You are to be commended for producing a fine historical chronicle of the Lower Skeena River.

Yours very sincerely

Michael A. Leisinger,
Chief Executive Officer

Foreword

♦ Norma V. Bennett

This is a history of Skeena country, centering around what is now Terrace, up until 1920.

The purpose of the book is threefold:

(1) To provide a background of the history of our area and of the events that contributed toward its settlement.

(2) To examine the quality of pioneer life through the media of pictures, newspaper excerpts and personal accounts.

(3) To assemble many of the scattered stories, articles, reports, etc., that have been written about this area and to make them available at a central location.

In some instances where a story has had its roots in our time frame, rather than cut it off at 1920, we have continued it to a more suitable termination date.

There are times when different versions of the same incident appear. In these cases all have been presented so the reader may better assess the situation from more than one viewpoint.

There are often different spellings of the same place name, particularly in those of Indian origin. We have retained whatever spelling was used at that time and it is interesting to note how the more modern version has evolved.

We have retained the original wording of some of these pieces, but in doing so we ask that our readers excuse the use of expressions that are no longer tolerated.

How this history came about has already been recounted in Volume 1 and does not require repetition. However, credits and acknowledgments should be repeated and sometimes added to until the final version has been completed.

From its inception to its final disposition *Pioneer Legacy* has been a community enterprise. As its compiler I desire to express my deepest gratitude for the assistance I have received in these important areas:

(1) MATERIAL: For permission granted by the owners of various newspapers to use any stories, articles, reports, etc., found relevant therein. I am especially grateful to the late Catherine M. Fraser of the Terrace *Omineca Herald*, who made available to me the earliest files of the publication, which she had so faithfully preserved. My thanks also to the Terrace *Herald*, the BC Archives and Records Service (formerly the Provincial Archives of BC), the Vancouver *Province*, the Prince Rupert *Daily News*, the Victoria *Times-Colonist*, the Vancouver Public Library, the Hudson's Bay Company Archives, *BC Digest* (now *BC Outdoors*), *Paddlewheels on the Frontier* (Vol. 1) and all others whose generosity and assistance I am happy to acknowledge.

A special salute to the pioneers of Terrace and area, those doughty originals who dreamed a dream of the future, the results of which others like myself have been able to enjoy. They have shared with me their trials, their hopes and their achievements and my association with them has enriched and inspired my life.

For additional information, confirmation and encouragement I am particularly indebted to the following:

Vina Eby, Floyd Frank, Clair Giggey, Ernest Hann, Jean Jefferis, Ted Johnston, Lloyd Johnstone, Edith Kawinsky, Ed Kenney, Ken Kerr, Onalee Kirkaldy, Emma Lindstrom, Gordon Little, Bill McRae, Edith Mitchell, Katie O'Neill, Adella Pohle, Hazel Schultzic, Mildred Skinner, Jack Sparkes, Gordon Sparkes, Kathleen Varner and Elsie M. Whitlow

(2) PICTURES: My thanks to all those who so graciously opened their albums and entrusted me with pictures that were priceless to them, to be copied and used as I saw fit.

To those who reproduced the pictures for me—Mr. Willard Ireland and later provincial archivists, Mr. J. Robert Davison and Ms. Share Mawson.

To Mr. Ken Fuergutz, local photographer, who was ever generous with his time, his encouragement and his expertise.

(3) PUBLISHING: And now to the final area in which I have received immeasurable aid:

To the small committee that got things going and never gave up despite innumerable difficulties—Helene McRae, Yvonne Moen and Casey Braam, I owe this book's very survival.

Helene, with her eye firmly fixed on the goal of publication, was our liaison to the Dr. R.E.M. Lee Hospital Foundation, which, through her efforts, agreed to sponsor our project. Her knowledge of pioneer days (she is a product of the Durham-Adams lineage) has proved invaluable. She has also put much of this material onto computer disks and is our contact to the printers.

Yvonne, with her buoyant energy and tireless enthusiasm, has constantly spurred us on and never allowed us to lag. Her ability to organize has been of the greatest assistance.

Casey, with his quiet common sense, his surprising background of pioneer knowledge, his perceptive eye and his fine artistic abilities, has been an irreplaceable member of our group.

My committee joins with me in extending our sincere appreciation to Pat McGinlay, who so generously offered to take on the onerous task of typing a considerable amount of this material onto the computer disks. It is a time-consuming operation and deserves our collective thanks.

The others, too, I must mention, who in one way or another gave of their time and advice—Jake Muller, Rod Link, Mike Rossiter and Ken Veldman.

(4) ADVERTISING AND MARKETING: Helene and Bill McRae, with their usual competence, have taken charge of this aspect of our project and with almost unbelievable success have more than achieved our anticipated goal. We are deeply indebted to them for their tireless dedication to our cause. We must also mention in this regard the generous assistance given by John Clift of Ev's Men's Wear, Jim and Norah LeCleir and Misty River Books.

(5) YOU, THE PUBLIC: As your response to our first volume has been so gratifying, I feel that I can address my thanks to you as individuals. I deeply appreciate your participation in our project by becoming book owners. I also want to express my thanks to those who bought in quantity—the City of Terrace, Skeena Broadcasters and Gail and George Munson of the Northern Motor Inn. I can only hope that the book has met your expectations and that your enjoyment of it is sincere.

Any monies received from the sale of these books will go to the Dr. R.E.M. Lee Hospital Foundation in support of Mills Memorial Hospital and Terraceview Lodge, as I desire no compensation for myself. I have already been amply repaid by the associations I have made and the friendships I have enjoyed.

Norma V. Bennett

Skeena Country

♦ Norma V. Bennett

When God created Skeena country, He did it with a prodigal hand. Range upon range of mountains march in seemingly endless parade, their snow-capped peaks glistening in the sunlight or rising semi-obscured through collars of chiffonous mist. Vast tracts of timber seep along the mountain slopes and across the valley floors, their bases matted with an almost tropical verdure—fern and frond, brush and bramble, devil's club and ivy. The trees rise straight and tall, reaching upward and ever upward, the light sifting down through their branches in cool, emerald shafts to narrow cathedral aisles, deeply carpeted with spongy moss. Tones of green are everywhere, punctuated only by the seasons.

In the spring the tender jade of unfurling deciduous leaf contrasts sharply with the darker hues of evergreens and the sombre green-black shades of balsam. In autumn the countryside is ablaze with every conceivable vivid hue, brilliant and breathtaking in its flamboyant beauty—a panoramic explosion of colour. Then the leaves fall slowly, lingering with whispered reluctance until finally only the bare skeletons of trees are left to await the next miracle of spring. The evergreens stand sentinel over winter—dark, silent and brooding—occasionally herringboned with new-fallen snow.

It is a land of waters. There are lakes lying cradled like gleaming mirrors, embossed with cloud pictures and snow-topped mountain crests, giving back in faithful reproduction a perfect replica of all that is reflected therein, but never once revealing the secret mysteries of their own unbounded depths. There are rivers, swift and impetuous in their rush to the sea, sometimes cascading through rocky gorges, straining like mettlesome steeds against their confines; sometimes sliding smoothly but powerfully with whirlpools sucking in dangerous undertow, carrying trees or logs or any other obstruction that bars their progress as they swell their banks to overflowing and threaten to spill their waters far out over the valleys; sometimes trickling amongst the sandbars in low water, bearing little resemblance in this momentary insignificance to the relentless torrent of flood days. There are creeks, somersaulting in gay and reckless abandon, rushing sparkling joyousness to their ultimate destiny—their complete loss of identity in the oblivion of greater waters.

Valleys, slung like giant hammocks, invite the herds to graze, the crops to flourish. It is as though this land, wooed by the warming winds, kissed by the ardent sun, charmed by the rune in the treetops at night, lay waiting. Waiting until the time when change, in the guise of white-skinned men, should at first gradually, then with a tempo so quickened as to be almost fearsome, transform it to a state scarcely recognizable. The promise of the land is for the future—food in abundance, materials with which to build, work for man's practical needs and beauty for his spiritual yearnings. Perfect sites for towns and settlements, offering space and peace and plenty; a land of opportunity requiring men and women of strength, of vision and of faith. It is indeed a time for sowing.

The First People

There in the shadows of the mountains, close by the mighty waters, dwelt the First People. Theirs the lands, the forests and the streams, and all the bounty of nature contained therein—theirs from time immemorial "for the use of Man in the Garden of Earth." To adequately chronicle the life and customs of these people requires the most intensive research and the most skillful pen. It is a subject unto itself and quite outside the scope of this simple presentation.

May it suffice, therefore, to acknowledge their presence, their culture and their rights.

SS Inlander *taking on wood.*
(20-B)

Riverboat Landings

Time to Come Ashore

◆ Norma Bennett

In Volume 1 we dealt in depth with tales of the Skeena River itself and the many sternwheelers that plied its unpredictable waters, allowing the travellers to recount their own experiences.

Riverboat days were glorious days spiced with adventure and the stimulus of danger, and sometimes with a bit of humour as an extra bonus. No one who made such a trip ever forgot it and many became one-time authors in their zeal to commemorate the event.

But what of those who manned the boats? Think of the responsibility of the captain who must know all there was to know of an ever-changing and sometimes treacherous river. He must rely on his crew to be ready and knowledgeable of how to line the craft through dangerous narrows and past submerged rocks.

The fireman must never lag, for unless he kept his fire going, there could be no progress, and the amount of wood required for this purpose

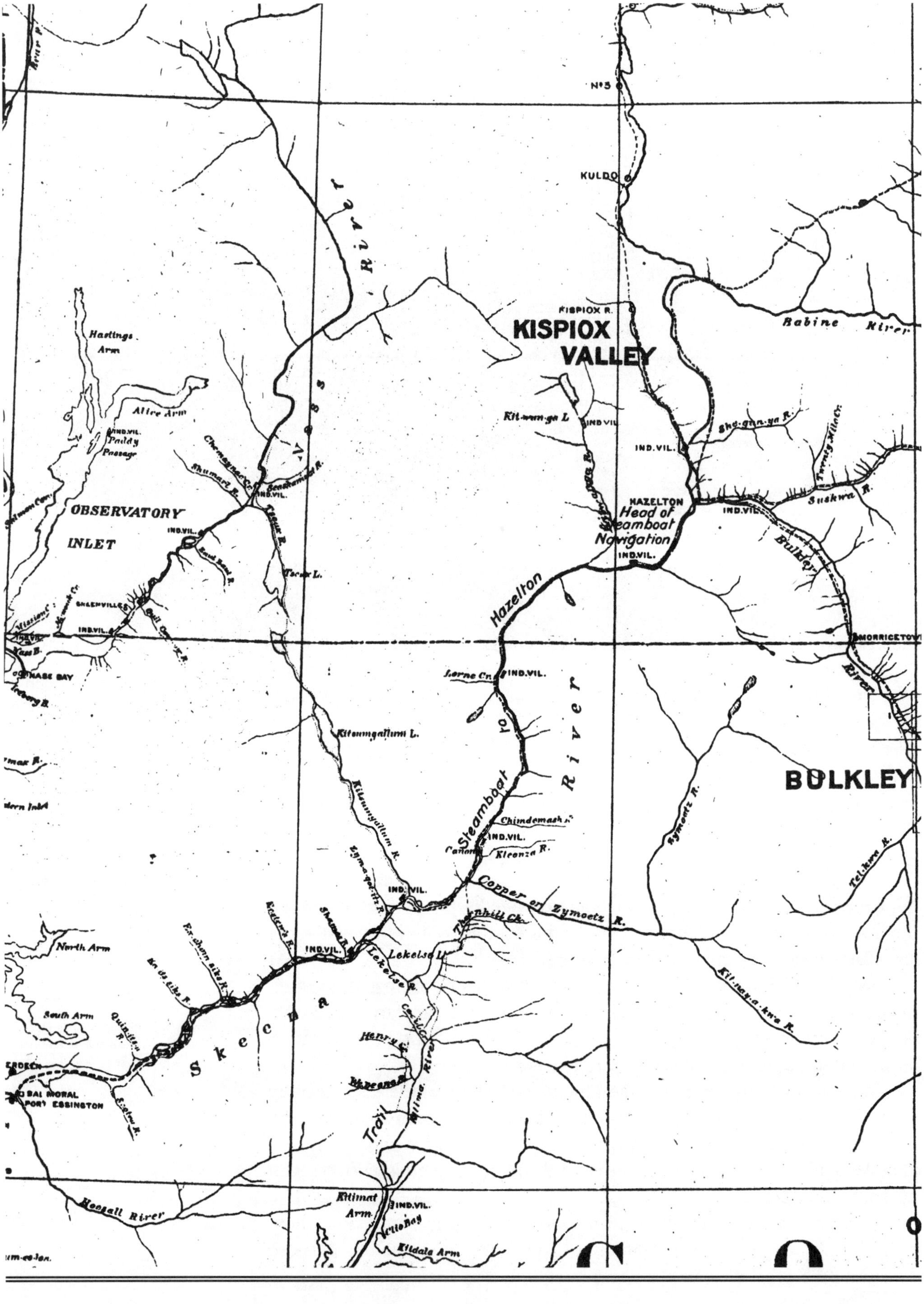
KISPIOX VALLEY
BULKLEY
KULDO
KISPIOX R.
HAZELTON
Head of Steamboat Navigation
Hazelton
Steamboat
River
Babine River
Bulkley River
Suskwa R.
MORRICETOWN
OBSERVATORY INLET
Hastings Arm
Alice Arm
Paddy Passage
Kitsumgallum L.
Kitsumgallum R.
Lorne Cr.
Chimdemash R.
Kleanza R.
Copper or Zymoetz R.
Thornhill Ck.
Lekelse L.
Lekelse R.
Skeena
North Arm
South Arm
Quinitsa R.
PORT ESSINGTON
Trail
Kitimat Arm
Kildala Arm
Hoogall River
Tel-kwa R.
Zymoetz R.
IND. VIL.
Henry L.
Kitwanga L.

was enormous. In fact it was so great that it gave many a man a good living cutting firewood for the sternwheelers. Huge piles of cordwood were stacked at intervals along the riverbank to supply this need. Crew and sometimes even passengers provided the manpower necessary to transfer it on board.

There are still to be found today, overlooking the banks of the Skeena River and also deep in the forest, long piles of cordwood left unused, mute testimony to someone's industrious enterprise so many years ago.

Some of the piles are fifty to seventy-five feet long and up to three to four piles wide. They have now rotted down to less than half their original height, but some of the end crosspieces are of split cedar and are still in fair condition.

These piles were placed high above the river for easy loading with a chute down to the riverboat. Wood was hauled by horse and wagon to the boat landings. Woodcutting was generally done during the winter and spring, then the woodcutters would go prospecting for the summer months.

Elizabeth Whitlow, nee Durham, an early pioneer of the Kitselas days, recalled: "Woodcutters were paid three dollars per cord and they were paid only for the cords loaded on board. I remember some of the old-timers saying there was competition among riverboat captains as to who could obtain the best wood. Drier wood made more steam for a faster trip!"

In inter-company rivalry it was a favourite trick to take a competitor's wood supply in the hope that the resultant delay would allow the aggressor to arrive first at their common destination.

Numerous stopping places developed along the river route to Hazelton. Thus on an upriver run, one might expect to stop at such places as Bateman's Landing, Eby's Landing, Stuart's Landing (later called Dobbie's), Copper River, Kitselas and Meanskinisht.

If an exchange took place—that is, wood coming on and supplies or mail going off—the landing might support a small community of settlers that might later grow into a town.

We will now examine some of these places where the riverboats stopped, and we will see what has developed.

Left: Cordwood at Kitsumkalum, June 1911. (20-B)

Right: Unused cordwood, almost ninety years later. (65-C)

EARLY SETTLERS

SS Hazelton *at Tomlinson's sawmill on north side of Skeena River, 1906. This was across the river from the village of Meanskinisht. (41-A)*

Remo, the small settlement seven miles west of Terrace, has been known by several names. In the steamboat days it was known as Bateman's Landing on the north bank of the Skeena, and as Neidhart's Landing on the south bank. Later, in 1908, there was Swanson's Landing and still later, Breckenridge's Landing. Farther west was Morris' Landing.

REMO

The Bateman Family

♦ as narrated by Emma Lindstrom to Norma Bennett in 1971

In 1905 my mother and father, Mr. and Mrs. James E. Bateman, with my younger sister Beatrice and myself, set out from Oregon, more to see than to settle the newly opening region of north central British Columbia. We boarded the *Princess Beatrice* in Vancouver and sailed up the coast to Port Essington, where we remained until the middle of July. We were then able to take the Hudson's Bay sternwheeler, the *Mount Royal,* up the Skeena River to Hazelton. I remember that we went right through the Canyon—we didn't get off and walk around—we went straight through Little Canyon and Big Canyon both, no trouble at all.

My mother and we girls remained in Hazelton for twelve days awaiting Father's return from a trip farther on. He travelled to the Bulkley Valley, where he filed a land application for a pre-emption there. But he wasn't too impressed. He got up one morning—in fact it was the first of July—and found ice on the water in the pitcher. That was enough for him. He returned to Hazelton, saw there was little hope of his making any money there for the winter, so decided to take us all back to Port Essington and thence to Oregon.

On the trip south to Vancouver we sailed aboard a CPR flat-bottomed

Mr. & Mrs. James E. Bateman with daughters Emma and Beatrice. (66-C)

freighter, the *Tees*. It took twelve days to reach Vancouver. We stopped at Massett, Port Simpson, the Nass, Queen Charlotte City and every cannery along the coast on the way down. We took on great quantities of canned fish and at Nanaimo loaded coal, the dust of which penetrated everywhere. Meals aboard the CPR boat were exceptionally good and we enjoyed many delicacies of the times, corn on the cob being one that I particularly relished.

The year 1906 found the Batemans back along the Skeena. Father came out alone in the spring and chose what is now known as Remo as his place of settlement. The "ice-in-July episode" had caused him to give up his idea of homesteading in the interior. When Mother, Bea and I were ready to follow, Father came down the river to meet us at Port Essington. He had left his tent, his clothes and everything he owned—except for what he had on—in his tent.

Mother was aghast.

"What in the world did you leave all your belongings back there for?" she asked. "Surely that was a foolish thing to do."

"Oh, no," Father replied. "It's all right, really. The Indians on the Skeena River are absolutely honest. They won't touch a thing."

Nor did they. Everything that he had left in the tent was still there when he returned.

There wasn't too much difficulty getting started. Father had built a cabin—a log house. He split shakes and put in partitions. There were two bedrooms and the living room. We cooked and lived in the one big room.

It was all so new to us. There was nothing at Remo at all. Up around Terrace there were a few bachelors. The nearest family was the Durham family and they were up at Kitselas. There were no neighbours. John Neidhart lived across the river and he was the only neighbour we had.

So we settled down into our new home on the river. Father wouldn't have been anywhere else, he liked it so much. The timber was too heavy for farming but he planned to make a living from the woods. He was an experienced timberman and figured on logging and taking the rafts down the river, which he did. My father took the first raft down the Skeena, as far as I know, from Captain Dick's Landing. He had two men working with him.

All supplies had to come in from Port Essington. That was the only place there was. The canneries, of course, supplied their own people, but they had nothing to do with anyone else.

No other settlers came in during that first lonely winter of 1906. However, we were not entirely cut off. Quite a few came who were travelling up and down the river and had nowhere to stay. We didn't have any place to keep them either; we were not keeping a stopping place. But there was six feet of snow on the ground that winter, so we took them in. They had to sleep on the floor, but everyone packed their own blankets in those days, so that was no hardship. We fed them and they got good meals. Then at bedtime our visitors unrolled their bedding, slept on the floor, rolled their blankets up again in the morning and that's all there was to it. When

Bateman's Landing. Riverboat passengers have just arrived. (67-C)

they left, they carried their blankets in their packsacks on their backs, as like as not.

I remember some of them quite well. There were the three men from the Bulkley Valley who were taking the ballot boxes down to Port Essington following an election. Mr. Durham came once, too, with his son George to see a survey crew or something like that. Anyway, they couldn't get back and had to pass the night with us. And there were several others.

Oh yes, and Mr. Dobbie. He froze his foot. He was the telegraph operator at Graveyard Point, just below us here, towards Rupert. He couldn't go out on the telegraph line any more so he came and stayed with us for, oh, about six weeks, I'd say. He was there until his foot got in shape so he could travel on it.

The first winter we were up here, we cut a hundred cords of cordwood and stacked it up on the bank. The second winter, my father cut cordwood, too. The first summer we were here, my father and two other men cut logs off of the sandbars. There were good trees, good timber lying on the sandbars, and they took these logs and formed a raft and took it down and sold it. My mother, my sister and I, we ran the camp—we did the cooking for the three men, Dad, Bates and Olson. They had their difficulties taking the logs down, as did most men who didn't understand the river too much. They lost a lot of their logs. Once a storm came up and their raft broke. But what they had, they took down to the sawmill—it would take any amount they had.

Three years later my father, together with Charlie Lindstrom and two other men, made another raft of logs, just the windfalls that were on the bars. So that was two rafts, and then we had this hundred cords of wood. My father sold that wood for $3.50 and $4.00 a cord. That cordwood was our first winter's grubstake up here. My father had gotten food from the storekeeper in Essington with the promise of putting up this wood. And we put it up! So that was that.

There was no other way of making a living here. That was the only way, except for those who had traplines. The Indians had their certain trapping districts too. They got mink, marten, beaver, lots of weasels—and I recall someone down below us here getting a silvertip fox, but I never saw it. There were some squirrels also, but not good enough to bother with.

My father didn't trap and he never hunted at all. We caught the odd fish with the nets, but that was all. Otherwise we lived, practically speaking, on bacon and eggs. Berries were plentiful. There were lots of blueberries if you wanted to pick them, but we never saw any raspberries until after the land was broken up.

If I were asked whether nature was our friend, I would answer yes—and no. In the summer it was the same as now. But in winter the heavy snow was a drawback. You couldn't do very much in three or four feet of snow.

In 1907 my father got a contract for cutting cordwood for the canneries. We now had two scows, one to put the cordwood on and the other to live on. My father had finished the contract and the towboat came out to get us. It brought a storm along with it. There we were in the middle of the river, my mother, my father and myself, as well as the crew of men he had working for him. We were on one scow and the cordwood was on the other. The tugboat came out to pick us up and they towed us out into the middle of the stream at Telegraph Point. The river is wide there. The tide changed, a storm came up and it got dark to boot. There we were out in the middle of the river with those two scows bumping together. My mother was so scared—oh boy! But I don't think she was as scared as my father was. I'll never forget it. Mother was just frantic but Father was worse. Charlie Adam was there too, just a helper on the tugboat. He wasn't very old at that time—just a young fella. Anyway, we got towed in the next day without any further trouble but they took the scow that we were living on and tied it to the wharf.

Usually we didn't get off the scow as soon as we got to Essington as we didn't have any place to go except a hotel, and we had all our stuff on this scow. Well, this trip, I went to visit my sister in town and Mother was left alone on the scow. She heard someone come aboard in the dark, and of course we had no flashlights then. Whoever it was missed the ladder and landed in the mud under the wharf. Had the tide not been out, he would have drowned there and then. His cries for help frightened Mother, who did go out and, together with the watchman, managed to get the poor soul

The steamer Northwest *was wrecked on a sandbar west of the mouth of the Lakelse River in August 1907. It broke up with loss of contents but no loss of life. The Batemans and Elof Olson were aboard. Elof said the doors jammed and many had to be pried open. His own door, however, was broken down by his friend Bateman, who told him to stand aside while he bashed it in.*

out of the mudhole. He must have been half soused because he smelled terrible!

All mail that winter was landed at Kitimat and brought over by dog team. It was taken to Hazelton by dog sled, and ours was dumped off at Copper River. Anyone coming down our way would bring our mail to us. It was just a custom of the country. There were so few people here and the mail was so welcome. It was left there and anyone passing our way became our mail carrier.

There was no Eby's Landing until—let me see now—1907. Then there was a hotel, a store, a post office and a telegraph office. It was the same time as Olson bought his place up here . . . 1907.

I recall a funny thing that happened shortly after we came. There were two Natives who had a railway tie contract and were cutting ties on the hill below here. They lived in one of their own little houses that they had built. One of them had a tool box full of the nicest carpenter's tools you could ever wish to see. My father used to go up there and he'd borrow these tools as he needed them to build our cabin. There was something he wanted— oh, an auger, I guess—I just can't remember what it was. Anyway, when he got through with the tools, he said to my sister and me, "You girls take these tools up to the Indians' cabin and give them to the Natives there." So we went up. I often think of it—I was about fifteen at the time and my sister was younger. When we got there, there wasn't a soul in sight and a half-drizzling rain had begun to fall.

I said to Bea, "There's a tool box in the cabin. I wonder if we shouldn't put these tools inside to keep them from getting damp."

So we did. We went in and I lifted the lid of the box and placed the tools inside and we came out.

Just then we saw the Indians. They had heard us talking and were looking down from away up on the hill. They came down, looking at us very suspiciously the while. I told them where we had put the tools my father had borrowed and why we had gone in and put them away. They never said a boo word—not one boo word did they say. They just stood there and looked at us. So we beat it for home as fast as ever we could. No doubt they were as surprised to see us as we had been to see them.

The Lindstrom Family

♦ as narrated by Emma and Charlie Lindstrom to Norma Bennett

Charles Lindstrom arrived in Prince Rupert in 1907 and settled at Remo in 1908. He had left Sweden at the age of twenty, landing in New York, where he spent some time. He then proceeded by train across the States, stopping here and there en route. He ended up in Seattle, where he was

Emma Bateman's and Charles Lindstrom's wedding day, 1909. Rev. Thomas Marsh officiated. (66-C)

obliged to wait two weeks to catch a steamer north to Alaska. He went to Skagway, Juneau, across the White Pass to Whitehorse and on to Dawson, following closely the old gold Trail of '98. From the Yukon he came down to Prince Rupert, where he and his companion readily found work for the entire winter. The new townsite was just being laid out and there was plenty for everyone to do.

When the work was finished, the camp closed. One day Charlie went into the boarding house to ease the pangs of his hunger with some good home cooking. My sister Bea and I were both working there. In those days everything was very roughly built and there were cracks in the walls big enough for us to peer through. It was a source of great amusement to us both to peek through these apertures at the unsuspecting diners within. Bea saw Charlie first and she thought, "Boy oh boy, there's a real fine fellow." I thought so too. As Charlie says today, it was I who won his heart and I've never let him go.

Charlie went up the Skeena the following spring in search of land. He found what he wanted at Bateman's Landing, now Remo, and returned to Prince Rupert to register his pre-emption.

Charlie and I were married at Kitsumkalum in 1909 with Reverend Marsh officiating. Bea was our bridesmaid and Mr. Morrison, the YMCA missionary, acted as best man.

On the day after our wedding we were amongst a group of people down at Eby's Landing watching a riverboat come over the Kalum Riffle. This was a very bad stretch of water among the rocks on the south side of the river. Two men were wrestling down on the freight deck, back and forth in front of a rope strung across the open freight door. As the spectators watched, the boat lurched in the Riffle, the wrestlers hit the rope, which collapsed with the force of the collision, and the two men, one Chinese and the other Native, fell overboard and were swept downstream to their

Emma and Charles Lindstrom on their Remo homestead with horses Daisy and Blonde. (66-C)

deaths before the horrified but helpless onlookers. What had been an amusing spectacle one minute had become a horrible tragedy the next.

Father and Charlie built our first house, my first married home. The lumber came from the first sawmill at Kitsumkalum, which, oddly enough, burned to the ground the very day we were married.

The Breckenridge family was among the first friends Charlie and I had. They arrived in 1908 and had lived in a tent at my father's place until such time as they got their homestead. Their cabin across the river saw many a good time for they were a happy, hospitable family and always had company who were glad to gather there.

We had a railway doctor here. When my oldest boy was born, Dr. Johns attended me. His territory extended from Kitselas down below here. I was lucky to have him. Of course my mother was with me too, so I didn't have too much to worry about.

Charlie and I were blessed with six children, three boys and three girls. Our sons are Charles, Otto and Bill, our daughters, Claire, Helen and Marie.

We have enjoyed a long and happy life at Remo.

Emma Lindstrom with son Bill. (66-C) Bill Lindstrom first saw the light of day aboard a Grand Trunk Pacific train bound for Prince Rupert. Emma didn't quite make it to hospital in time, but with the assistance of a lady passenger who acted as midwife, a healthy baby boy was delivered. Bill returned the favour many years later when he changed a flat tire for the same lady—Mrs. Bussie!

The Breckenridge Story

◆ Emma A. Lindstrom

Among the land seekers who came up the Skeena in June 1908 was a family from Oregon. Why they unloaded settlers' effects at Bateman's Landing would be hard to know. But land they did, and they became the second family there—Mr. and Mrs. Harry Breckenridge and baby son, Harry Jr., and Mrs. Breckenridge's grandmother, Mrs. Starr, then eighty years old.

Mr. Breckenridge had brought a large tent, and he soon had it up and his family settled in it while he looked around for a homesite.

Like everyplace else on the Skeena, the mosquitoes were plentiful and Bateman's Landing was no exception. The newcomers were the targets. Fly Tox was only in the dream stage at that time, so their only protection was a smudge by day and cheesecloth tents over their beds at night.

Mr. Breckenridge located a pre-emption on the riverfront on the south bank of the Skeena, directly across from Bateman's Landing, and there he built a log house for the family.

Grandma Starr, as she quickly became known, was a real pioneer. She had been born in Pennsylvania and as a bride had come around the "Horn" in a sailing vessel to make her home in Oregon. She could—and did—tell many tales of her pioneer days near Portland, where she raised her family.

The Breckenridge home soon became a gathering place for the set-

The Breckenridge piano was transported across the river by loading it on a deck floated by two canoes.

tlers. They had brought a piano as part of their "settlers' effects" and Mrs. Breckenridge was the pianist at these gatherings, with Mr. Breckenridge leading the sing-songs. They had been faithful members of the Methodist Church in their hometown, and the songs were mostly hymns and were really enjoyed by us all. I can still see them in memory—the pleased and happy expression on Grandma Starr's face as she sat in her rocking chair with Harry Jr. cuddled closely. But as time passed she grew more feeble, and she passed away quietly late in the summer of 1909.

There were no caskets to be had on the Skeena in those days and so some of the neighbours helped to make one out of the materials they had. Dr. Johns, a railway doctor, prepared her for burial.

Next day we all gathered at the Breckenridge home for the first—and to this day the last—funeral to be held at Remo, as the settlement is now known.

Mr. Marsh (later Canon Marsh) of the Kitsumkalum settlement was not at home to come down for the funeral, so one of the young settlers who had a prayer book read the burial service, and Grandma Starr was laid to rest a few yards to the south of her last pioneer home.

The Skeena has flooded over its banks several times since then and the old pre-emption has been logged and tractors have taken the logs off. The location of the last resting place of Grandma Starr has been obliterated, and likely none knew of, or had ever heard of, the lonely grave in the shade of the cedars and hemlocks beside the river.

Mr. Breckenridge became Remo's first postmaster in 1909, although it was named Breckenridge Landing and was that name until 1918 when Mr. John Neidhart, who was postmaster then, had it changed to Remo in memory of his hometown in Germany.

> Tom Regan was an undertaker-on-call up and down the river in the early days. His home may have been at Port Essington. However, he was the one to contact when there was a death or fatal accident at the many camps along the river. He also sold coffins to the bereaved families.
> He was said to be quite a religious man. One day he was travelling with Mr. Bateman in a canoe when it drifted down onto a sweeper (a log hanging out over the river). Down went Mr. Regan to his knees in the bottom of the boat. Mr. Bateman wielded a cudgel and told him to get up and paddle, or else. The latter was taking no chances on what Mr. Regan's prayer might be about.

Bill Lindstrom Reminisces

♦ Bill Lindstrom

There were many people who came to the area in the early days and stopped as squatters for short periods, never leaving a reason to remember their names. They either left for greener fields or for World War I, and never returned.

Many of the first settlers originated from the gold rush in the Yukon. Most were returning, looking for a place to settle. The opportunities offered along the Skeena attracted their pioneering spirit. Some stopped on their way up to the goldfields and lacked the means to go on.

Dates of residence of these early settlers are uncertain, as time has dimmed the memories of many of the old-timers. To add to this, when one has no particular event with which to link his movements, then the year seems to have little significance.

The pioneers who settled in the remote settlements along the Skeena have to be classified among the hardiest, both in physical health and in spirit. Some of us will never understand why they left their homes in more developed societies to reside in seclusion and fight the elements that challenged them.

During the summer the riverboats brought communication and supplies. They also bought their cordwood. This hinged on water conditions—if the water was too high, the boats had difficulty; if it was too low, there was not enough water in the shallow sections. One of these boats, the *Northwest*, went aground just west of Remo and broke in two. The passengers and crew spent the night on a sandbar.

The summer brought such "friendly little creatures" as mosquitoes and black flies. The accepted repellent for them was smoke or bacon grease mixed with turpentine and applied on all exposed areas.

Food was plentiful as the river ran full of fish. Wild berry patches were numerous and the gardens grew well.

The winter presented an opposite condition. When the ice prevented travel on the water and the last boat had passed, they knew there would be no more until the ice was gone again the next spring. The winter's supplies had to be stored before this. They had to consist of products that would last the winter without spoiling in root cellar or on a shelf in the cabin. It does not take much imagination to list the menu—salt pork, bacon, ham, fish, dried fruits, onions and commodities for bannock. These were bolstered by the garden vegetables and game that the land provided.

Some mail came through with adventurous winter travellers by dog team or by foot, or by canoes that braved the drifting ice in early spring or late in the fall.

When a job was to be done, such as building a cabin or clearing a garden patch, all a man had to work with were hand tools, and the only power was that of his own muscles.

Some of the pioneers who resided at Remo are listed here. I make no pretense of this list being complete or the dates exact, but I do offer it with respect and with the honour due these hardy folk who have helped make this a better place for me to live today.

Dr. Johns also tried a little barbering on the side. However, one day as he was cutting a customer's long hair on top, he managed to take the knuckle of his own finger along with it. The blood flowed, and the doctor promptly fainted.

John Neidhart

Came to Remo about 1905. Lived on the south bank of the Skeena. Remo was named for the town in Germany from which he came.

Charles Swanson

About 1905. A farmer-fisherman; married; had great skills in a rowboat and would cross the Skeena at any stage of flood. Remained at Remo until World War II, when he left for the coast. He later died of exposure after a boating accident.

Dick Carr

1906–1935. A bachelor who lived on a small farm south of the river. Veteran of World War I.

Tom Laird
: 1906–1942. A bachelor-farmer who lived on the north side, two miles east of the old station. Came here from the Klondike.

Bob Laird
: 1907–1918. Brother to Tom Laird; died in his cabin. It is said that he was buried under the floor one cold winter.

Arthur Carr
: 1910–1918. Became road foreman and helped build the old Remo road, which still exists on the south side of the Skeena, linking Remo and Terrace. Later made his home in Terrace.

William C. Breakenbury
: 1913–1918. Married, with two children; lived on south side of river. Worked for the railway as section foreman. Moved to Kitwanga, where he retired. His family, George and Violet, still live in Kitwanga.

Elof Olson
: 1907–1944. Emigrated from Sweden; a bachelor-farmer. Worked in canneries at the mouth of the Skeena before settling at Remo.

H. L. Hulbert
: 1908. Bachelor-farmer; a friendly old gentleman. Came in from the Klondike.

Jens Earlandson
: 1913–1965. Emigrated from Norway; a bachelor-trapper. Made snowshoes for all the community. A good fisherman who gave most of his catch to his friends. Very generous with his possessions and extended a free helping hand anytime. Like to play solo (cards).

Emil Jopp
: 1914–1980. A bachelor-farmer who stayed on at Remo; a good neighbour.

Dan Klatter
: 1910. A bachelor-prospector from the Yukon. Carried mail along the river by canoe and dog team.

Joe Lapley
: 1910. Lived on the south side of the Skeena on Alwyn Creek. Had no occupation, but people said he lived off the gold he found. If he did, no one knew where he got it.

    He was killed by wolves about 1921 or 1922. He was on his way home from the store and was overtaken by a man driving a team of horses. Lapley did not accept a ride for himself, but he did give his pack to the driver, asking him to drop it off at the fork in the road. This the driver did, but it was never picked up, nor did Lapley arrive home. It was not until two or more years later that his headless body was found in the woods, his scraps of clothing bloody and torn. It is assumed that he was attacked by a wolf.

Remo people knew the legend of the Split Mountain. It seems a hunter unexpectedly came face to face with a hungry bear. In the nick of time, the mountain split in two, leaving one on each side. Thus both were saved.

EBY'S LANDING– KITSUMKALUM

Edward Eby

♦ A.E. "Ted" Johnston

Ed Eby and Billy Bruce came into the area about 1905. They built a hotel with bar, a store, a post office and a barn for freight horses with a blacksmith shop to shoe horses and repair wagons, etc. There was also a Dominion Government Telegraph office at this location.

It was known as "Eby's Landing" and was located about a quarter of a mile south of where Henry Frank built his home.

Ed, of medium height and quite stout, was a married man. He brought his wife and infant son, Vernon, into the country after getting settled. Ed and Billy Bruce operated the landing until 1912 or 1913.

Ed had two or three teams of horses he used for freighting. He had the contract to haul the telegraph wire and supplies for the crew that was building the telegraph line through to Alice Arm, Anyox and Stewart. This line went up the Kalum Valley to the Nass River, then over the mountains to Alice Arm.

The road to Kalum Lake at that time was just a trail cut through the woods. Stumps were low cut to allow the wagons to go over them. There was no grading except on side hills and even then, no more than necessary. There was no gravelling, so during the wet seasons it was mostly a sea of mud. Consequently, it was practically impossible for wagons to go through during the wet weather. As the freight had to go, they used what was called a "jumper," a sleigh-like affair made all of wood (the runners were made of hemlock mostly, with a natural crook for them and two cross beams made with about twelve inches of ground clearance). There was no iron on these, so they would slide over gravel, stumps or mud with a minimum of friction.

Because of the long distance to Kalum Lake and the rough type of road, they needed a halfway station, so Ed and Billy Bruce each staked a pre-emption at Lost Lake, about Mile 9 on the Kalum Road. This solved the halfway problem, as pulling the jumpers about ten miles a day was all horses could stand. Also, when using wagons on these rough roads, there were many breakdowns and it was handy to have a place to do the repairs or stop for the night without having to go all the way back to Eby's Landing.

The supplies for the telegraph line were hauled to Mud Lake or to the foot of Kalum Lake, whichever was the easiest, depending on the condition of the roads. From there it would go by boat to the north end of the lake, then by pack horse to where they were working.

When the railroad construction was finished and trains started to run, Eby's Landing was finished. Ed Eby then moved into Terrace. In partnership with his brother, Sam, they built a store on Kalum Street. The material for the building was from the old Kalum Store and Hotel. Ed later sold his share to Bill Sparkes.

The Ebys

♦ as narrated, in part, by Vina Eby to Norma Bennett

Edward A. Eby left Elmwood, Ontario, for Victoria in 1896. He worked there at his carpentry trade. His wife, Vina, whom he married in 1904, was born in Wisconsin. She was one of a family of thirteen and what she learned from this experience—homemaking and practical inventiveness—stood her in good stead when she accompanied her husband to pioneer in the still-desolate country of the Skeena River in British Columbia.

Mr. Eby had a look around Port Simpson, then went on to Port Essington in 1905. In 1906 he came upriver to Kitsumkalum, where he established himself at what became known as Eby's Landing. He built and

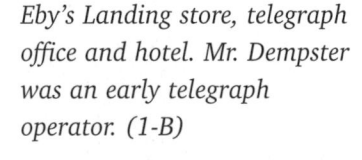

Eby's Landing store, telegraph office and hotel. Mr. Dempster was an early telegraph operator. (1-B)

operated both a store and hotel. Later he kept horses for freighting on the telegraph line to Stewart. His pre-emption was at Lost Lake on the Kalum Lake road. There he built a large stable for the horses as a halfway point on the freight haul.

Ed Eby hired men to cut cordwood for the riverboats and hauled it out with a team of horses.

One of daughter Vina's early memories centres about the root house where they kept the homemade bread for the mail carriers who came through with the dog teams. The cool dark interior both attracted and repelled, its mysteries never completely solved even by bright sunlight.

Vina relates that one egg cost a dollar. Her maternal grandmother, who lived at Blaine, sent up four chickens, which were put in the root cellar for warmth. When skunks sought to investigate, Mrs. Eby at first mistook the marauders for kittens.

Sometimes her mother would call from the window, "Vina, look," and Vina would rush to part the curtains and watch caribou swim across the river.

Mrs. Eby was an excellent seamstress and Vina remembers the lovely lace on the children's dresses, as well as the intricate embroidery and crochet work to be found in the parlour.

Mrs. Eby was an all-round pioneer woman who could turn her hand to many different things. She was a good hunter and is known to have shot goats. She also "hunted" with a camera and developed her own pictures.

The Ebys moved to Terrace about 1911 or 1912. The store and hotel at the Landing were torn down and the lumber used to build Eby's cottage in Terrace, as well as the Marsh house. The telegraph office stood at Kitsumkalum until the 1936 flood.

Ed Eby served overseas in World War I, leaving Terrace in 1915. He was a sergeant with the 102nd Battalion, CEF.

During his absence the family remained on what is now known as Eby Street, the site on which Mr. De Jong later had his farm. In town, Mrs. Eby was able to indulge in her favourite pastime, playing tennis. Her two friends, Evelyn Large and Annie Noonan, often played with her.

Shortly after the war, the Ebys moved to Smithers, where they lived to celebrate their fiftieth wedding anniversary. Ed Eby was a life member of the Masonic Order, Omineca Lodge No. 92. He was also a life member of the Smithers Curling Club

Mr. & Mrs. Ed Eby, 1910. (16-C)

The Thomas Marsh Story

♦ Thomas Brown Marsh

The late Canon Thomas Jabez Marsh proceeded as a missionary from Kitimat on snowshoes with an Indian and two dogs, over the Kitimat Trail en route to his new Anglican parish, in March 1908. He had come from fifteen years of pioneer missionary work with the Indians at Hay River on Great Slave Lake. His new charge was a dot of a place called Eby's Landing on the Skeena River, two miles west of present-day Terrace. Had not the river been blocked with ice, he could have gone by riverboat up the Skeena instead of following the tote road from Kitimat to Copper River, then the Dominion Government Telegraph line to Eby's Landing.

At the Landing, Ed Eby operated a hotel, a store and saloon. The population consisted of fourteen settlers and many construction workers building the Grand Trunk Pacific Railway. When Mr. Marsh tried to enlist help to build a home for himself and his wife and family, who would arrive by riverboat later in the spring, the men informed him they did not want any damn preacher in the country. Old Dad Weeks, however, gave him shelter in his tent.

The next day Mr. Marsh purchased at Eby's store a crosscut saw, a double-bitted axe and a broad axe and began falling trees and squaring timbers alone on the church lands. His years in the North had taught him self-reliance. The scoffing men then changed their attitude and pitched in to help him raise timber for the building.

Soon his wife, Alberta Jane, arrived on the riverboat with Mrs.

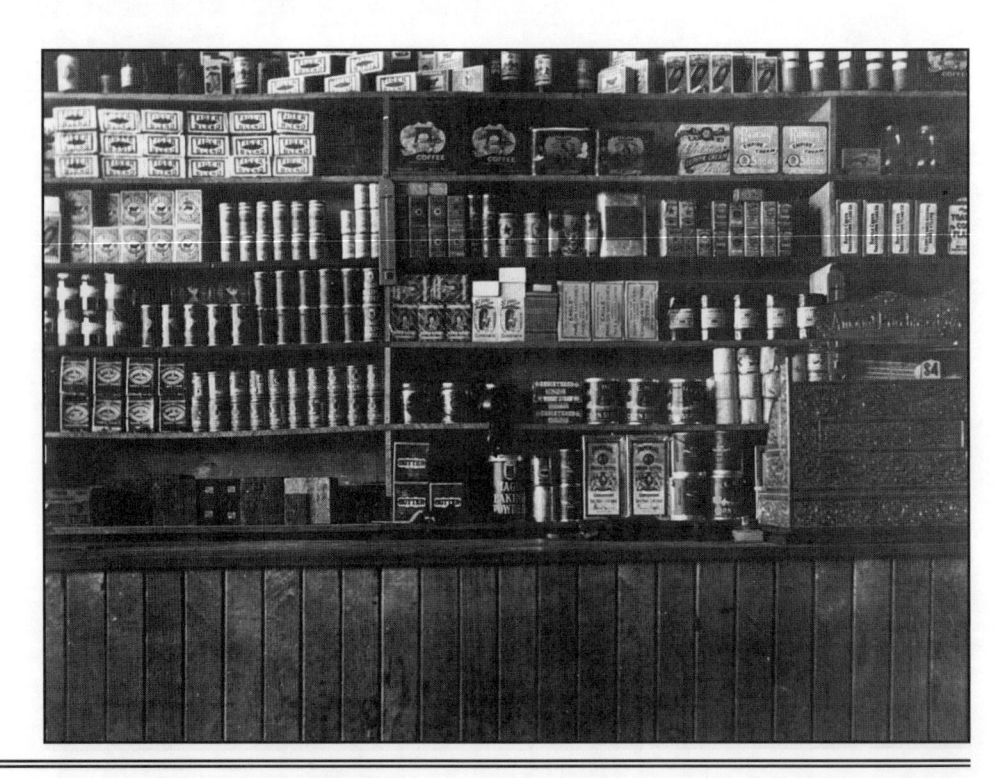

Inside of E. Eby & Co. store. (51-C)

Marsh's sister, Rose Deacon. They, too, lived in Dad Weeks's tent until the sturdy two-storeyed house was ready.

R.L.McIntosh, first postmaster at Prince Rupert, had donated the land to the church and bought it back years later, using the log house for a summer home.

The Marshes became good friends with the Frank family, who had settled at the Landing before them.

Mr. Marsh gave local services and gradually extended his ministry among the reluctant railway workers' camps; the men soon grew fond of him. He had studied medical books and could often recommend simple remedies, as well as pull aching teeth. Not until the men requested a sermon did he preach one; after it, the men insisted on passing the hat. Soon he was preaching in camps from Kitselas to Remo, indeed, from Kwinitsa to Cedarvale.

A crisis arose when it became necessary to run the line through an Indian graveyard on the bank of the Kitsumgalum River. The Indians refused to move their graves. A constable armed with a gun asked Mr. Marsh to go with him to tell the Indians the lines would be pushed through in any case. The minister insisted the guns be left at home. The Indians trusted him and consented to move their graves and the railway went through.

Soon the riverboats no longer ran. Mr. Eby sold his old hotel to Mr. Marsh, who tore it down and hauled the dry lumber to Terrace, where he built a spacious three-storeyed home on ten acres of land. For many years this home was the centre for gracious hospitality.

While the minister helped the newcomers find homes, firewood and other needs, his tiny wife nursed the sick and brought countless babies into the world; her only medical training was what she had read in books.

Copy of advertisement in Omineca Herald, 1908:

*KITSUMKALUM HOTEL
Kitsumkalum, BC*

This splendid new hotel lately opened at Kitsumkalum, situated on the Skeena River and Grand Trunk Pacific Railroad about 80 miles east of Prince Rupert, offers every accommodation to the travelling public at reasonable prices. Choice brands of liquors and cigars always on hand. Well-stocked store in connection.

—E. Eby & Co., Props.

SS Skeena nearing Eby's Landing. (51-C)

St. Matthew's Anglican Church was built on a hill, under Mr. Marsh's supervision. A memorial window bore the name of Thomas Marsh.

Mr. Marsh served the church until the final breakdown of his health. He was made an honorary canon on retirement. He was now almost completely blind, but liked to tap his way around the town with the aid of two canes and greet his friends. He died in 1930 and was buried in the cemetery on the hill behind the town.

Mrs. Marsh died at age eighty-eight in 1955 in Montreal, where she had been living with her daughter, Mrs. James Farquhar. A son, Thomas Brown Marsh, for many years a member of the old Provincial Police Force, lived in Squamish, where he was employed by the PGE Railway. His son, Thomas (Reid) Marsh (the third), carried on the old family name, and his daughters, Etonda Jean and Margaret, attended UBC. The old Marsh home in Terrace was sold and later completely destroyed by fire.

Henry Marsh, a nephew of the late Canon T.J. Marsh, became Bishop of the Yukon. Many times in his sermons he made use of stories from the exciting days of "Uncle Tom's" ministry on the Skeena.

Henry Frank– Early Settler at Kitsumkalum

♦ Floyd Frank

The Frank home at Kitsumkalum, 1909. Mattie Frank is in the yard with the children. Etonda Marsh is on the left. (1-B)

In 1898, when the government decided to open a trail from the Little Canyon to Kitimat, Henry Frank was engaged to do the work. It was over this trail that many of the later pioneers trekked when coming to the valley.

He drove his location stake to take up a pre-emption in the Kitsumkalum Valley in the spring of 1905, the first location stake driven in the valley, with the possible exception of Thomas Thornhill's. The pre-emption was situated on the bench, with the vocational school now situated on the pre-emption's northwest corner, Alex Houlden's home on the northeast corner and the old Kitsumkalum cemetery on the southwest corner where the location stake was driven.

In 1906 Henry Frank purchased a sixteen-acre homesite close by the Skeena River, registering it in the name of his wife. This property, south of the railway and west of Frank Road, is where the family dwelling—and later on, all the farm buildings—were built. This was Lot 365A and a twenty-acre piece of property lying just south

♦ Early Settlers ♦

of the sixteen acres was known as Lot 365B. Jimmy Adams and Walter Noble, who were living in Port Essington, wished to purchase a piece of property in the Kitsumkalum Valley, and Henry Frank arranged for them to buy this twenty-acre lot. Directly south of here was the Ed Eby property, possibly five acres, on which the Eby Hotel and Store was built. The Frank homestead was Lot 363.

In 1922 the twenty-acre parcel of land, Lot 365B, was offered for sale through Kenney Real Estate and Henry Frank purchased it for $672.65, this odd number likely including a charge by the real estate company for incidental expenses or commission. The property was registered in the names of Ivan and Floyd Frank. River erosion over the years, especially the 1936

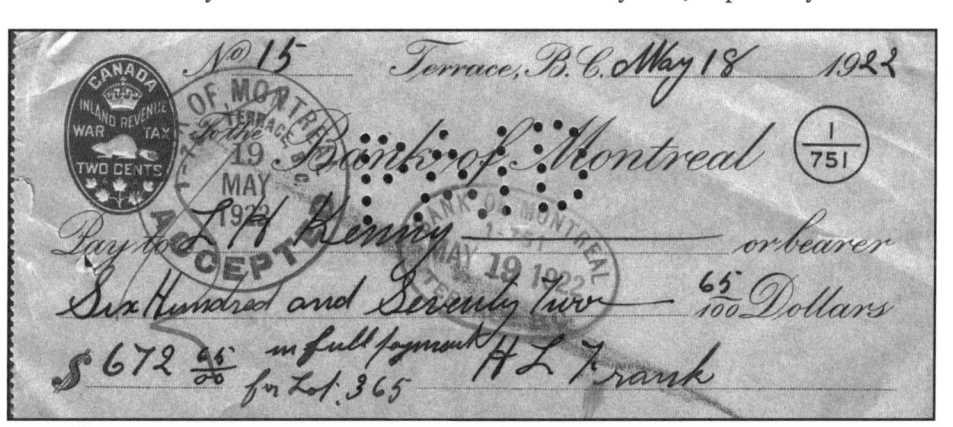

Mrs. Frank with Miss Fayette (Mrs. Eby's sister) with children (left to right) Vernon Eby, Belle Frank, Jack Frank, Morrison boy, Floyd, Ella and Ivan Frank, another Morrison boy. (1-B)

♦ 39 ♦

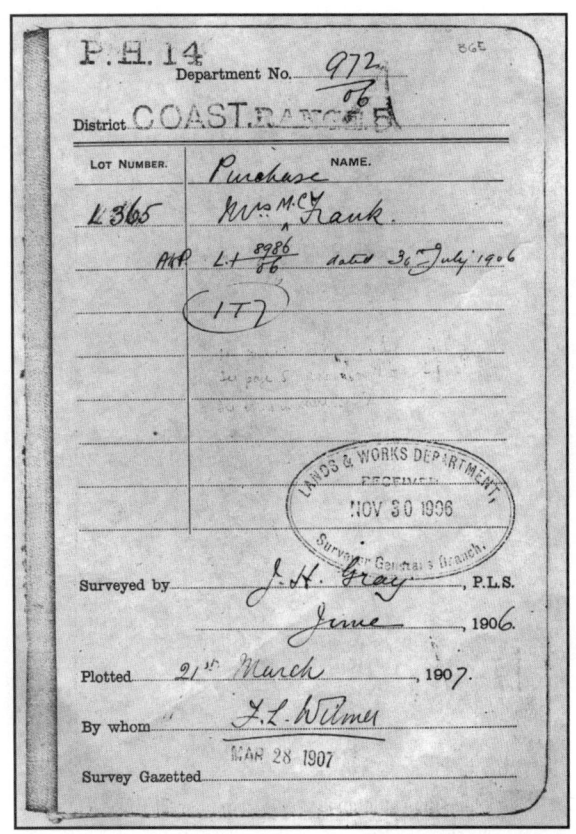

"super flood," has taken all but about six acres of the thirty-six acres originally contained in lots 365A and B.

It was in the late summer of 1905 and Henry Frank was standing on the dock in old Port Essington at the mouth of the Skeena River, watching an old tramp schooner unloading its cargo, when a middle-aged fellow walked up and engaged him in conversation. He had worked his passage up on the schooner and, like many others at that time, was interested in the new country that was opening up in the North. He had no money, nothing but the clothes he wore, but what did that matter? Wasn't this a new country where, if a man was willing to work, he could at least keep from starving to death? Anyway, he wanted to go upriver and stake land so Henry agreed to take him on his next trip and help him to stake a pre-emption. This is how S.C. Weeks arrived in the district, and he located to the west of the Frank pre-emption. Later, when the district needed a site for a cemetery, he gave an acre of his land along the brow of the bench. Although a bachelor, he somehow acquired the nickname of "Dad" and as "Dad Weeks," he was known to everyone in the district.

After staking his land, Dad went upriver for a season and cooked in a mining camp. Then he went over to the Queen Charlotte Islands for a year or more. Meanwhile, Henry worked in Port Essington in the winter and in summer patrolled the Skeena and its tributaries as fish warden, clearing a bit of land on the bench and putting up a shack in his spare time. In the spring of 1908 he moved his family up from the coast to take up permanent residence in the valley.

The Giggeys

♦ Clair Giggey

At some time during our stay at Kitselas, my father had met a man named Weeks, more popularly known as "Dad Weeks." He had a pre-emption that fronted on the railway right-of-way at Kitsumkalum and he named several others—Harry Frank, Billy Goodwin and R.L. MacIntosh, who all owned land at Kalum, as he called it—and they were all of the opinion that the railway would certainly build the station there. He also said that Ed Eby had a hotel and store at the steamboat landing and there was a government telegraph office. Mr. Weeks also stressed the fact of the large Kitsumkalum Valley directly north and the Lakelse Valley across the

Skeena to the south, and there was no doubt but that Kitsumkalum would be the town of the future. One other item of importance that Dad Weeks failed to mention was that, during the rush of railway grade building, Mr R.L. MacIntosh had erected a very substantial log house on his property adjacent to the railway and had also built a small frame building to be used as an Anglican church. The Rev. Thomas J. Marsh, with his wife, Alberta, had arrived at Kitsumkalum from Hay River Mission some time in 1908. They had two children, Thomas Jr., and daughter, Etonda. Mr. and Mrs. Macintosh were staunch Anglicans and by virtue of this, they delegated the use of both the house and the little frame building: the house for Mr. Marsh and his family, and the other building to be used for church services.

I think Mr. Marsh had likely met my parents at Kitselas. At any rate, he was at the steamboat landing when we arrived there from Kitselas. He very kindly asked whether we had made any arrangements for a place to live. When he got a negative answer he suggested that my parents look at a fair-sized log cabin located about a hundred yards back from the house where they were living. He explained that he had no authority, but that the cabin had been built by the YMCA, and after the railway grade was completed, the YMCA had moved further up the line and the cabin was empty. He also pointed out that the cabin was on Mr. MacIntosh's property and he was sure it would be all right for us to occupy it for the coming winter at least.

Mr. Marsh said that Mr. MacIntosh was the postmaster in Prince Rupert and that they had their permanent residence there. My folks were sure thankful for the use of the cabin. It was about sixteen by twenty-four feet, well equipped with windows and a good floor. There was a spring just a few feet from the door and an abundance of timber for fuel. My stepmother could make a place homelike even though there wasn't much in the way of furniture. She would cover a few boxes and packing cases with whatever and presto, it was a home!

Mr. Ed Eby, who owned the hotel and store at the Landing, had a contract to supply cordwood for the river steamers. Eby's was a regular stop en route, both up and downriver, so it was a natural for the boats to "wood up" here.

My dad took on a job of cutting this cordwood for Mr. Eby and I worked along with my father. This work lasted for a couple of months, and then for the balance of the winter, and until early summer 1911, we worked together hacking railway ties for George Little. Mr. Little had quite a number of "tie hacks" working for him and also several teams hauling ties from the woods to trackside. Mr. Little allotted my dad a patch of timber directly south of the present site of the Kalum School.

We continued in this work until 1911, when other things developed and we prepared to move into Terrace.

"Dad" Weeks

Samuel Charles Weeks (1845–November 13, 1925)

♦ from the Terrace *Omineca Herald,* November 27, 1925

"Dad" Weeks's cabin at Kitsumkalum, 1908. This is where the Marsh family first lived. Pictured are (left to right) R.L. McIntosh and son; Mattie Frank with Belle on her knee, Luella and Floyd on her right, Ivan on her left; Mrs. Lillesberg; other ladies from camp and "Dad" Weeks with broom. (1-B)

"Dad" Weeks, as he was commonly known, came in 1905 to Kitsumkalum, which in the early days was one of the largest settlements on the lower Skeena River. There he took up a pre-emption close to the river, where for many years he combined the duties of postmaster with those of the farm. The ranch itself he developed into the largest producer of strawberries in the valley for a number of years.

Generous to a fault, "Dad" held a warm place in the hearts of many travellers up and down the line during the days of railway construction, and great was his never-failing hospitality. His ability to entertain with stories of the pioneer days gained him many and varied audiences. The people of Terrace and Kitsumkalum have particular reason to be grateful to Mr. Weeks, who donated a portion of his farm for what is now used as a cemetery for the district. A more beautiful location could not have been chosen, nor could a more generous impulse actuate its giving.

♦ Early Settlers ♦

Kalum Lake. In this group are Elsie Dover, Jean Dover, Mrs. Annie Ross of Rosswood, Velma Greig, Frank Nightwine, Walter Warner and George Hipp. Joe Felber photo (27-C)

North to Kalum Lake

Settlement spread north from Kitsumkalum in those early years, and it wasn't long before cabins—mostly belonging to bachelors—sparsely dotted the landscape, concentrated along the Kalum Lake Road and the north and south ends of the lake. They made the (at that time) tedious trips to Eby's Landing at Kitsumkalum to stock up on supplies at Eby's Store, to call for the mail, to watch a riverboat in or out and to exchange gossip with

Kalum Lake Hotel, community gathering. (17-A)

♦ 43 ♦

Pack train leaving for Kalum Lake with mail and supplies. (10-C)

acquaintances at the landing. Many had come in to work on railroad construction and remained to pre-empt land all along the way to Kalum Lake. They often took jobs hacking ties or building roads to eke out their incomes until their land began to produce. One of the most colourful personalities to settle at Kalum Lake was a lady, Mrs. Annie Ross, who came up the Skeena about 1909.

The Ross Story

♦ Robert Ross Jr.

Annie Ross was born near Minneapolis, Minnesota, and at the tender age of fifteen married Robert Ross, a Canadian from Prince Edward Island who had come down with his two brothers to homestead land on the St. Croix River. It being timberland, Robert Ross went into the logging business.

From that marriage—and it was her only one—there were eight children born. The oldest three died shortly after the birth of the third child of the dread black diphtheria that swept their community in an epidemic wave. The other five children were born later.

In early 1896 Annie and her family of five arrived on the Pacific coast following an accident in which Robert Ross had lost his life. They settled first in Tacoma, Washington, but later moved to Everett and still later to Lowell, Washington.

In late 1909 Annie went up to British Columbia, where she had heard there was free land available. She was a true pioneer type, and life on a homestead held a strong appeal for her. With well-grown sons she felt she could make a good home for her family in the wilderness territory that was just beginning to open up.

She travelled to Prince Rupert on the old steamer *Cottage City*, then up the Skeena on one of the riverboats, to disembark at Kitsumkalum. While waiting to look things over, she lived in one of the Lillesberg cabins and cooked at Eby's Hotel at the landing. In due course she filed a pre-emption at the head of Kalum Lake and went to live there with her daughter Inez.

Her sons Tom and Frank also pre-empted land nearby. Annie's place later became known as Rosswood and she was the first postmistress. The post office was opened in 1912, with the mail coming out from Terrace, sealed in a bag. It operated for five years, closing in 1917. You can imagine the feelings of the settlers around Kalum Lake when they found they no longer had to make the long trip to pick up their mail.

It also gave Annie Ross the opportunity to know the neighbouring settlers even better. She became the repository of many a confidence as she always found time to chat with the men coming in off their lonely pre-emptions in the hope of finding that magic envelope bearing their name. She understood their anxiety when letters were long overdue and many times dispensed sympathy or joined in the exuberant spirits of those who shared their precious news with her. She knew, too, those who had trouble reading or writing and often lent assistance to smooth out such difficulties.

Tom Ross became known as an expert handler of horses. He freighted with a team during the days when the telegraph line was going north from Kitsumkalum to Stewart. When that was completed he logged with his horses for George Little.

Robert Junior was the son whose diary so well describes work on the telegraph line north from Kitsumkalum. It is to him, also, that we owe credit for much of the information on the Ross family. In a letter to Norma Bennett he says: "When I was in Terrace, 1910 to 1914, I worked for George Little in several different jobs. I worked in the mill and I drove team in the woods—pulling logs to the loading ramp and loading them on the sleighs. Then I worked in the store with Lindsay Morrison for a time. I enjoyed all of these jobs. I also worked for a time hauling rails for Dan Stewart, a subcontractor on the railroad being built. We hauled from New Hazelton to Stewart's Camp near Fort George—eight days going out and six days coming back. It, too, was in the winter. Once, the temperature got down to fifty-six below zero (Fahrenheit)."

Robert Ross was a very sensitive young man and one can deduce from his writings that he was deeply impressed by the beauty of this country. He has remained something of a philosopher throughout his long life and one can sense that nothing has shaken the conviction of his faith nor blunted the keen sense of humour that so often surfaces in his written accounts. The following excerpts are from his diary, recording his arrival in this area:

October 20, 1910
Arrived at Kitsumkalum, a small Indian village near the mouth of the river of the same name.

October 29
We arrived at Kitsumkalum Lake today after spending a couple of days on the trail. The lake is about seven miles long by about three miles wide at the widest part. It is a beautiful lake with sandy beaches at the northern end. Along the edge of the lake are towering cliffs, with hardly a place to land a boat except at the middle of its length, where a small stream that flows into the lake has built up a sand bar. This is called Maroon Point. I do not know how it got its name. The forest is very dense along the west side of the lake and comes to the very edge of the water. All around may be seen the mountains, snow-capped and towering. The sun, shining on the snow, makes them look like a huge sugar pile.

October 30
We woke this morning in time to see the sunrise. It was an impressive sight. As the sun rose from behind the mountains to the east, it cast a shadow of those mountains on the ones on the western side of the valley. This shadow gradually crept down and down on the mountains until finally it disappeared altogether as the sun appeared over Goat Peak, a lonely mountain to the south. The land throughout here is a great glacial deposit and consequently very rocky. The timber is quite dense but small. Jack pine, cedar, spruce and many cottonwoods are the principal trees. A few balsam are found in places. There are several small streams through here, and some small rivers. Lakes, too, are part of the landscape.

December 8, 1910
We went up Goat Peak today, hunting goats, but the snow was so deep and the footing so precarious that we decided to return without hunting. On the way back we came down Hall Creek and there saw the beautiful falls in the creek. This falls is about sixty feet high and drops straight down the entire distance. The creek itself rushes its turbulent way in and out among the rocks and finally empties into Kitsumkalum Lake.

May 21, 1911
Time is slipping by with a speed that is frightening. We left Rupert for Kitsumkalum on May 3 and got to the lake two days later. After staying on the ranch for a couple of days we again went to Kalum and brought out a pack to the cabin. The folks arrived at the cabin two days after we got there the first time. We cleared land for several days, went hunting and fishing and enjoyed ourselves immensely. The sunsets were glorious . . .

In 1914 Robert became ill and had to return to the US so he was out of touch with the happenings in the Terrace area and at Rosswood. In 1918 he acquired a merchandising business in Lowell, Washington, and his mother, Annie Ross, used to spend all or part of her winters there. He was thus able to hear something of his old friends and from time to time visitors dropped in to see him bearing news of Kalum and Rosswood.

Before Robert left the lake in 1912, Annie had started to build a larger house, which she intended to use as a hotel. She had sold two five-acre tracts of land on the south portion of her homestead—one to her nephew, Henry Conroy, and the other to two Frenchmen named Couture and Gendron. Annie's homestead was sold after her death by her daughter Inez to Mr. Joe Hart, from Everett, Washington.

Clair Giggey pays tribute to this fine woman who had become a close friend to his family. He says, "She was one of the old school whose philosophy was 'Paddle your own canoe'—so sadly lacking in this day and age. She took her pre-emption when the only connecting link between Kalum and what was to become Rosswood was a rough trail. On several occasions Annie took over the cooking at my sawmill camp and in 1931, owing to Mrs. Giggey's illness, she very graciously accompanied her to the Mayo Clinic and stayed with her for the several weeks until her return.

"Yes, Annie Ross was 'rough and ready'—all wool and MANY yards wide!"

Kitsumkalum

♦ Belle Watt (nee Frank)

Come walk with me by the Skeena
Just for an hour or so—
I'll tell you of Old Kalum,
And the life we used to know.

By the Kalum River Village
Where big salmon jump and play;
Chief Nelson and his wife lived there
Long before we came to stay.

Up the Skeena was Eby's Landing
Where riverboats brought in pioneers;
A store, hotel and telegraph
Served the folks for just ten years.

Then the Grand Trunk Pacific whistled past
And the sternwheelers ran no more;
We got our mail from the stations,
And not dog teams as before.

Oh, the letters the bachelors wrote
To the *Family Herald*'s Primrose page;
And the lovely widows responded
Bringing in children of school age.

Rev. Marsh brought us his message,
His sweet wife nursed us when ill;
From T. Eaton we ordered our clothing
And managed without the pill.

I still see Hell's Gate canyon
Where the devil dared to play
His nasty tricks on riverboats,
As they would buckle, bend and sway.

And there's our Sleeping Beauty—
She's one who will never change;
While guarding our Skeena Valley,
She rests on yon mountain range,

Come and drive above our valley
And admire the beauty below,
And think again of those pioneers
Who made trails through these woods and snow.

COPPER CITY– COPPER RIVER

Stuart's Landing–Dobbie's

♦ A.E. (Ted) Johnston (from *Pioneers of the Area*)

Heading upriver, the next stop after passing Little Canyon was Stuart's Landing. Here prospectors disembarked and firewood was loaded, along with fruit and vegetables in season.

A Scotsman, David Stuart, came to the Copper River area, prospecting and trapping in the early 1880s. David had worked as foreman for Cunningham and Inverness canneries around the mouth of the Skeena River (Spokeshoot, as it was known in the early days). There he met Jane Smith, whom he married in 1885. Their daughters Jemima and Mary were born in Port Essington.

Around 1890 he brought his family up the Skeena to homestead on the north bank of the river, about three miles above Little Canyon. They cleared a large piece of land, planted a fine fruit orchard and grew vegetables and hay for their livestock. Two more daughters, Janet and Pricilla, were born at Copper River.

GTP visitors to the Stuart Ranch, summer of 1908. Pictured (left to right) are G.A. MacNicholl, purchasing agent; J.B.L. MacDonald; David Stuart, seated; Mr. Morrison, evangelist; M.A. Roby, writer; C.C. Van Arsdol, asst. chief engineer; T.M. Baird, office engineer. (68-C)

Jane Stuart died in 1900 and David Stuart remained on the homestead until his death in 1912.

Simeon Wilson Dobbie, a tall, blond, slender man from Ontario, left home at an early age. He worked his way west through the United States and up into the Cariboo country, where he spent some time before coming to the Skeena Valley. He came to the area in 1898, first working at a gold prospect at Lorne Creek. Later he worked for the Dominion Telegraph and while travelling along the line, he met Jemima Stuart.

He married Jemima in 1905 and after living at Graveyard Point and Kitselas for a time, they eventually purchased part of the Stuart property and the Landing was changed to Dobbie's Landing. Here the Dobbies continued to farm and raise their family and saw much activity during the riverboat days until the completion of the railroad.

A Lady Takes a Look Back into the Past
♦ Rita Rogerson (from the Terrace *Omineca Herald*–August 14, 1958)

Left: GTP railway track and a steamer on the Skeena, 1910. (25-A)/BCARS 29353

Right: SS Inlander *at the head of Kitselas Canyon. (20-B)*

Mrs. Jemima Dobbie looked back into the past. After being married in Vancouver in December 1905, she and Mr. Dobbie arrived in Port Essington on their way to Graveyard Point. Then they travelled up the Skeena River by canoe. They spent the first night with Wiggs O'Neill and Walter Flewin at Telegraph Point. It was snowing on the Skeena and Telegraph Point was a welcome sight. They continued on their way the next day. The river was frozen over at Salvus, so they had to portage their canoe half a mile, and they spent the second night camping out on Hudson's Bay Flats. The third night they reached Graveyard Point, which is a little south of the Shames River.

♦ Early Settlers ♦

At the Dobbies. Pictured (left to right) are Jemima Dobbie with sisters Janet and Mary, Paul Post (Mary's husband), Sim Dobbie and the Dobbie and Post children. (69-C)

Mr. Dobbie was the telegraph operator at Graveyard Point where riverboats stopped for cordwood. They spent two years there. While hiking around, they explored the mountain on the right-hand side of the river. On this mountain they found a cave containing graves—Indian bodies in boxes. Whether these bodies were mummified as others that have been found in caves on the coast or not, Mrs. Dobbie had no idea. Right near the Shames River, there was Indian village that was old fifty years ago. Now it seems all grown up with jungle brush.

It was in December when they moved to Kitselas Canyon by canoe, where Mr. Dobbie was to be the telegraph operator. It was just at the start of Kitselas town at the foot of the canyon. Paterson had a store at Kitselas and a hotel for prospectors and such. There were men working the tunnels who used to frequent the bar in the hotel. Sometimes the take of the bar would be a thousand dollars a night.

The Durhams lived on their ranch between the tunnels, and Charlie Durham was the ferryman at Kitselas. Kitselas grew—four stores, two rooming houses and two poolrooms. The Dobbies stayed there about six months, then moved to Copper City (Stuart's Landing), where they remained.

Mrs. Dobbie remembers when a certain "old timer" was a gay young purser on the riverboats. On this occasion, the purser landed at Copper City dressed in his best grey suit. He knew Mrs. Dobbie and her sisters. He also knew a new trick on how to break an egg. The trick backfired and ruined

"Buck" the ox, destined for the Frank's at Kitsumkalum. The ox was forgotten on the riverboat until it got to Dobbie's Landing. From there it made it to the Durham ranch at Kitselas. Riding Buck are the Durham girls, Nellie, Paddy and Irene, with Barney Phillipson, GTP trainman, "putting on the brakes." (65-C)

his nice suit. The girls ran to his assistance with cloths, but the spot remained.

At Copper City they cut cordwood for the riverboats and there was a crew of a hundred men cutting ties. This was most fortunate when in 1912 there was a huge forest fire. This fire jumped across the Skeena River and roared across the flats. It burned the barns and chicken houses. The hundred men watched the ties and the house. It seemed as if it would go in spite of all their efforts when the wind suddenly died.

Yes, Mrs. Dobbie has seen a great deal of activity on the Skeena River. Copper City is the quietest now that it has ever been. The Dobbie place is one of the beauty spots of the Skeena district.

Note: Unfortunately the old Dobbie home burned to the ground in later years and with it went many photographs and interesting paper clippings about David Stuart and the early days. Also burned in this fire were many interesting photographs of Simeon Dobbie and his home in Ontario.

COPPER RIVER– SKINNER'S LANDING

♦ from the Terrace *Omineca Herald* files

Across the river from the Dobbie ranch, on the south side of the Skeena River, was a small settlement known as Copper River and sometimes as Skinner's Landing.

There had been great activity in the area as early plans had been for the railroad terminus to be at Kitimat rather than at Prince Rupert. The railroad would then go through the Telkwa Pass to Telkwa or meet the Grand Trunk Pacific survey at Kitselas. The grade was actually started and a series of rock cuts was completed near the mouth of the Copper River.

Here the Creeches had a seventeen-room hotel, and in 1908 Percy R. Skinner started a store, setting up his business in a tent. He was joined later by his brother, Leslie G. Skinner, and together they operated the Skinner Brothers General Store. This became an important supply depot for prospectors as they held the only explosives agency in the area and also became a sub-mining recording office

The landing was also a distribution headquarters for dogs, supplies and equipment. Dog teams with mail from Hazelton and Kitimat often met and exchanged their loads in winter.

On January 11, 1916, Percy married Mildred S. Sparkes and brought her to the Creech Hotel. They lived at Copper River for four years. Son Ralph was born in October 1916 after a long and difficult delivery. After several days, they finally had to send to Prince Rupert for a doctor and engaged a special train to bring him to Copper City. Mildred's sister-in-law, Mrs. Will Sparkes, went by boat to Dobbie's and sent the wire from there. In the meantime they continued to work over Mrs. Skinner. After what seemed centuries of waiting, they heard the train coming. It stopped, and with fate's unexplainable irony, just as the new doctor was walking in the door, the baby was born. Five years later Murray was born and had a far less spectacular entry into this world than his brother.

Copper River, deserted Skinner store. This was once a centre of activity. (70-C)

COPPER RIVER POST OFFICE

Harvey Creech, postmaster, *February 1, 1909, to July 28, 1914.*
Percy R. Skinner, postmaster, *September 1, 1914, to May 19, 1920.*
Leslie G. Skinner, postmaster, *August 1, 1920, to February 4, 1956.*
Closed.

MEANSKINISHT– CEDARVALE

The Holy City

♦ E.M. Whitlow

Cedarvale, formerly known as Meanskinisht, or the Holy City, was founded by the Reverend Robert Tomlinson in 1887. Mr. Tomlinson was an Irishman who had attended a medical college and was sent to Victoria by the Church of England Missionary Society in 1867.

After a short stay in Victoria he went up the coast to Metlakatla to work with the famous and controversial missionary, William Duncan. He was soon transferred to carry on missionary work on the Nass River, and during the first year on the Nass, Mr. Tomlinson made a trip to Victoria by canoe to marry Alice Woods. The Tomlinsons worked among the Native people on the Nass for twelve years and established a mission at Kincolith. Their next mission was at Ankitlas, seven miles above Kispiox Village, where they spent three years. The Tomlinsons had nine children, six of whom survived. Friction had gradually developed between the missionary and his bishop, and Reverend Tomlinson and his family moved to Metlakatla, where they spent the next five years with William Duncan.

When William Duncan left the Church of England and moved to Alaska with his followers to establish a new village, Tomlinson decided to do the same on the Skeena and went upriver to Kitwanga, where the family spent the winter of 1887.

In March 1888 the Tomlinsons and their six children (Robert, eighteen; Alice, fourteen; Lily, twelve; Richard, ten; Annie, eight; and Nellie, four), together with Samuel Bright and his wife; Edward Stewart, his wife and small daughter, Esther; Peter Hep; and Moses Hep and his wife, journeyed down the ice on the Skeena with dogs and toboggans to establish a Christian village.

They chose Meanskinisht, this word meaning "at the foot of pitch pines." There was land suitable for cultivation and most important, a small stream nearby with a waterfall for the sawmill that was to be their main source of revenue.

It was a non-sectarian community and the rules were strict: no liquor, dancing or working on the Sabbath. Gradually, new converts joined the community that eventually reached a population of eighty.

A sawmill was built by the missionary out of his own meagre

Rev. and Mrs. Robert Tomlinson Sr., Meanskinisht. (48-B)

resources, land was cleared on a small island, a horse and bull were purchased at Hazelton and walked down the riverbank, and a heifer was brought upriver from Port Essington by canoe. Poultry and sheep also were added in time to the little settlement's farming resources. The missionary's house was at one end of the village and a log church with its bell at the other so that the missionary and his family would have the furthest to walk, thus setting an example to the rest of the congregation. Money was scarce. Robert, the eldest son, ran the sawmill and the men of the village who worked in the mill were paid on scrip and received goods at the community store. Supplies for the store were purchased from Robert Cunningham at Port Essington at the mouth of the Skeena. Lumber from the mill was sold at Hazelton, Skeena Crossing and Lorne Creek, and vegetables were sold to the miners at Lorne Creek, the Methodist Church Girls' Home at Fort Simpson and to the steamboats on the Skeena run from Port Essington to Hazelton. The settlers also hunted and fished to augment their food supply, and smoked and salted meat and salmon for the winter.

When the child population of the village increased, school was held in the church. Mr. Tomlinson was the first teacher. A schoolhouse was built in the centre of the village and over a period of years the teachers were Lily and Anne Tomlinson, a Miss Kemp and a Miss Day. The government eventually built a new school on the other side of the river on land donated by William Thompson.

The village was administered by a council of elders and a jail in the centre of the village served as a warning to those who would break the rules of the community.

In 1905 a beautiful little church was built with lumber from the village mill and all the labour was donated. Edward Wilson built the pulpit and communion table, and Samuel Bright and Robert Tomlinson Jr., the pews. Only the stained glass windows, furnace and hardware were purchased. The church burnt down in 1950.

The first church at Meanskinisht—probably the first on the Skeena River. (47-B)

Second church at Meanskinisht, 1907. Rev. R. Tomlinson was the pastor. (18-C)

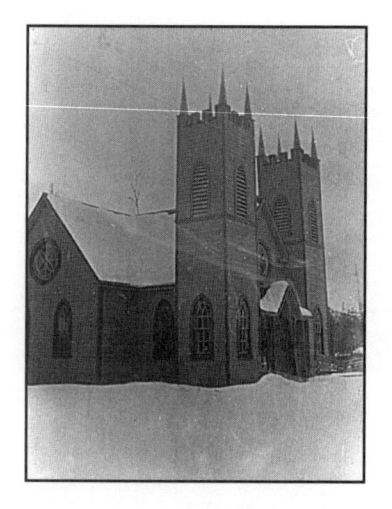

Annie told me about the early hardships and struggles of Meanskinisht pioneers and how, when the horses died, Richard, Lily and herself pulled the plough while her father ploughed the furrow.

"That year," she laughed, "the furrows were not very deep but we produced a crop until we got another horse."

In the fall of 1903 William Duncan persuaded Mr. and Mrs. Tomlinson and Robert, the eldest son, to join him at New Metlakatla. Richard was left in charge at Meanskinisht. They stayed with Duncan for three years and returned in 1912. Mr. Tomlinson died there on September 18, 1913, and Mrs. Tomlinson died in 1933.

The inscription on their grave reads as follows:

"In memory of Rev. Robert Tomlinson, 1843–1913, 46 years medical missionary in Northern BC and SE Alaska, also Alice Mary, his beloved wife and co-worker, 1851–1933."

Several years after the death of the founder of the village, a religious crisis arose and the village was divided by personality conflicts. Richard Tomlinson joined the Salvation Army and that group bought the old log school to use as their headquarters. Mrs. Philip Sutton led a non-denominational group and the remainder of the people supported the United Church. Services were held by visiting ministers from Terrace and Kispiox in the church built in 1905, and Mrs. Moberly taught Sunday school for eighteen years. Although there were different congregations, it is interesting to note that they all attended the same church if a visiting missionary conducted the service.

This is by no means a complete history of Cedarvale, a community founded by a dedicated couple who endured great hardships. Reverend Tomlinson defied his church, but only to minister to the Native people in a way that he felt was best suited to their needs.

Life at Meanskinisht

♦ Robert Tomlinson Jr. (as told to his wife)

In the year 1887, after getting William Duncan and his people settled in Alaska, our family returned to British Columbia and the Skeena River.

Father was an ordained medical missionary. He had worked with the northern Indians since 1867. He knew the language and the people. I was seventeen and the eldest of six children.

We spent the first winter in the Indian village of Kitwanga. Early in the spring we travelled down on the ice about twenty miles, where an old

Kitwanga Indian had given us his hunting ground as the site for a Christian village. There were eight Indian converts with us.

Indians arrived from the surrounding heathen villages where Father had conducted services. The village grew. A sawmill was built and log cabins were replaced with frame houses. A beautiful church with stained glass windows was the pride of the village people.

Self-government was set up by the Indians in their own village council. One of the rules was that no one left the village on Sunday and all work ceased. Another was that no tobacco was to be used in the village. Meanskinisht was for many years dubbed the "Holy City."

The country was heavily wooded. There were no roads. As far as white neighbours were concerned, we might just as well have been in the jungles of Africa.

Our living had to be carved out of the wilderness. The river supplied us with fish, and game abounded in the forests. The earth was black, rich and fertile. After clearing and planting, we were able to grow all the vegetables we needed. The Indians followed our example. Each home had a well-kept vegetable garden, and flowers to gladden the eye. Our village was a going concern that sold lumber up and down the Skeena.

The only way to go places for many years was by canoe in the summer and by snowshoes in winter. Then came the sternwheelers.

One night there was a knock at the door. We were happy to welcome the Rev. Thomas Crosby from Port Simpson. He had arrived by canoe with a group from his congregation. He told us he had come as far as he could by steamer, now tied down the river because the water was too low. The captain had hoped that the river would rise so he could get his freight as far as Hazelton.

"We were lucky enough to get a canoe at an Indian village," he told us, "and here we are."

Mr. Crosby and his Indian friends were making this hazardous journey to evangelize. Crosby could preach a soul-stirring sermon.

That evening, we attended a service in the church. After church, the Indians were taken to the homes of their clansmen. Mr. Crosby went home with Father and the family while I busied myself getting a crew together.

We had decided to go down the river the next day in the hope that the steamer *Hazleton* would still be tied up. We were anxious to get our freight and also the mail for our village and the upper Skeena country.

Next morning, we were up bright and early, Amos, the captain, Joe and myself.

"Be sure you get the box of drugs," Father called to us as we were leaving.

EXCERPTS FROM A LETTER FROM ROBERT TOMLINSON JR., KETCHIKAN, TO STAN ROUGH, KITIMAT:

We took the first winter mail from the interior, through to Kitimat, after finding that the Nass route was not satisfactory for taking out the winter mail . . . While the Meanskinisht boys carried the winter mail from Hazelton, it never once missed connecting with the CPR boat at Kitimat.

I have myself written a good deal about the early days on the Skeena. I spent most of my life in that country. I have canoed up and down, and learned the tricks of that old river as a crewman and later took the responsibility of Skipper. Then came the steamboats. The first time we heard the steamboat, we were planting potatoes. We all stopped and rushed down to the riverbank, for we could hear the engine plainly—still we waited a long time before she came into sight. There was an upriver wind and the sound carried a long way. There are some interesting stories to be told about those first steamboat days, and of the fine men who manned those boats. Captain Bonser was one of the best, and a real friend, not only to me, but to everyone along the Skeena. He was loved by all. He was especially kind and considerate to old Indian people, and they in their turn, did all they could to repay him.

It was always exciting going downstream. Avoiding the dangerous places was the captain's responsibility; Joe and I had to paddle to give him enough speed to make the rapids safely.

The Big Canyon was smooth as glass and we made it through easily. When the water is high, it is a seething mass with whirlpools that swallow great trees. The Little Canyon, too, was child's play.

Soon we arrived where the steamer lay pulling at her lines as if anxious to be on her way back to the coast. Captain Bonser welcomed us warmly. We had a good dinner and slept that night aboard the boat.

In the morning the canoe was loaded with care. The sheet iron, which we needed badly to make stoves for the winter, was placed below the floorboards. The mailbags were stored away on the bottom of the pile. The box of drugs was also tucked away carefully.

Mr. Crosby had asked us to get Mr. S.S. Osterhout, who was aboard the *Hazelton*, and bring him back with us. He was to take charge of the Methodist Mission at Kispiox. Young Osterhout decided to return to the coast. His guardian angel must have been whispering in his ear that day.

When she was eighty-one years old, Mrs. Annie (Tomlinson) Moberly recounted her memories of life at Meanskinisht and it was recorded on tape. Her niece, Mrs. Kathy Johnson of Kitwanga, has kindly given permission for its use. In the following memoir, Mrs. Moberly's own style of speaking has been preserved as much as possible.

Memories of Meanskinisht

♦ Annie Moberly

Now I was born at Ankitlas and I was three years old when my father went to England to explain that the Church of England religion was no good to Christianize Indians. He favoured a plainer service. So he went off to England and they said to him, if you can't preach the way we want you to preach, you'd better quit. So he came back and he quit.

He went down to Old Metlakatla where Mr. Duncan was. He was working for the Church Missionary Society. My father was a missionary doctor and he worked for Mr. Duncan for five years. I think most of his work was in the sawmill—Mr. Duncan had a sawmill. Of course I think he preached, too.

Well, when Mr. Duncan decided to go over to Annette Island, my father decided to come up the Skeena River. There were some Indians, old ones—I could give you the names of them—that wanted him to start a mission. So we came up in the autumn. In October we came up the river and we spent the first winter at Kitwangar. Then in the spring, the tenth of March, Father and some of the Indians who wanted to be Christianized came down the river on the ice, looking for a place where they could start a mission. They nearly started it at Woodcock, but what stopped them from doing this was that the stream at Woodcock was too far back in the woods and Father wanted to have a sawmill. Father had no money. He had to earn all his money. So they came on and came on until they reached Meanskinisht. There was a lovely stream over on the other side with a beautiful waterfall and it wasn't too far back. So he made a mill over there and built a small house.

They built just a sort of shack at first, with cedar bark around it and an open fireplace in the middle, with a hole in the roof for the smoke to go out. The few Indians, seven of them, that came with Father, they had one side of the cabin and Father and Mother and us six children had the other side.

Then they built a log house. I can't quite remember, but my recollection is that it was about sixteen feet wide and about twenty-four feet long. It was all split shingles—oh, there was no lumber—split poles! Then they said to Father, you've got your family and the children while we are just ourselves. You have this house.

Then they built another, a small one-roomed log house. There lived Edward Stewart and his wife and little girls . . . one was the same age as I am. That was the first starter of Meanskinisht. I was eight years old then. The year was 1888.

Before Father went to Kispiox, he was at Old Metlakatla and then they sent him to Kincolith up the Naas River. There my brother and my sister and another sister and my other brother were born. There was ten years between my oldest brother and me. Then the Church Missionary Society sent him up to Ankitlas, which was an Indian village. There's none there now. One little baby was born up there after me, between me and my youngest sister. This little baby lived only a few days, I think. It's buried up there at Ankitlas.

Well, there was nothing here . . . absolutely nothing but trees . . . nothing. There wasn't a house, there wasn't a thing . . . nothing but trees. These they slashed down, but wherever you went were trees, nothing else.

I can remember as a kid my mother and my elder sister in the spring used to walk up and down the ice for exercise. They used to leave me and my sister, who was four years younger than I, to keep an eye on the fire because it was in the middle of the cabin, you see.

I can remember having a quarrel with my sister. There was a birch tree that had been cut down and I said to my sister, "I am going to smooth it so I have a planing bench." I had a little axe, but my sister said, "It's mine," and I said, "It's mine," and she put her fingers down. I said, "Take your fingers away or I'll chop them," . . . so I chopped them and my father had to stitch two stitches there and two stitches here . . . just grazed this one . . .

Another time Mother and my elder sister were out for a walk. They said, "Now look after the fire. If it rolls out, don't touch it. Call us!" And I, naughty girl, said to my sister, I said, "Oh how I'd like to see them run!" We were to ring a bell if the fire rolled out, so I rang it. I rang the bell and up they came—"What's the MATTER?" So I got a spanking, I can remember that.

You see the fire was on the earth and there was a hole in the roof for smoke. It was an Indian-style house . . . the first house there was in the Indian style. It wasn't more than about twelve by twelve. We had no cookstove . . . all we had to cook on was that thing for a starter. Later they went to Hazelton and brought down a cookstove over the ice on a sleigh with dogs.

I will tell you how the sawmill was started. My mother's father and mother died. They lived in Victoria, and they died and left six hundred dollars to each of their children. So my mother got six hundred dollars. She said to Daddy, "Here, take the six hundred dollars and start a sawmill . . . you can have it." So he started with that.

Years ago everything had to come up in canoes, big canoes. There were no steamboats, no railways, no anything. When you bought things, you had six months to pay. You bought groceries and you had six months to pay for them. You went to Essington and bought from R. Cunningham, and I think that's the only store there was in Essington. Then these things were brought up in canoes.

That spring we cleared a little piece of land that was on the island. We started there as Father said it was the best place. We put in some potatoes, so that year we had potatoes. Well, the next year we increased our place. Soon we could grow enough and more than we needed for our own use. The Indians made their own gardens up at Anakwawa, two-and-a-half miles up farther. There's a sort of flat and they had their gardens there. Of course there were no animals, so we didn't have to fence. As soon as we could grow enough potatoes and things, Father got in touch with the Girls' Home at Port Simpson and he took down a big two-ton canoe loaded with our potatoes, which he sold.

We canned our own fish. We got the cans they had, but had to make them up. I mean they were cut in the right length, but they weren't soldered together and had no lids on. We had to buy the machine, that was the thing, and my oldest brother was really good at it. He put the can together, soldered it, we filled it with fish, he put the lid on and soldered that.

Then we had a big—what they called—Enzam stove. It's a long trough with an iron bottom and it sits on rocks and you push wood underneath it, set the fire, and that boils it. Then we put the cans in that thing to cook.

We canned some of our fish and salted some, but we didn't dry any. We generally put up two great big barrels about this size. We salted only the bellies, we didn't salt the backs . . . we didn't like the backs. We threw them away. Of course there were no laws then. You could catch all you wanted. One time we canned twenty-one cases. Father wanted to send one case to Mother's married sisters who lived together. Another case was to go to Mother's married sister who was a widow with five children. We had to eat the rest ourselves.

The trough? It was, I would say, about six feet long and about three feet wide. It sat on rock and the earth was scooped out so a fire could be pushed underneath it. It had a wooden lid in two halves . . . too heavy to move. We put the cans on trays that we made ourselves and we boiled the fish for three-and-a-half hours, I think it was. Then we had to take them out and tap them. Now why, I don't know, but you had to. You don't do it when you're canning nowadays. You had to tap them and then let the air go out and solder that hole. It was all done by hand, every bit of it. It really was no trouble . . . it was just a little bit of a hole, you see, like a punch hole. But why we had to do it if you don't have to now, I don't know.

Yes, we left Kitwangar the tenth of March, 1888, as I said, and came down to this shack that they had built. Before long, before the winter came, they went up to Hazelton to get the cookstove. We cooked grouse, the blue grouse . . . no moose, but caribou. It's only since the railway went through that the moose have come and it's only since the railway went through that the deer have come. There are a few deer around, but not many, but there's caribou. I don't know how many caribou are now in this country.

Sometimes we would go out in the hills and pick berries. We picked huckleberries, raspberries, wild gooseberries and saskatoons, and that's about all. And there were those little bits of—I don't know what you'd call them—the Indians call them "mielle." They grow on a little tree, little bunches of berries, and they are blue.

You ask if the Indians ate any wild roots of any kind. I think they did, but I'm not sure. We never did. But for medicine they did . . . they used Devil's Club . . . boiled it down for medicine. We never did that either as Father was a doctor and we didn't have to, you see.

Of course there were no roads. If you had to go anywhere, you had to go down on the beach—the island didn't come right up to the house. We went diagonally down to get onto the island and of course we had a little canoe . . . a little what we called "melanshuks." I don't know what you would call them in English. Canoes . . . a canoe is made out of cedar and melanshuks is made out of cottonwood. It is smaller and they used it only for fishing. It would be about four feet wide and sixteen to eighteen feet long. We used it for crossing backwards and forwards to the island.

The next incident that I can remember was that Father decided to build a better house. The first house was on a flat; this was on a little rise. He built this house with a lean-to to it. It had a living room and at the far end it had a small room that Father used as a study and to keep his medicines in. It had a door into the lean-to and a passageway. Under the lean-to was Father and Mother's bedroom and all round this way was where Lily and I slept. It had an upstairs and my elder and younger sisters slept there.

Before we moved into that building, somebody in England gave Father some money and told him to build a schoolhouse because, you see, there was no school. Mother had to teach us. The schoolhouse was about sixteen

Reverend Tomlinson's home in Meanskinisht, 1906. Pictured are Rev. R. Tomlinson with son Robert Jr., and his daughter Alice (Tordiffe) with wee Hazel Cook. (18-C)

by twelve feet. Mother taught us from the middle of October (not before) to the middle of March. That's the only schooling we got because we had to start getting the garden ready and everything else, so we couldn't have more. She just taught us two hours a day, just the three of us, Nellie, Rich and me. Lily and Alice had been sent down to Victoria to stay with the aunties and go to school. Robert got very little schooling. In school, Father would often come in and say, "Oh, I'm so busy, let Annie go and water the animals, never mind any more schooling." I'd go like a shot . . . I was always wanted, so I had very little schooling . . . I don't think I got to more than grade five. Mother was wonderful . . . though my Father was well educated, Mother was a better teacher and she tried to bring us up with learning. Yes, we learned a lot of things from the life around us—practically, you see. Of course we didn't have all the things they have now in school. Mother just taught us ordinary. You must remember that that was seventy years ago. There was no school for the community because there was no community, there were no children . . .

So we moved into the house. Well that was a misfortune, and I'll tell you why. The steamboats were beginning to run on the river and now we could get our freight upriver. It was pretty high, sixty dollars a ton to bring it up, so you can imagine how we had to scrimp to find money. Well, they were fixing their furnace on the steamboat this day and they threw away on to the beach some fire bricks. Father asked them if he could have them and they said yes. Father wanted them for his fireplace. This was built of stone, but the back of the fireplace . . . he used it there as a lining to make it look nice. It must have been too close to the wall . . . anyhow one night—well, at four o'clock in the morning—the house went up in flames. It was eight below zero (Fahrenheit), the twenty-eighth of November. There was no water but the river water and we hadn't much in the house. Hardly anything was saved—some medicine, Father's money box and the little piano we had. I didn't even save my clothes, so of course before any help could come the whole place was burned to the ground. My sister Lily broke a window and threw out her blankets so they were saved, but otherwise there was very little.

We moved then into the schoolhouse and you can imagine how much room there was—Father and Mother's bed here, Nellie's bed there, Lily and my bed here. We had built a little store and Robert and Richard slept over at the store.

The mill was running then because the store was built with lumber from the mill. It had no fire in it, no stove. We only went there to sell, we never stayed in the store. If anyone came and wanted to buy something, we served them. The reason we started the store was to please the Indians who wanted one. Father said, if I pay you cash I can't have the store. If I don't pay you cash —and in those days $1.25 was a day's work —I'll write it out on a piece of paper. Then you go down to the store and whatever you get is put on the back of that paper until you finish that and that's done, you see.

After that, all the houses that were built had the chimneys made with bricks. Father started a brick mill over on the other side of the river. There was lovely soil there for bricks and the chimney of our new house was made with bricks.

Now I'll tell you of an accident that happened. Father and my brother, Richard, and my sister, Lily, they went over to get a load of bricks. They were going to build the new house. The mill was running. Robert ran the mill with the help of two Indians, Joseph and another man, those were his helpers. He ran the mill and of course we sold the lumber. Nearly all these houses were made with lumber from the sawmill. You go to Kitwangar—nearly every house built there had the lumber brought from here. You go to Skeena Crossing and nearly every house there, the lumber was bought here. You go to the old part of the hospital at Hazelton and you'll find the lumber came from here. Of course that brought us in some money to buy food and decent clothes.

My mother's sisters, down in Victoria, were very, very good. They used to send us up a box of clothes, second-hand clothes, you see. They were given to us and we used to be delighted.

Well, to get back to the accident. One day Father and my brother and sister, they went over to get a load of bricks. They put them in the canoe. There was a nice wind and they had the sail up. They had a wheelbarrow in which they had been wheeling the bricks down over the hill to place in the canoe and they started coming across the river. They got nearly to this shore when there was a gust of wind that shipped the sail too much and the bricks shifted over to one side of the canoe. The canoe upset.

Mrs. Robert Tomlinson Sr. writes of a time when the Indians risked their lives to get the freight back to the mission before the high water, when all other canoes turned back because they knew provisions would be badly needed. The night before the canoe arrived, the family had eaten everything they had. One of the girls asked their dad what they would eat the next day and he said they would have to dig up the potatoes they had planted. The Indians arrived that night. Mrs. Tomlinson writes: "Can you wonder that working with and for such people for a lifetime has brought satisfaction and friendships beyond description. The Indian people are a wonderful race and oft times mistreated by those who have not tried to understand them."

Now all the bricks went into the river. Father went in too, as did Richard and Lily.

My eldest brother was coming down the road and he had a door on his shoulder. He happened to look up and see the canoe go over. He dropped the door and ran back to the man he had got it from, who had a wood shop on the bank here. He said, "Come quick, they're drowning." They jumped into a melanshuks and down they went, down the river.

Well, the first one they picked up was Father. Poor Father had got hold of the wheelbarrow but he had got the wheel end of it and it kept flipping over. He was nearly worn out but they managed to get him ashore.

Then on they went to look for my sister. When they got down to the whirlpool, which is about a quarter of a mile down, they saw the mast of the boat going round and round in the water. They went and pulled that up and there was my sister hanging on to the mast. They put her ashore . . . she was still alive.

Now my brother. They went on. They could not see where the melanshuks had gone, so they kept going. They picked up my brother about two-and-a-half miles down. He couldn't get ashore. He was sitting on the upside-down melanshuks and he could not get ashore as he didn't have a paddle. He was just going down, down, down the river hoping he'd go ashore somewhere. He couldn't swim. None of us could swim—we never learned how.

So all our bricks were gone. Otherwise no one had any bad effects from the accident. You see, they managed to get Father before he was too worn out, but he was nearly so. You see, he was too far out to swim, and he didn't know how anyway. He was a short, short, stoutish man. But it was a real wonder seeing that mast in the whirlpool going round, pulling it up and there was my sister hanging on to it!

Oh, I'll tell you another incident. After we had been here about, I think, two years, a friend of Father's down at Essington gave him a present of a young heifer. So Father went down with a crew. The crew always consisted of five—the captain, a bowman and three on the towline. Well, Father went down extra and they brought that little heifer up the Skeena River in the canoe. Where Father could walk her, they untied her and Father walked her along. Where the bank was steep and the walking too rough, they put her back into the canoe. They brought her home and we had her here all winter.

The next year Father went to Hazelton and he bought a bull and he walked that down from Hazelton. He had to—he couldn't put the bull in the canoe. He was too big. There was no road, there was only just quite a little pathway. We were the first ones that ever had any animals here.

Another incident, later on . . . I think it may have been about five years after we came here. Father said we've got to get a horse, we've just got to. So they went up to Hazelton and they bought a horse to plough with, and we put in our potatoes. Well, the coming year, after we got the horse, the horse disappeared. It was before the ploughing and Father said to us kids, whoever finds the horse I'll give them twenty-five cents. So we hunted and we hunted and we hunted for that horse and we couldn't find it. It wasn't until about four days after the horse was lost that we found it, but it was dead. It had caught its foot in the fork of a tree and couldn't get it out. It had fallen over and died. Here we were passing to within twenty feet of where it was lying, but the brush was so thick we couldn't see it.

Well, we couldn't afford another horse so Father hitched up three kids, Richard, Lily and I, onto the plough and he held the plough and we pulled. I tell you, our garden wasn't extra good that year. We three kids pulled the plough . . . we had to . . . we couldn't afford another horse. As soon as we could afford one, we got another.

We enlarged the clearing a little bit more each year, but think of all those stumps! Those cedar stumps had to be taken out all by hand, pulled out and dug round . . . what a job! The Indians didn't do anything round the house as a rule. They were not very spry doing anything. They left everything to grow. Of course they chopped down trees for wood and they grew their potatoes.

We didn't clear anything more than just a little bit around the house. All our vegetables and everything else were grown on the island. The animals were on the island and a barn was built there.

I never made any pots out of clay or anything like that. I never wove any cloth either, but I did make Indian braids. You know, Indian braids for pack straps. I do have the stick for making the Indian braid.

I was twenty-five years old and I went up to Hazelton to work for Dr. Wrinch's wife for a year. This was years afterwards, you see. I promised to stay a year. While I was there, in the evenings I made Indian braids. I made twelve of them because I had made up my mind that when my year was up, I was going to take a trip to Victoria. I had never been out in the world before—Hazelton was as far as I had ever been. So I made these braids and I left one braid in the stick.

When my year was up I came home here to Meanskinisht and I stayed three days. Then I took the steamer, the *Mount Royal*, and I went away. This was the trip when the *Mount Royal* was wrecked in the Kitselas Canyon.

I was on the island with the others. We were there for three hours before a big canoe came and took us off. They took six at a time and put them on this side. They had two ropes. They tied a rope to one end of the canoe here and they tied a rope to the end of the canoe there and they took six across. Then they pulled the thing back, you see, put six more in, pulled it back and so on. The captain's wife came to me and she said, "Let's go before they get too tired." I says, "Oh no, let's be the last, then we can sit in the canoe right through and we won't have to scramble through all that brush." I said, "Who wants to scramble through that . . . your shoes won't be fit to wear." So she went and told the captain. The captain thought that was a very wise idea. So we were the last to go and we sat in the canoe and we went right through the canyon, the last six . . .

The telegraph lines were busy. Miss O'Neill, Wiggs's sister, she was the telegraph operator here and she got word first that there had been a wreck and all passengers were drowned. A little after that, she got word that the passengers were all saved but all the crew was drowned. Some hours afterwards Mother and Father wired down to me to know what I was going to

Katie O'Neill, telegraph operator at Meanskinisht. The snowshoes were given to her by the Tomlinson's at Christmas, 1906. (18-C)

do. I said I was going to go on, and so away I went the next day. Our passage had been paid on the boat, so the Captain hired a boat from Kitselas with two men in it and he said to take me and a Mrs. Phillips and the captain's wife. We were the only three women on the boat. We were to be taken down to Essington to catch the boat for Victoria.

They were instructed to stop for nothing. Well, we went down about thirteen miles, I think it was, when there was a man waving his hand, so they called ashore and he said, "I want to go on this boat. Take me!"

"Can you row?" they asked and he said yes, so they took him. Well when we got to tidal water, the tide was against us and we had to stop. We stopped and called at a little fishing boat. The captain of this boat was very good to us and he gave Mrs. Phillips and me his own room so we could have a sleep. We had to start off at four o'clock in the morning. We made it to Essington to find that the boat had left about four hours before. So we were stuck at Essington for two weeks—Mrs. Phillips up at the hotel while I was with the Methodist minister and his wife.

Well I got down to Victoria all right and when I got to my sister's she gave me a dress. I only had one. She gave me a coat, lent me them, and she gave me some money as I had lost my money and everything else in the wreck. I hadn't been there more than about a week or so when I got word from my father and mother to come back, that they had to go to Metlakatla, you see. I hadn't intended to stay very long, but back I had to go. Father and Mother and Robert all went off to Metlakatla, Alaska, leaving me, my brother Richard, the schoolteacher and the lady telegraph operator, Katie O'Neill.

The schoolteacher's name was Miss Day. I was to look after the house and do the cooking for them—board them. Miss Day only had to pay for her food, not her room, because Father had promised a room for her with the BC government when they sent her as a teacher.

Miss O'Neill paid for her food, but she didn't pay for her room—we gave her the room for nothing. Miss O'Neill stayed on—that was in September—she stayed on until the following spring, then she resigned. They sent someone else but this other person lived on the other side of the river. We didn't have to board him at all. But Miss Day, she stayed on until the school closed. You see, she had come for the term.

Then I wrote to Mr. Loring, the Indian agent at Hazelton, and I asked him if I could teach school and he said yes, if you can tell them what a mountain and a river and a stream are, you can teach it, he said. I taught the Indian school for three years. Do you know what the wages were then? Just $33.50 a month, that's all a schoolteacher got, teaching Indians. Of course there were nothing but Indians. Well, I taught it for three years. When Father and Mother came back to Meanskinisht, Father said to me,

"Now I'll teach the school in the morning and you can teach it in the afternoon and we'll divide the pay." I said, "Nothing doing, you can get a maid to come and help you and she can do the housework." I'm going off to earn my living, is what I told him.

The meaning of Meanskinisht? "Mean" is foot, and "skinisht" is mountain—foot of the mountain. And we were on the foot of the mountain, you see, and that is why it was called Meanskinisht.

When the steamboats began to run, Father told them that they could not load wood (we used to sell wood), or land any freight on Sunday. They thought Father was very strict and called it the "Holy City."

When did it become Cedarvale? Oh, when the post office came. We didn't have a post office until the railway came, and the railway was through in 1913. They may have wanted a different name because the post office was on the other side of the river, you see. The only reason I can imagine why it was called Cedarvale was because there were so many cedar trees. Otherwise, it was Meanskinisht until the Grand Trunk Pacific went through. Some people put "Cedarvale" on their letters and some put "Cedarvale, Meanskinisht."

Well, then they decided they'd make a prison . . . yes, they had a prison. Do you know where Mrs. Sutton lives? Did you notice a hollow as you are going up the village here? Well, that's where the prison was, just off the road there and it was made eight square. It had one window up too high for anyone to climb through and it had bars across it. It had one door.

Oh yes, everybody had to keep the rules if they didn't want to go to jail. Was anybody ever put in jail? Why yes . . . there's one man I know of was put in jail because he kept running after a girl and he wasn't supposed to, you see. It was against the rules, so she was locked up in a house and he was locked up in prison . . . I think they were there two weeks.

School at Meanskinisht. This building was used as a school from 1906 to 1909. (18-C)

Jail at Meanskinisht, 1906. (18-C)

The judges were the heads of the village, men like Samuel and Father, you see. Father, of course, was the boss. He would call in the elders and they would all decide what should be done. As people came after, there were elders too, like Stephen Morgan and Amos Williams . . . they're dead now. A jailer? Oh, no, no . . . somebody had to feed the man there, that's all, usually one of the Indians. They just took him along, locked him in, and left him to lie on the bed or to read.

The law of Cedarvale was no smoking, no drinking, no work on Sunday. Everybody that could was supposed to go to church three times Sundays.

There was a service at eleven o'clock, one at three o'clock, and after this service, anyone who wanted to stay could remain while we sang a few

Annie (Tomlinson) Moberly (left) and Katie O'Neill in 1967—lifelong friends. Friendships formed in those early days lasted throughout the years. (18-C)

hymns. Then there was a service again at seven o'clock in the evening—three times—and then in the middle of the week there was a service, Wednesday night. It was really to fill up their Sunday that there were so many services because they had nothing to do, you see. This helped to keep them out of mischief and they were only too glad.

After I had been here about, oh, I'd say three years, I could speak the Indian language just as good as they did and I understood it. Then I went away to work and I was gone for twenty years and I forgot all about it. Oh, I know the odd word here and there, like I know a horse and a dog and a sheep and things like that, but otherwise, if a man was talking, unless he was telling a story, I would not really know what he was saying if he was speaking in Indian. But if he was talking a prayer . . . I'd know.

Long ago we couldn't get mail in the winter . . . no mail came at all. So Father wrote the government and asked them would they pay two men to go over the trail to Kitimat to bring the mail in for Hazelton, Meanskinisht, Kitwangar and other points. So they went and we had two mails in the winter, then after a while there were four mails in the winter. In the summer months the mail came up the Skeena by steamboat. There were always two men and they had a dog team. Sometimes my brother went. We used to look forward to the mail, but the letters were often months old. However, we got used to it and it didn't worry us kids for long.

Nothing ever worried us for long. Of course we were brought up to behave. If we couldn't behave we had to stay home and we all wanted to go to church. When Nellie was little we two stayed home and Mother taught us. It was over half a mile to walk, you see. Lily and Richard and Robert and Father went in the evening, but we went in the morning and afternoon and stayed for the singing. There were no kids to play with, you might as well say there was nothing—no picture shows. I've only been to two picture shows in my life . . .

When the first steamboat arrived, everyone was so tickled to see it. We'd know it was coming because we'd hear it about two miles down. If we had an order of groceries on it, we'd hope it wasn't Sunday. If it was, the steamboat had to go right on by to Hazelton as this was the Holy City.

Once years ago when we were kids, my sister and I were tired of washing the living room floor so we said to Daddy we'll cut cordwood for the steamboat and we'll pay for the oilcloth for this floor. Daddy said, "I'll pay for the freight," so we went . . . My sister, my youngest brother and I, we cut down trees and we hauled cordwood. We got three dollars a cord until we had earned enough for linoleum for our living room floor. I can even tell you the year—it was the year Queen Victoria died, if you can remember that . . . 1901? Well then it was in 1901 when we cut cordwood for the riverboats.

These were the tough old days, I'll tell you right now. But somehow, on looking back, they were the good old days too.

Note: Anna Moberly (née Tomlinson) passed away September 1969 at the age of eighty-nine.

Obituary

Pioneer Missionary of Cedarvale Dies

Last Sunday, August 8, 1954, in the churchyard at Cedarvale, was laid to rest the mortal remains of Thomas Richard Tomlinson, aged 76, who passed away on August 6. The late Mr. Tomlinson was a member of one of the oldest pioneer families in the North and played no small part in the development of these parts.

The deceased was the son of Rev. and Mrs. Robert Tomlinson who founded the village of Meanskinisht, now Cedarvale.

In 1865 his father married Miss Alice Woods and brought his bride by canoe all the way up the coast to Old Metlakatla. One of their stopping places was Alice Arm, named after Mrs. Tomlinson.

The elder Rev. Tomlinson belonged to the CMS and was in charge of the mission boat at Kincolith, when Richard was born.

In the spring of 1888 the Tomlinson family, with various Christian Natives, founded the settlement at Meanskinisht. Richard at the time was a young boy. Here he had lived ever since.

In 1917 he married Ensign Agnes Parr of the Salvation Army, a lady who was ever ready with sympathy and aid when the occasion arose. She passed on in September 1951.

At one time Richard and his brother, Robert, carried the mail from Kitimat to Dobbie's Landing, over practically the same route being followed by the railway now in the course of construction.

He leaves a family of three: Mrs. Johnson (Kathleen) of Cedarvale, Walter of Winnipeg, Mrs. Seline (Mary) of Florida, one sister, Mrs. Moberly of Cedarvale and one brother, Robert, of Ketchikan, Alaska, as well as seven grandchildren.

Rev. Robert Tomlinson, Jr. (1959)

A pioneer missionary in BC's Skeena District, Robert Tomlinson, was buried Thursday in Ketchikan, Alaska, where he retired in 1939.

The 88-year-old Methodist Church missionary died Monday in Ketchikan. Born in Kincolith on the Nass River, he was raised by his missionary father among the Indians and learned to speak in the Nishga tongue before he mastered English.

His father was the Rev. Robert Tomlinson Sr., a contemporary of the famed William Duncan who founded Metlakatla, BC.

The younger Tomlinson worked with his father among the Indians both in Alaska and in BC until the latter died in 1913. He then joined the Rev. Walter Rushbrook on the northern coast Mission boat, the *Northern Cross*.

During this time, he met and married a girl working for the Methodist Church Girls' Home at Port Simpson. He left the Anglican Church and entered the Methodist service, taking charge of the Mission at Kispiox on the upper Skeena from 1913 to 1924.

He later served as manager of the Hazelton Hospital farm until 1932 when he accepted a call to take charge of the church at New Metlakatla, Alaska. He served there until he retired.

He is survived by his widow, Roxana, three daughters and a son in Washington State, and a sister, Mrs. Annie Moberly, of Cedarvale. His first wife, Ethel Collins, died in 1919.

Philip Sutton

♦ as narrated to Stan Rough in 1961

Mr. Sutton was born in Cedarvale, his father being one of the first settlers to join Reverend Tomlinson's new village. He has a great respect for the Tomlinson family and the work they carried on amongst the Native people.

He told us of his great joy on being able to read as a boy and the first words he read were from Genesis: "And God said, 'Let there be light' and there was light." As he repeated these words several times, those of us in the room were moved by his sincerity and great love of his faith.

In his youth Mr. Sutton was a member of his uncle's five-man canoe crew and later became a canoe captain on the Skeena, carrying freight and supplies to the various river settlements.

He worked in the Tomlinson Co-Operative sawmill for twenty-five cents an hour, was a deckhand on the riverboats and was employed on the construction of the Grand Trunk Pacific Railway.

For ten years he worked on the section gang of the railroad and then worked in sawmills and cut poles. At seventy he retired from the pole business as he felt he was getting too old to cope with the mechanical changes that were taking place.

In 1908 he married the daughter of Samuel Bright, one of the original Cedarvale settlers who assisted Reverend Price and Reverend Tomlinson in translating the New Testament into Getsan, the language of the people of the Upper Skeena.

The Suttons live in a house back from the road beside the river and have a fine garden and a number of fruit trees. Recently Mr. Sutton visited Kitimat for the first time in fifty-eight years. It was a thrilling experience, he said, travelling a distance in several hours that used to take days.

He was confused at first when he arrived, but as he was driven to the dock he began to recognize old landmarks and to point out places where several of the early settlers' cabins once stood. Time did not permit him to go over to Kitimaat Village, a trip he is looking forward to.

Mr. and Mrs. Phillip Sutton wedding at Meanskinisht, February 20, 1908. Katie O'Neill made the bride's gown (18-C)

Note: Philip Sutton passed away in Terrace Hospital January 4, 1968.

One of Three

♦ Edith M. Essex

The old post office and store at Meanskinisht (later named Cedarvale). (47-C)

People who have travelled across the river on the reaction ferry at Cedarvale will recall the old grey building on the north side of the Skeena, situated close to the ferry landing. It has been photographed hundreds of times.

This is one of the remaining three original buildings that were constructed by the missionary, the Rev. Robert Tomlinson, when he founded the village of Meanskinisht. The other two are on the south side of the river.

The building has witnessed many historic events and has had a varied career. It is also a part of CNR history. It was built before the turn of the century by the Reverend Tomlinson for his oldest son, Robert, and his bride. The right-of-way for the GTP (now the CNR) was purchased from the Reverend Tomlinson and the building was moved back closer to the riverbank as it would have been too near the railway track.

It has gazed with awe upon the huge freight canoes manned by expert Native crewmen that have passed by its windows. It has watched the steamboats on their way up and down the river, and has seen the launching of the first ferry. It trembled with fear during the great flood of 1936 when the murky waters of the mighty Skeena lapped hungrily against its walls.

First used as a home, it was surrounded by a white picket fence enclosing a garden and flowers. In 1906 it served as a telegraph office in riverboat days. Later it became a ferry house, and then a post office and tiny store when the post office was relocated in 1918. For many years it had the only telephone connection with the outside world and was the centre of business for the small community. It also saw service a few times as a polling station during elections. Now with the passing of time, which brings many changes, it is slowly going into a decline.

Still, memories will remain. The laughter and quarrels of school children coming in for their small purchases. The tears it has seen when expected letters failed to arrive. The happy voices of teenagers waiting to meet the mail train. The excited voice of a small tourist boy saying, "Look, mom, a store, just like out of the movies!" The "Oos!" and "Ahs!" . . . how quaint, how neat . . . delightfully different comments from tourists. All these and many more. Memories—just memories, but from these, dreams are made. Ah me, what stories the walls could tell if they could only speak!

Stolen

♦ Edith M. Essex

It has gone from the wall where it hung so long—
The old Sweet Caporal sign.
Stolen away in the dark of the night
By a sneak afraid to face the light—
Gone from its Skeena River home.
Could not the old sign have been left alone?
The only bit of colour the old grey wall had
Its loss arouses feelings both angry and sad.
Fifty-four inches long by nineteen inches wide
Not a thing one could easily hide.
Therefore it was stolen in the dark of the night
By a sneak afraid to face the light.
Where has it gone, the old Sweet Caporal sign?
Your ventured guess is as good as mine.
To Vancouver or some other city far away—
Even perhaps to the USA.
Thirty-five years or more it hung safely on the wall
Only to be stolen at night by a thief this fall.
The lass on the sign had a Scottish air
With her eyes of blue and her flaxen hair;
And she scorned the moustache scratched upon her chin,
The disfigurement her proud bearing could not dim.
A Collector's prized possession she now will be
A prize other collectors will rally to see.
And not one of them will ever know the tale
Of the Sweet Caporal sign stolen from the old
Post Office at Cedarvale.

The old Sweet Caporal sign. (47-C)

THE TALKING WIRE

Terminal Station of Collins's Overland Telegraph, New Westminster, BC, sketched by F. L. Pope. (25-A)/BCARS 9359

THE COLLINS OVERLAND TELEGRAPH

Date Capsule

It may at first appear improbable that the dream of a quiet, unassuming American visionary by the name of Perry McDonough Collins could possibly have influenced the opening up and eventual settlement of our own Skeena country —but it did!

To better understand the sequence of events leading up to the first ventures by sternwheelers on the Skeena River and to establish a quick time orientation, the following date capsule is presented:[1]

1843—First public telegraphic line in England (London–Slough).
1844—First telegraphic line in America (Washington–Baltimore).
1846—First telegraphic line in Canada (Toronto–Hamilton).
1860s—By the early 1860s Europe and eastern North America had a network of lines.
1861—Transcontinental line in US completed to San Francisco.

Intercontinental communication would require submarine cables.

1851—Cable laid, Dover–Calais.
1854—Several cables in use between England, Ireland and the Continent.
1857—First attempt at a transatlantic cable failed.
1858—Second attempt had short period of success, then failure.

These failures led to the idea of an overland telegraph to link Europe and United States via British Columbia, Alaska and Siberia.

1860—Perry McDonough Collins lobbied in Britain, then Russia, to get approval for his dream. He got it! A long interval of financing and legal negotiations followed.
1864—the SS *Union* made the first attempt to navigate the Skeena River—ascended about 60 miles.
1865—By this year the telegraph line going north from San Francisco had reached Oregon.

> **1865**—On April 18 of this year, the line reached New Westminster, BC.
> **1865**—the SS *Union* was chartered by the Collins Overland Telegraph to transport supplies inland. Sailed up Skeena River approximately 90 miles.
> **1865**—On September 14, the line reached Quesnel. The speed of this part of the construction was due to the fact that the Cariboo Wagon Road was already in use.

From Quesnel northward lay unexplored territory. Which route should they now follow toward Alaska?
 Meanwhile, work was going ahead well both in Alaska and in Siberia.

> **1866**—the SS *Mumford*, designed especially for the Skeena River, transported supplies for the Collins Overland Telegraph. Ascended the river approximately 110 miles.
> **1866**—On July 25, the announcement of the success of the Atlantic cable was made. The Collins Overland Telegraph project was doomed

Construction in BC reached about 25 miles beyond Fort Stager, a company supply depot situated at the junction of the Skeena and Kispiox rivers.

> **1867**— On March 27, the official order to halt work was given. The Atlantic cable was now an established success.

> **1867**—Alaska work parties did not receive the stop-work order until four months later.

The Pioneer Telegraph Survey of British Columbia

♦ P.J. Leech, CE (from the *BC Mining Record*, August 1899, Vancouver Public Library)

I was engaged by the Western Union Telegraph Company in the year 1866 when they were constructing the line with the intention of carrying it through British Columbia and Alaska to Behring Straits, crossing Behring Straits with a cable, and continuing to St. Petersburg, Russia.

 I left Quesnelle on the 6th June, 1866, in company with Conway (the superintendent of the work); T. Elwyn (who was sent by the Government at the request of the Telegraph Company to act as stipendiary magistrate); and W. Burrage (one of the quartermasters of the Company).

 The working party were then about sixty miles WNW of Quesnelle.

My duty was to survey the line, make a reconnaissance of the country through which the line passed, determine the latitudes and longitudes of the several stations which were to be twenty-five miles apart, make regular meteorological observations and report generally on the nature of the country. We caught up with the working party on the twelfth of June.

The previous year (1865) several exploring parties had been sent out to select the best line of route to be followed, bearing in mind that the line was to be as near the coast as possible for the purpose of getting supplies to the several stations by means of the rivers, but to keep clear of the coast range of mountains.

Out of the lines which were explored, that selected by a man named Burns was adopted. He had explored from Quesnelle to Fort Fraser, a distance of about 135 miles, and at the time that I joined he was exploring from Fort Fraser to the Skeena River, a distance of about 270 miles.

The line of route having been selected, a surveyor (J. McClure) having a rough sketch of the country went ahead with two or three axemen and blazed the trees, keeping as straight a course as the nature of the country would permit. Then came the choppers (about eighty men) who cut down all the trees within a width of twelve feet, next a man who paced distances of seventy yards, and at the end of each distance drove a stake in the ground; after him came a party of Chinamen, who dug holes where the stakes had been driven; then a party of axemen, who cut poles on which to string the wire; next the polesetters, whose duty it was to nail the bracket on the pole, place the insulator on the bracket and set the pole upright in the hole, filling in the earth and stones and stamping it well down; lastly came the wire party, who strung the wire on the poles.

Thus at the end of each day we had telegraphic communication with civilization.

In addition to the parties mentioned above there were others employed making trails, building bridges over streams and making rafts at the crossings of rivers.

Our supplies were brought from Quesnelle by trains of mules and horses. We had a band of horned cattle with us, so that we had plenty of fresh meat.

At the end of September work was stopped for the season, we having reached a point on the Kispyox River about fifty miles WNW of the Indian village of Kispyox, which is situated at the confluence of the Wastenqua or Bulkley River with the Skeena. Kispyox is about 130 miles from the mouth of the Skeena. We built a large house at Kispyox and called it Fort Stager. Burns had explored about fifty miles beyond the termination of the line, and had got to what he considered was the Naas River. Our object was to strike the Stikine River, near the mouth of the great Canon, which is about 170 miles from the mouth of the Stikine.

The country lying between Quesnelle and Westroad River is heavily timbered, gradually rising from Quesnelle. From Westroad River to Lake Tchinkut the country gets more open and park-like, and continues so to Fort Fraser.

From Fort Fraser to the Skeena the country becomes still more open in some places, the grass (red top and blue joint) grows so high that horned cattle cannot be seen in it, and it was so thick with pea vine that it was hard work to walk through it.

I counted twenty-four different kinds of fruits growing wild. Raspberries, strawberries, serviceberries, gooseberries and currants were amongst them.

On the stopping of work the whole party returned to Kispyox and an exploring expedition was then organized to proceed by sea to Stikine, up the Stikine River to the great Canon and then to explore in the direction of the Yukon River, and from the Stikine in an ESE direction to strike the point where Burns had struck the Naas.

Excerpt, "From Pack Trail to Radio and Then What?"

◆ S.A. Cunliffe[2]

In that period of British Columbia's history from the middle to the end of the last century, although seemingly remote and cut off from the rest of the world, events occurred that linked her most definitely with world affairs.

Those stirring days saw the Cariboo gold rush, the coming of the Royal Engineers, construction of the Cariboo Road, the uniting of the crown colonies of New Caledonia and Vancouver Island into the Province of British Columbia, the entry of that province into Confederation in 1871, and the construction of the CPR, which tied the province into the rest of the Dominion.

Most of these happenings, while affecting the southerly part of the province directly, only had an indirect bearing on the north.

The one event in the history of the white men in the north that links up the country with the rest of the world was the attempt to establish telegraphic communication between New York and Europe.

Previous to 1866 several attempts were made to lay a cable from Europe to America, but these failed on account of no ship being large enough to carry a sufficient length of cable to span the Atlantic. To that time no method of splicing a cable on the high seas was known.

After the cable failure of 1858 a company was formed to build a line through British Columbia and Russian America, connecting by a short cable across Behring Straits, with a line across Siberia to St. Petersburg. This company was a branch of the Western Union Telegraph Company and was known as the Collins Overland Telegraph. Collins was a clerk in the United States consul's office in Vladivostock and he acted as intermediary between the Russian government and Western Union on this side.

The company responsible for the attempt and final laying of the Atlantic cable was the Atlantic & Pacific Transit & Telegraph Company. This company was also to connect British Columbia with Canada, but wanted extensive guarantees and subsidies from the Imperial, Canadian, British Columbian and Vancouver Island governments. These were not forthcoming as the Collins Overland Telegraph had approached the legislative council in 1864 and offered to build the line, asking no bonus or aid. The necessary legislation was passed and in 1864 a start was made from Yale, BC, under the direction of Colonel Bulkley. By 1866 the line was completed and in operation as far as Quesnel, while for hundreds of miles farther north the route was laid out and cut one hundred feet wide.

The country was little known and had to be explored in order to locate the most suitable route. Colonel Bulkley was engineer-in-chief (on leave of absence, US Regular Army), with the other principal officers as follows: Mr. Lewis, assistant engineer; Captain Scammon, chief of marine; Major Wright, adjutant; Major Chappell, chief quartermaster; Dr. Fisher, surgeon-in-chief; E.K. Laborne, interpreter and F. Whymper, artist.

The route was so well chosen that when the Dominion government later carried the line from Quesnel to Dawson in 1898, it was found impossible to improve on it.

During 1865 and 1866 the immense distance that lies between the southern boundary of British Columbia and the mouth of the Amur River in Siberia was the scene of very extended operations. Not less than five hundred skilled men, besides bands of Cossacks in eastern Siberia, Chinamen in British Columbia and Indians everywhere were engaged in building telegraph, exploring the route or transporting goods and materials.

When it was finally decided that the Bulkley Valley to Hazelton and Kispiox was the logical location, one large and two small river steamers were operated on the Skeena River, as well as other steamers on the Naas and Stikine Rivers.

The first materials—wire, implements, supplies—arrived at New Westminster on board the *Milton Badger* in June 1865. These were distributed to such good effect that by June 1866, Fort Fraser was reached by wire. When the season of 1866 closed, the telegraph existed from the southerly boundary of British Columbia to a point twenty-five miles beyond Fort Stager, a supply depot at the confluence of the Kispiox and Skeena rivers named after the general superintendent of the Western Union Telegraph.

Meanwhile, the ship *Great Eastern* was built and successfully laid a cable across the Atlantic Ocean, thereby accomplishing what the overland telegraph builders in British Columbia were trying to do. No further work was done in British Columbia after the fall of 1866, and in 1868 Mr. McCutcheon, an operator, abandoned Fort Stager, bringing out with him thirteen large canoes loaded with provisions and clothing. The tons of wire and piles of material left behind were a great source of supply for the domestic requirements of the Indians for manufacturing nails, fish spears, traps, toboggans and even for the construction of rude suspension bridges.

The remains of one such bridge at Hagwilget was once visible from the fine modern suspension bridge built by the Department of Public Works in 1931.

The parties working up the Alaska coast did not hear of the successful laying of the cable until July 1867. These parties had about fifteen thousand telegraph poles made and these were abandoned to make campfires for the wandering Natives.

In their disappointment, the men who had endured the hardship of the work for years hung black cloth on the telegraph poles and put them in mourning.

The immense sum of $3 million had been sunk by the Western Union Telegraph Company into this undertaking.

Upon abandonment of the line it quickly fell into ruin from Quesnel to Fort Stager and to the northern limits of the work. The remainder was operated for many years, forming the origin of the present system of the northern interior of British Columbia.

Barkerville became the centre of the Cariboo district mining operations during the famous gold rush, and the Canadian government subsidized the Collins Overland Limited for additional construction between Quesnel and Barkerville, thereby establishing telegraphic communication between the mines and the coast.

As previously noted, the work on the northern line was abandoned in 1866.

Capt. W.F. Butler, in his journey across the north in 1873, came upon remains of the telegraph line in British Columbia. He reports that "we reached a broadly cut trail which bore curious traces of a past civilization . . . this trail with its ruined wire told of the wreck of a great enterprise."

Note: The author of the above article wishes to express his appreciation for the help given by Dr. W. Kaye Lamb, provincial librarian; John Dore, Esq., of the Dominion Telegraph Service; and others who have provided local anecdotes and colour that will perhaps disappear in the passing of the years as men grow older and memories fade.

> **TELEGRAPH CREEK**
>
> *It is interesting to note that although the exploring parties reached Telegraph Creek and recommended that the wire cross the Stikine River there, it never actually arrived. Construction halted too soon. The name, however, has lived on to this day.*

Telegraph Trail

♦ from the *Shoulder Strap*[3]

Through the primeval forests of northern BC the party cut a wide swath, sometimes reaching a maximum width of fifty feet and at others narrowing down to half that because of the rugged terrain. For nearly eighty years this scar on the natural symmetry of the country has been known as the "Telegraph Trail." Aviators look for it as a landmark. Trappers, traders and hunters welcome its easy travelling. So well did these early explorers of the telegraph company choose their route that today, near the boundary between BC and the Yukon, the new Alaskan Highway merges with the old Telegraph Trail.

An Enormous Task

Some idea of the enormity of the task and the speed with which the work progressed is revealed in the account by Willard F. Ireland, BC provincial archivist:[4]

> All material and provisions must now be transported by boat and pack train. The trail must be surveyed, and cleared to a width of between twelve and twenty feet; bridges must be built over all streams which could not be forded; swamps must be "corduroyed" and hillsides too steep for pack animals "graded from three to five feet wide." Telegraph poles cut to specified dimensions, must be erected sixty-three paces apart and strung with wire; at all large rivers—and the party had to build boats before they could navigate these—double wires must be stretched. Every twenty-five miles a station must be erected: a log house with a fireplace, chimney, door and windows. To accomplish all this, Conway had only a comparatively small party. It averaged, he says, sixty white men, thirty-two Chinamen (who were employed as cooks, pole-men and wire-men), and twenty Indians, employed mostly as boatmen and in the transportation of supplies. But the

THROWBACK

The reader is referred back to the journal of Charles Morrison, which is given in the riverboat section of Pioneer Legacy, Volume 1. Morrison came up the Skeena on the SS Mumford and was in the employ of the Collins Overland Telegraph Company. His account was included there to provide a greater depth of perception into conditions as they existed at that time. This is an instance where a story belongs in more than one category and a choice must be made as to where it may be the most effective.

Lineman's cabin, sketched from original painting by J.C. White during Western Union Telegraph Expedition in 1865. (25-A)/BCARS 56517

> **OLD TELEGRAPH ROAD**
>
> PENETRATING NORTHWARD THROUGH THIS POINT, TOWARD WILDERNESS AREAS OF BRITISH COLUMBIA AND ALASKA, A TELEGRAPH LINE WAS PARTIALLY BUILT IN 1865-1867 TO CONNECT NEW YORK WITH LONDON VIA A BERING STRAIT CABLE AND A LINE ACROSS RUSSIA. A SINGLE-WIRE POLE LINE FOLLOWED A FIFTY-FOOT CLEARING THROUGH HEAVY FORESTS AND ACROSS FROZEN TUNDRA. WESTERN UNION TELEGRAPH COMPANY DROPPED THIS PROJECT ABRUPTLY IN 1867 WHEN SATISFACTORY TRANS-ATLANTIC CABLE SERVICE WAS ESTABLISHED. RUSSIAN-AMERICAN CO-OPERATION IN BUILDING THIS LINE FACILITATED OUR PURCHASE OF ALASKA IN 1867.
>
> ERECTED BY - HISTORICAL SITES AND MARKERS COMMISSION
> STATE PARKS COMMISSION

Historical markers such as this one at Bellingham, Washington, commemorate the valiant attempt to build an overland telegraph. (63-C)

organization, "military in character," was highly efficient: the strictest discipline was enforced, and a magistrate accompanied the party into the wilds; all trading with the Natives was forbidden; and no "spirituous or intoxicating liquors" were allowed in camp. In less than four months, without working on Sundays, they were able to complete 440 miles of trail and 390 miles of wire, to erect 9,246 poles and build 15 stations.

Success or Failure?

Although the monetary loss at the time of cessation was great, the knowledge obtained through the opening up of vast tracts of wilderness, the detailed information left by the surveyors and the notes of Colonel Bulkley in his ledger, have proven invaluable in later days. It is also a recognized fact that the Collins Overland Telegraph venture expedited the purchase of Alaska by the United States from Russia.

Collins himself seemed doomed to oblivion. Many places were named for members of his party, for example, Bulkley River, Kennicott Mountain, Burns Lake, Decker Lake, etc., but nothing commemorates this intrepid man himself. It is said that the Kispiox River was for a time named for him, but this did not last long. It was soon back to its original name.

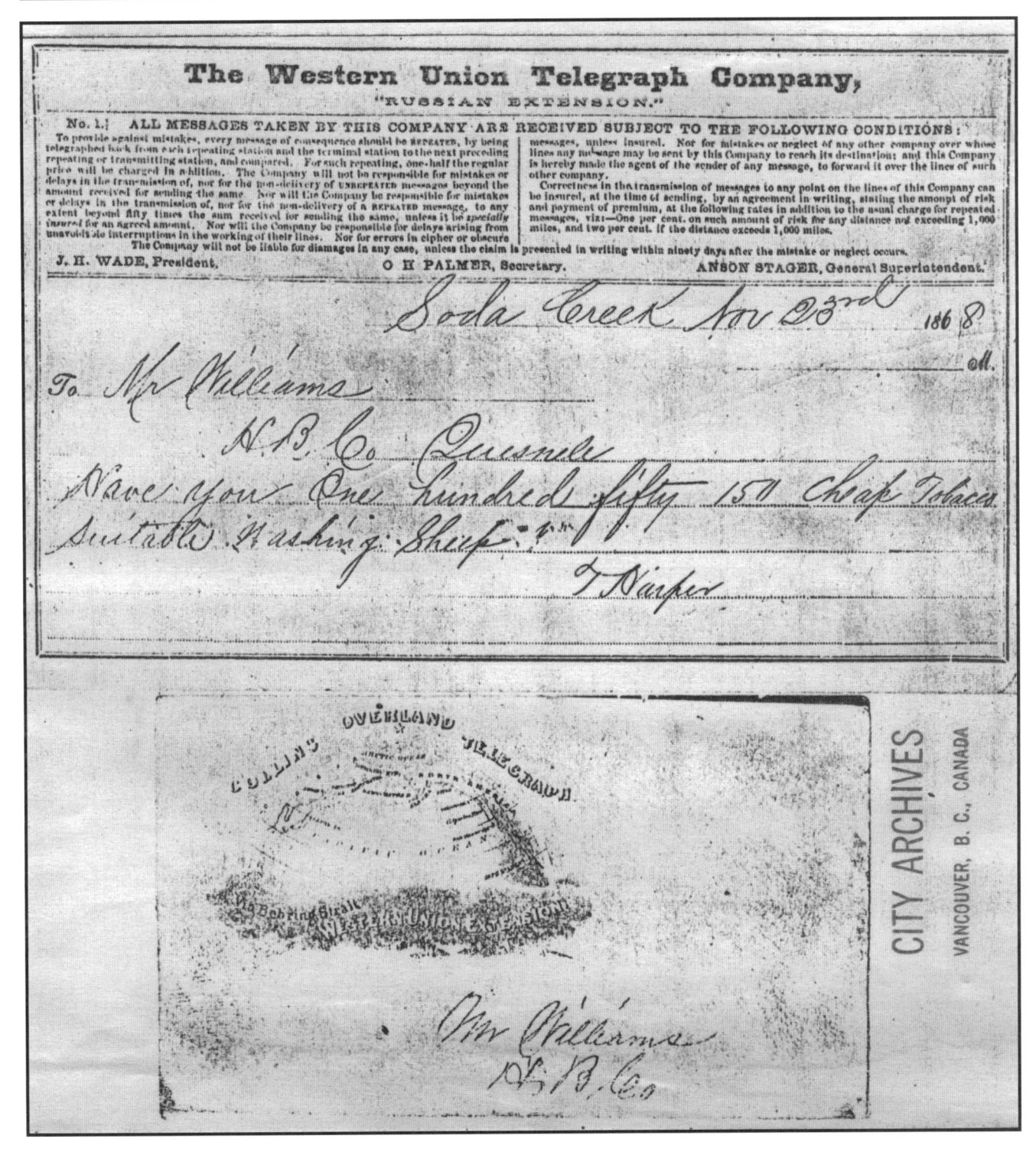

Collins's niece founded a $550,000 scholarship fund and left it to the New York University in his memory. Eventually even the recipients of his bequest did not know the history of the man behind it. Now, through research and time, we acknowledge his endeavours as successful because we are aware of their results, although his initial project may be considered by some to have failed.

There is a memorial to the Collins Overland Telegraph on the riverbank at Quesnel.

Langevin's Report, 1872[5]

By the Act completing the union of Columbia with Canada, the telegraph lines of that Province became the property of the Dominion, and are a charge upon it. These telegraph lines extend from Swinomish in Washington Territory (US) to Barkerville, at the extremity of the Cariboo Road. There is, besides, a branch from Matsqui to Burrard Inlet via New Westminster, in addition to a telegraphic right-of-way over the line belonging to the Western Union Telegraph Company from Swinomish to Victoria, which comprises two submarine cables. This line of telegraph is 569 miles long, in addition to the submarine portion, which is a mile-and-a-quarter in length; it originally cost $170,000. Besides this line, there is that from the mouth of the Quesnel to the Sabine, but this has not been kept up and is abandoned.

... the line is under our control in virtue of a lease for ninety-nine years, to which the Government may put an end by giving a month's notice. The telegraph line is a charge upon the Government, which has to maintain in a good state of repair, and at its own expense, the portion under water; and in consideration of this, all messages between Victoria and Swinomish are to be transmitted by the Western Union Company without charge.

Hazelton

The year 1866 saw the arrival of the work parties for the Collins Overland Telegraph Company, and the first real invasion of the district by the white men. As we know, their effort was short-lived, but some of the men engaged in the project stayed in the area to prospect, and a few of them wintered at the Forks. In 1868 this small settlement on the banks of the Skeena was given the name of Hazelton from the profusion of hazelnuts growing there.

THE YUKON TELEGRAPH

A Short History

♦ Norma Bennett

After the discovery of gold in the Klondike in 1896, the sudden influx of people made it a matter of prime concern that a quick and efficient means of communication with the "outside" be established. Ottawa finally bestirred itself to build a line from the Yukon-Alaska border—at the point where the Yukon River crossed over into American territory—down to Lake Bennett. Here it met the White Pass & Yukon Railway from Skagway. This line was completed early in 1899, thanks to the diligence of the largely French-Canadian crews sent out from the East to handle the job.

Telegrams could now be sent by the White Pass & Yukon to Skagway, then south by steamer. This, however, did not prove to be too satisfactory as many messages were delayed or lost altogether.

Eventually Ottawa was prevailed upon to extend the line south to connect with the Canadian Pacific Telegraph at Quesnel.

Surprisingly enough the old Collins-surveyed route was found to be the best and once more came into use. The line followed the Skeena River from Hazelton to Kispiox, then the Kispiox River for some twenty-two miles, and once again back to the Skeena.

By the autumn of 1899 the work crews operating out of Lake Bennett reached Atlin. Late in 1901, about 117 miles north of Hazelton, the final connection was made, this despite the fact that the two crews advancing toward each other had taken different passes through the mountains and so had originally bypassed one another.

There was little fanfare at the conclusion of the nineteen-hundred-mile line, the cost of which had been stupendous. This, however, was peanuts compared with the cost of maintaining and operating the line in years to come.

The first winter was the hardest for the men, who had to put up with inferior cabins, meagre food supplies, distances that were too long between cabins, as well as all the other hazards that could not be foreseen or prepared for. Later, "halfway" or "refuge" cabins were built, and sometimes even "quarter-way" cabins between each cabin and "halfway." With a daily 8:00 p.m. roll-call system, the men were able to look forward to some means of checking and communication. Supplies were brought in by annu-

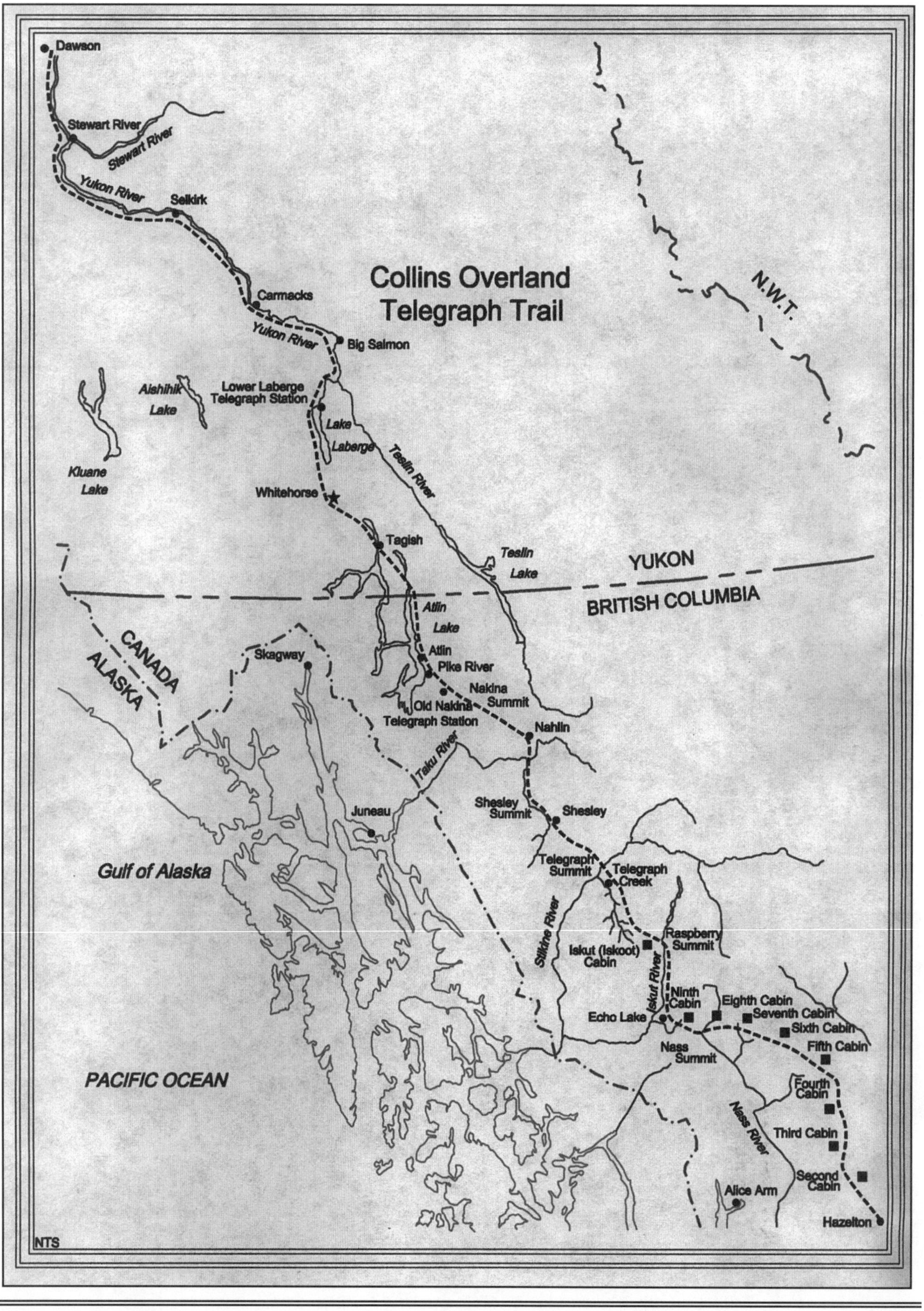
Collins Overland
Telegraph Trail
Dawson
Stewart River
Stewart River
Yukon River
Selkirk
Carmacks
Yukon River
Big Salmon
Aishihik
Lake
Lower Laberge
Telegraph Station
Lake
Laberge
Teslin River
Kluane
Lake
Whitehorse
Tagish
Teslin
Lake
YUKON
BRITISH COLUMBIA
N.W.T.
CANADA
ALASKA
Atlin
Lake
Atlin
Pike River
Skagway
Nakina
Summit
Old Nakina
Telegraph Station
Nahlin
Taku River
Juneau
Shesley
Summit
Shesley
Telegraph
Summit
Telegraph
Creek
Gulf of Alaska
Stikine River
Raspberry
Summit
Iskut (Iskoot)
Cabin
Iskut River
Ninth
Cabin
Eighth Cabin
Seventh Cabin
Sixth Cabin
Echo Lake
Nass
Summit
Fifth Cabin
Fourth
Cabin
PACIFIC OCEAN
Nass River
Third Cabin
Second
Cabin
Alice Arm
Hazelton
NTS

al pack train and as time went on, these were increased. The mailman, too, became an important link with the outside.

In the stories that one may read of life as a lineman or operator on the Yukon Telegraph—and some are first-hand accounts—one cannot help but marvel at the hardiness and intrepid courage of these men. How they could stand the everlasting loneliness, to say nothing of the everyday obstacles that continually cropped up, is more than the average person can comprehend. Cold, blizzards, ice, flood, sickness, accidents, death on the trail, danger from wild animals, fire, etc., were all commonplace to them. And what boggles the mind even more is the admitted fact that most who came for one season only, remained for years. The "spell of the North" is no idle fantasy.

Early in 1905 business fell off so alarmingly that Ottawa considered cutting down on staff. This decline was due to the US having laid a cable to Skagway, thus establishing a far more reliable service.

In 1936 short-wave wireless was introduced experimentally. Gradually, with the use of better and stronger sets, parts of the old land line were abandoned, superseded by a modern and efficient means of communication. The line from Hazelton to Telegraph Creek was let go first—how many tragic tales it might have told—and next, the part from Telegraph Creek to Atlin. Eventually a complete conversion was made.

In 1953 the Canadian National took over the old Yukon Telegraph, and it was no more.

Excerpt, "From Pack Trail to Radio and Then What?"

♦ S.A. Cunliffe

The (Collins Overland) telegraph trail lay deserted and abandoned until the Yukon gold rush of 1898, when several parties came into the country by the Skeena River and north from Hazelton. The Indians of Hazelton or Kitenmax (the people who fish by torchlight) and Kispiox (the people of the hidden place) used the trail to the north, but during the gold rush the Dominion government wished a connection from Quesnel to the Yukon. Supplies were again brought to Hazelton via the Skeena, Nass and Stikine rivers.

Investigation showed that the old trail was the best route and by 1900, construction was again in full swing. As a link with today, there are numerous old-timers in the north, revered and highly regarded, who were on the construction of the line. Two of the men with ranches in the Bulkley Valley today (1940) are Messrs. Barrett and Sealey, who after packing sup-

H.B. Birch (Hughie). Long-time lineman and operator on the telegraph line north of Hazelton. (65-C)

Pack horses leaving Hazelton, heading north, 1910. Supplies were brought in by riverboats sailing up the river from Port Essington and Prince Rupert before the GTP was completed. (65-C)/WWW—HHL 4005

plies into the Yukon, came to Hazelton with their pack trains and packed supplies and material both north and east.

Cabins were established twenty miles apart for the operator and lineman, with a halfway cabin and a shelter at the five-mile point for the use of the lineman. At first these men lived together, but dissension crept in, culminating in a murder over the position of a salt shaker on the table. After this, two cabins were erected and the men lived apart, sometimes not seeing each other for weeks. These men were up on the trail for three years before obtaining a furlough. Their supplies were packed in to them by the government and their salaries paid into the bank. In addition to this, most

Little Iskoot Refuge Cabin, 1906. (65-C)/WWW 1275

Government Telegraph cabin north of Hazelton, about 1910. Note the roof made with interlocking split logs and wood pegs. (65-C)/WWW 95720

of the men trapped and so added to an already substantial stake against the time of vacation.

The problem of keeping operators and linemen supplied with the necessities for a year was a large one. As many as seventy-five pack horses were used at a time, this large train making two, sometimes three trips to supply the cabins.

The picturesque pack trains as well as the men on the line disappeared in 1936, when radio communication was established between Hazelton and the north. So passed an interesting and historical phase of British Columbia's development.

Hughie Birch's dog: "My tough little packer and true friend 'Sandy'." (65-C)

Jack Wrathall sitting in front of Seventh Cabin with his dog, on the Yukon Telegraph line in 1909. Jack's brother, William W. Wrathall, came to the area in 1907 to work on the telegraph line and was the photographer who captured so much of the region's early history on film. (65-C)/WWW 95734

Excerpt from *The New Garden of Canada*

♦ F.A. Talbot

We had gained the top of a hillock. Masses of poplar, willow and open patches surrounded us. But there, in the middle distance, was a shimmering, irregular blotch on the prevailing green. We hustled our horses and in a few minutes were among bushes fringing Tsinkut Lake. But a more conspicuous feature compelled our attention. Just above our heads trailed across the azure of the sky a thin, dull-grey thread, festooning regularly along the trail through the forest. We could not suppress a strange thrill. We were shaking inanimate hands with civilization stretching in an unbroken line from Vancouver to the far north, threading dense forests, jumping wild ravines, spanning roaring rivers, climbing and dropping over lofty storm, rain and snow-swept mountains, until at last Dawson City is gained. It is a slender link, bringing isolated, distant Klondike into direct touch with the restless throbbing pulses of the world, as surely as London is connected with New York—the YUKON TELEGRAPH.

Of the many stories in which the Yukon Telegraph played a part, we consider the following to be one of the most unusual and interesting.

The Long Trail to Home Sweet Home

♦ J. Wellsford Mills (from *The Shoulder Strap*, Summer 1941)[6]

The vast city of New York terrified tiny Lillian Alling. She walked along the brick and stone chasms that men called streets and though millions of people swarmed around her, she felt a loneliness in her heart that could not be stilled. This was America, the mecca for thousands of her race, but she, a true Russian, yearned once more for the rugged steppes of her native land.

She wasn't a big woman, nothing like the popular conception of Russian women. She was small, well knit, and very smart in appearance and manners. Only her hands showed that she had worked hard. The skin of her face was smooth and clear, her hair black and shiny. She still wore her native clothing, a heavy skirt, a blouse and a shawl over her head.

New York had been kind to her in its way. She had worked in many fine homes and gathered a few dollars. These she had saved.

But she had not reckoned on the loneliness of a strange land. The swift tempo of life here bewildered her. The hurrying people, the speeding automobiles, the screech of horns, all of these things unsettled her. She must get back to Russia. There she would be among her own folks. She could almost smell the barnyards, the newly whitewashed farmhouse. She could hear the excited gutterals of the peasants as they thronged around the marketplace and listened to the latest edicts of the commissar. An overpowering wave of nostalgia swept over her. She must go at once.

The little Russian woman soon learned that steamship tickets cost a great deal more than she had earned. Others less determined than she would have resolved to go back to work and save for their fare. But she knew she could stand it no longer. If she could not go home by ship, she would find other means. There must be a way.

Though Lillian was a Russian and of peasant stock, she was not ignorant. She knew that Russia was a vast country and that North America was not far from Siberia. She studied a map and after a careful survey arrived at a startling conclusion. She would not pay a steamship company to take her home. She would walk.

Her decision to walk is not as ridiculous as it sounds. Though it would mean a walk of at least six thousand miles overland, the only water obstacle was a mere fifty miles or so across Bering Strait in Alaska. If she could reach the shores of Bering, she knew that somebody would take her across to Siberia. From there on it would be easy.

To think was to act. Lillian set out at once. She laid her course from New York to Chicago; from there to Minneapolis; and then she would strike into Canada at Winnipeg, Manitoba. From there she would work her way westward to British Columbia.

Once she reached the coast province, she would go north to Hazelton and then to Telegraph Creek. The route would be perilous but effective. She would cross into Alaska and reach the straits. Then on to Siberia.

This doughty little women, no more than thirty years of age, reached Winnipeg. She left there, and the next heard from her was when she passed Second Cabin on the Yukon Telegraph Line, beyond Hazelton.

Constable Wyman of the Hazelton detachment, BC Provincial Police, received a telephone call advising him that a woman had passed Second Cabin and was heading north. Wyman was a veteran in that part of the country. He glanced at the calendar. It was the month of September, 1927. The summer was practically at an end and the North would soon be in the cruel grip of winter. Surely, the constable thought, a woman must be out of her mind to be wandering northwards at this time of the year. He went out at once and brought the woman in to Hazelton.

Sgt. W.J. Service, in charge of the district, began to question her. After ascertaining her name, he asked where she was going.

"Siberia," was her calm reply.

"What!" Service exclaimed in astonishment.

"I am going to Siberia," the little woman replied with dignity. "I will cross the Bering Straits at Alaska. I am able to do it."

Sergeant Service rubbed his chin. Here was a matter requiring some thought. He had no right to interfere with the woman, no legal right, but he knew the dangers she was facing.

"You have no food, no clothing. You cannot go at this time of the year. You will freeze or starve to death."

"I have bread, three loaves; and some tea," Lillian Alling told him. "I must go. You must not stop me."

She had the tragic dark eyes of a Russian. They were now filled with the haunting light of appeal. Service felt himself slipping. In another moment he might have turned her loose to go on her way. But the thought of that freezing weather and the sudden storms of the North steeled him. He gave orders to lock her up.

A matron was called to search her. She found two ten-dollar bills and an iron bar, about eighteen inches in length. It hung beneath her skirt like a policeman's baton.

"Why were you carrying that iron bar?" Service asked her severely.

"To protect myself," she answered.

"From bears?"

The little woman looked away.

"No," she replied, "bears are not bad. I carry it for men."

There was, Service decided, only one thing to do for this woman's protection and that was to charge her with vagrancy and recommend a fine more than she was able to pay. She would then be sent down to Oakalla Gaol, where she would have good food and lodging for some time. When she was released she might have forgotten her idea of walking to Siberia.

On September 21, Lillian Alling's trek came to a temporary end when she faced Justice of the Peace William Grant in the Hazelton Police Court. She was fined twenty-five dollars and costs, or two months in gaol. Since she did not have the twenty-five dollars she was sent to Smithers and then down to Oakalla Gaol.

The little woman's stay in gaol did nothing to dampen her resolve. She had said she was going to walk to Siberia and nothing was going to stop her. As soon as she was released she told the gaol officials that she would work a little while and get some more money and then start out once more. It was summertime soon, she said brightly, and the police could surely have no objections.

At the end of June 1928, Sgt. A. Fairbairn at Smithers was warned that Lillian Alling was coming his way. On July 19 she arrived in Smithers. Fairbairn was astonished.

"Did you ride on the train or did somebody give you a ride in their car?" he asked.

"I have no money to ride on trains," she replied. "I do not go in cars. I have walked."

Fairbairn began a lightning calculation. He soon discovered that this wisp of a woman appeared capable of making between thirty and forty miles per day. However, he wasn't altogether satisfied that she had travelled unaided.

"I have told you the truth," she said with a world of dignity in her voice. "I do not tell lies."

The sergeant assured her that he hadn't doubted her word. He just couldn't see how a little woman like her could walk so far in a day.

"Well," Fairbairn told her, "I guess you can walk all right, but I can't see how I'm going to let you go up into that country. If anything happened to you I'd never forgive myself. You have no food."

"I have enough. I can live off leaves and fruit. You must let me go. You must. I am able to walk that far. I will cause you no trouble, but you must not stop me. Please do not stop me."

Fairbairn thought the matter over. She had pleaded so strongly that he didn't have the heart to prevent her from carrying out what seemed to be her dearest wish. She had proven herself capable of travelling long distances without help. There was no question as to her desires. She wanted to get to Russia.

Despite her rough travelling garb, Fairbairn could sense a certain daintiness about her and he hated to disappoint her. Suddenly he came to a decision.

"I will let you go on one condition," he said.

"What is it?" she asked, leaning forward eagerly.

"That you report to every cabin along the Yukon Telegraph Line until you get to Telegraph Creek," he said.

"I will do that. I give you my word," she said solemnly.

"Then wait until I have told the boys you will be along."

Fairbairn immediately got in touch with the men of the Yukon Telegraph Line, that slender strand of wire across a wilderness. He advised them that the little Russian woman was coming their way and asked them to give her whatever assistance she may require.

The replies came rushing back to the police office. Every man along the line was more than willing to help the brave little woman who was willing to dare the perils of the North Country alone. The cabins were fifteen to twenty miles apart, but the men agreed to meet her halfway and escort her in.

Such generosity touched Lillian Alling. Tears welled in her eyes as she thanked Sergeant Fairbairn and set out on her long journey. He watched her diminutive form vanish and then went back to his office.

"We'll soon find out how far she can walk in a day," he said to himself. "There's no hitchhiking along that trail."

Word of her progress came back. It was astonishing. She was making twenty to thirty miles per day over the roughest kind of country. The news came from First, Second and Third cabins, and at last the Seventh Cabin reported her arrival.

Jim Christie and Charlie Janze occupied two cabins at Eighth. They didn't get the chance to go and meet the little Russian woman. She walked in on them between seven and eight o'clock one night, a pitiful sight.

Her clothing consisted of a thin skirt and blouse. She was wearing ordinary low running shoes. They were in shreds, her clothing in rags. Her face was swollen by poison fly bites and burned by the sun and wind.

"She can't go on in those rags," Christie told his partner. "Here's where we go into the tailoring business."

Off to town with the furs. John Jensen and Charlie Janze, linemen, at Eighth Cabin on the BC/Yukon Telegraph line. They spent many years working together on the line. Janze spent the years 1917 to 1936 as lineman and operator. Dogs played a big part in a lineman's life. (25-A)/BCARS HP 72875

Christie gave her his cabin. He furnished her with bathing facilities and then began to remodel a pair of riding breeches for her. He and his partner managed to locate a pair of good boots that fitted her. A shirt was then made over and the little woman had a new outfit of clothes that would be serviceable in that rugged land.

She stayed at Eighth Cabin for three days, resting and eating nourishing meals. But at no time was she communicative. She told nothing of her past.

At last she announced her intention of going on. Christie knew the loneliness of that country. He gave her a dog as a travelling companion, then he looked toward the north.

There was a summit there reaching more than eight thousand feet into the clouds. The line ran right over it. Christie knew that there were times when even he and other linemen became lost in the sudden fogs that swept up until it was impossible to see the narrow trail. In some places a single misstep meant death. He couldn't let this inexperienced woman go over there alone.

Christie accompanied the little Russian woman more

Lineman's cabin at Echo Lake on Yukon Telegraph line. (25-A)/BCARS 72863

than twenty miles along her route. He left her at the now abandoned Ninth Cabin to rest before going farther. There was wire trouble somewhere between Eighth Cabin and Echo Lake. Christie set out to locate it.

Just about this time Scotty Ogilvie, a robust Scotsman who occupied Echo Lake Cabin with Cyril Tooley, was preparing to go out and meet the little Russian woman. He bid Tooley good-bye and, taking two of his dogs with him, went singing down the trail toward Eighth Cabin.

The weather was bad. As Scotty travelled he felt the cutting wind on his face, but he sang, nevertheless.

Scotty's real name was Drysdale Ogilvie. He had come into the country with the old Grand Trunk construction outfits, and when the Great War broke out, he went overseas with the 1st Pioneers. Though a veteran of the North, he had never lost his rich, native burr. He had returned from the war and had taken the job of lineman with the telegraph company.

In view of what happened later, and at the risk of being charged with digression, a little description of Scotty will not come amiss.

He was a rugged son of Scotia, a man in whose veins ran the rich, virile blood of the Clan Ogilvie. Like many of his kind, he loved the free

Sled dogs at Thirty Mile Refuge Cabin north of Nahlin Station on Yukon Telegraph line. (25-A)/BCARS 72841

life of the far places. As a singer of Scottish ballads and songs, it is probable that he had no superior. In those harmonious get-togethers of the North Country, he excelled. His rich voice rolled out without the artificial aid of accompaniment. It was a resonant voice, deep and compelling, and it was always at its best when he sang "The Auld Forty-Twa." Generous and always willing to aid others even at great cost to himself, he went his way singing and rejoicing, a man's man in a man's country.

So Scotty swung along the rough trail in the pouring rain. He came to the raging waters of the Ningunsaw River, now in full flood. He looked at the usual river crossing, a cable, but it was now deep under water. He must find another place to cross the boiling torrent and walked along the edge of the bank, upstream.

Tooley was worried. Scotty had not returned. Christie now shared Tooley's anxiety and they set out to look for Scotty. They followed his trail to the bank of the Ningunsaw and noted the submerged cable. Then they saw Scotty's tracks leading upstream. Just then they heard his Huskies howl. The dogs were in a refuge cabin where Scotty had spent the night, but there was no sign of Scotty.

The two men followed his trail along the edge of the bank and they saw that it had been undermined by the rushing waters of the river. A few feet farther on, they saw the trail end. A part of the bank had collapsed.

There was the whole tragic story. Scotty had been going along there and the bank had collapsed and precipitated him into the water. He wouldn't have had a chance to save himself. The two men turned and walked downstream.

A quarter of a mile downstream they found him, his body jammed against a huge cottonwood snag. His head and shoulders were submerged. Scotty Ogilvie had sung his last song.

The two men finished the melancholy task of bringing Scotty's body ashore. They soon got in touch with the Provincial Police at Telegraph Creek. A short time later they were ordered to gather Scotty's personal effects and send them on to Telegraph Creek. They were also ordered to bury the body.

Back at the Ninth Cabin, Lillian Alling heard the story of Scotty's tragic death. Her dark eyes filled with tears. This man had given his life for her. She didn't know him, hadn't even seen him, nor had he ever seen her, but because of her, he had lost his life. She bade Christie a sorrowful goodbye, took her dog and walked out along the lonely trail.

Seven miles from Echo Lake the little Russian woman stopped at a clearing near the telegraph line. There was a mound of fresh earth there. She stood silent, tears coursing down her cheeks. The wind sighed through the trees as if chanting a requiem for the soul of Scotty Ogilvie. The woman listened, then turned into the bush.

She came out later. She was holding a tiny bunch of wild flowers in her work-hardened hands. She approached the grave, slowly, reverently. She looked at the grey skies above. Her lips moved, then she knelt beside the grave. She placed the pitiful little bundle of flowers on the grave gently, her lips moving in whispered prayer. Then she clasped her hands and beseeched God to take care of Scotty's soul. Her prayer ended. She raised her bowed head, made the sign of the cross, then rose to her feet. For a moment she stood there, then she turned and walked toward the line. She stopped, turned slowly, took one last, long look at the lonely grave, then struck out on her long journey.

A report came back later that she had reached Dawson. That was the last ever heard of her. Extensive inquiries have failed to discover her eventual fate. No one seems to know whether she reached her beloved Siberia or not. She walked from that grave in the clearing out into the unknown so far as we have been able to learn.

Other authors have added but little to this story. It seems that some accident befell the dog given Lillian by Jim Christie. When she arrived at Atlin, she had skinned the animal and stuffed the hide with grass.

At Dawson she worked as a camp cook for the winter, otherwise keeping very much to herself. In the spring she fashioned a crude craft and took to the Yukon River. She was seen passing through Tanana, and actually arrived at Nome, where she left the boat and purchased a few necessities.

An Eskimo reported seeing her somewhere between Nome and Teller. She had constructed a makeshift cart, and the dog hide covered the few possessions she pulled in it. There, the trail ends.

Again we are faced with the intriguing queries: Did she reach Siberia? Was her tremendous effort worthwhile? Somehow we cannot help but hope that it was.

THE DOMINION GOVERNMENT TELEGRAPH SERVICE

Branch Line–Port Simpson to Hazelton

PORT SIMPSON TO HAZELTON

from the Victoria Daily Colonist

OTTAWA GOVERNMENT DECIDES TO BUILD A TELEGRAPH LINE THIS YEAR

Ottawa, January 24, 1901: The Government decided today, in addition to completing this year the telegraph line from Ashcroft north to connect with the Atlin and Yukon country, to build a line 200 miles in length from Port Simpson on the coast eastward to Hazelton, where it will connect with the line constructed last year.

There seems to be very little information available on this part of the Telegraph line. However, the Public Archives in Ottawa was able to answer the following questions from the records and Annual Reports of the Department of Public Works, which was the department responsible for the line:

Q. When was the Government Telegraph connecting Port Simpson and Hazelton started?

A. The construction of the branch line from Port Simpson to Hazelton (199 miles) was started in March 1901 (RG11, Vol. 1403, letter No. 228857). Note that only a registered précis of this letter is known to exist.

Q. When was the line finished and in operation?

A. The construction was ended in early June and the line was put into operation on 13 June, 1901 (Annual Report 1901).

Q. Was the construction from one or from both ends?

A. The line was constructed from Port Simpson to Hazelton (RG11, vol 1397, letter 227226).

Q. Did the line follow the Skeena River?

A. The line was built on the north shore of the Skeena River (RG11, 1397, letter 227226).

Q. Where were the telegraph stations located along the way? What were the names of some of the early operators?

A. A copy of a list of employees by branch line on the Yukon system as found in the Department of Public Works' Annual Report of 1904 is enclosed. The stations of particular interest to us were at:

HAZELTON
    G.M. Swan, operator, salary $100.00 per month
    E.R. Cox, lineman, salary $100.00 per month
    J.C.K. Sealey, lineman, salary $75.00 per month
    E.E. Charleson, foreman, salary $150.00 per month

MEANSKINISHT
    E. Tomlinson, operator, salary $50.00 per month
    R. Tomlinson, lineman, salary $75.00 per month

SKEENA CANYON
    A. Daoust, operator, salary $75.00 per month
    C. Durham, lineman, salary $70.00 per month
    F. Dresser, lineman, salary $70.00 per month

LORNE CREEK
    A.J. West, operator, salary $75.00 per month
    J.E. McIntosh, lineman, salary $75.00 per month

TELEGRAPH POINT
    W. J. O'Neill, operator, salary $75.00 per month
    C. Peterson, lineman, salary $75.00 per month

GRAVEYARD POINT
    S.W. Dobbie, operator, salary $75.00 per month
    J. D. Wells, lineman, salary $70.00 per month
    A.E. Johnston, lineman, salary $70.00 per month

The following is a copy of a letter from J.B. Charleson, superintendent of public works, Yukon division, to A. Gobeil, deputy minister of public works, relative to the construction of this line:

Vancouver, BC, May 27, 1901
A. Gobeil Esq.,
Deputy Minister of Public Works,
Ottawa.

Sir:

Your letter of May 20th received. Your quotation of my instructions is altogether wrong. You say that paragraph fourth reads as follows: "For the construction of a line from Port Simpson following the course of the Skeena River to Port Essington." No such paragraph appears in my instructions, but paragraph fourth reads as follows: "For the construction of a telegraph line from Port Simpson following the course of the Skeena River to Hazelton." Those were and are your instructions, but if your instructions meant that I was to build to Port Essington, it would have been utterly impossible to do it except by the way proposed by me in my telegram to the Minister.

    I think that you and I discussed that matter and I showed you, if you remember, that there would be just two ways of building that line, one way was from Port Simpson to Metlah-katlah, which was not feasible at all as we would have to pass Tuck's Inlet and it would increase our distance about 50 miles. The other way was the way that we came, starting from Port Simpson, crossing a 5 1/2 mile portage to Work's Channel, then following

Vera Frank's father, Archie McInnes, worked on this line during construction days, along with his brother, Neil. By the time they reached the Bulkley Valley, the brothers had decided to remain, take up homesteads and pioneer the area.

SESSIONAL PAPER No. 19

GOVERNMENT TELEGRAPH SERVICE.

YUKON LINES.

Names of employees and monthly salaries, &c., Yukon Telegraph Service, which includes Port Simpson, Barkerville, Quesnelle and Lillooet branches.

(Compiled from pay sheets of June and July 1904.)

Number.	Office.	Intermediate Distance.	Positions.	Salaries per Month.	Tariff.	Night Rate.
				$ cts.	$ cts.	$ cts.
1	Ashcroft		C. E. Gooding, manager	60 00		
			R. B. Rochester, operator	42 00		
			G. L. Hall, operator	45 00		
			T. R. Clark "	45 00		
			G. H. Dean "	45 00		
			S. Pritchard, lineman	75 00		
			P. R. Quinn, Dist. Supt. Clerk	83 33		
			J. T. Phelan "	175 00		
2	Pavilion	40	F. C. Schanz, operator	60 00	25 and 2	25 and 1
3	Lillooet	22	S. A. MacFarlane, opr.&linem	60 00	25 " 2	25 " 1
4	Cash Creek *	4	Accommodation office, lineman	50 p.c. com.	25 " 2	25 " 1
5	Clinton	26	A. LeBourdais " "	60 00	25 " 2	25 " 1
6	115 Mile House	55	S. Hannah " "	60 00	25 " 2	25 " 1
7	150 "	35	T. S. Hall " "	60 00	50 " 3	30 " 2
8	Harpers Camp	33	S. H. Patenaude " "	40 00	50 " 3	30 " 2
9	Bullion †	27			50 " 3	
10	Quesnel Forks	4	O. Landry office, lineman	66 66	50 " 3	30 " 2
11	Soda Creek	42	C. H. Smith " "	60 00	50 " 3	30 " 2
12	Alexandria	28	G. A. Broughton office, lineman	60 00	50 " 3	30 " 2
13	Quesnel	26	T. F. Murphy, operator	60 00	50 " 3	30 " 2
			O. Earley, lineman	60 00	50 " 3	
			J. Mooney "	$3 per day	50 " 3	
14	Lafontaine‡	46	Cariboo Consolidated Co	50 p.c. com.	50 " 3	
15	Barkerville‡	15	J. Stone, operator and lineman	60 00	50 " 3	
16	Blackwater	53	J. McNeill " "	70 00	75 " 5	
17	Bobtail Lake	45	J. W. Howison, operator	75 00	75 " 5	
			J. A. Holder, lineman	70 00	75 " 5	
18	Stoney Creek	35	W. F. Manson, operator	75 00	75 " 5	
			J. D. Charleson, lineman	70 00	75 " 5	
19	Fraser Lake	35	G. N. Proctor, operator	75 00	75 " 5	
			M. McNevin, lineman	70 00	75 " 5	
20	Burns Lake	69	W. Heinz, operator	75 00	75 " 5	
			B. Lashbrook, lineman	70 00	75 " 5	
21	South Backley	30	N. McInnis, operator	75 00	75 " 5	
			E. Barrett, lineman	70 00		
22	North Backley	25			100 " 7	
23	Buckley Roach	27	L. Broughton, operator	75 00	100 " 7	
			H. Fink, lineman	70 00		
24	Morricetown	35	T. F. Cowan, operator	75 00	125 " 10	
			W. J. Toneri, lineman	70 00		
25	Hazleton	40	G. M. Swan, operator	100 00	125 " 10	
			E. R. Cox, lineman	100 00		
			J. C. K. Seeley, lineman	75 00		
			E. E. Charleson, for'man storekr	150 00		
26	Meanskinisht§	35	E. Tomlinson, operator	50 00	125 " 10	
			R. Tomlinson, lineman	75 00	125 " 10	
27	Skeena Canyon §	47	A. Daoust, operator	75 00		
			C. Durham, lineman	70 00		
			F. Dresser "	70 00		
28	Lorn Creek §	24	A. J. West, operator	75 00	125 " 10	
			J. D. McIntosh, lineman	75 00		
29	Telegraph Point §	53	W. J. O'Neill, operator	75 00	150 " 10	
			C. Peterson, lineman	70 00		
30	Aberdeen §	4½	G. Coutu, operator	75 00	150 " 10	
			B. F. St. Amour, lineman	70 00		

*Br. from Ashcroft.   †Br. from 150 Mile House.   ‡Br. from Quesnelle.   §Br. from Hazleton.

4-5 EDWARD VII., A. 1905

GOVERNMENT TELEGRAPH SERVICE—Continued.

NAMES of employees and monthly salaries, &c., Yukon Telegraph Service, &c.—Con.

YUKON LINES—Continued.

Number.	Office.	Inter-mediate Distance.	Positions.	Salaries per Month.	Tariff.	Night Rate.
				$ cts.	$ cts.	
31	Port Simpson§	39	M. W. O'Neill, operator	50 00	150 „ 10	
32	1st Cabin	27	H. A. Cullon „	75 00	125 „ 10	
			Hugh Taylor, lineman	70 00		
33	Kuldo	28	G. T. Carpenter „	70 00		
			G. W. Smith „	70 00		
34	3rd Cabin	25	Chas. Martin, operator	75 00		
35	4th Cabin	20	P. Burnell „	75 00		
			J. McMenamin, lineman	70 00		
36	5th Cabin	20	E. A. Hawley, operator	100 00		
			C. E. Loucks, lineman	$3 per day		
37	6th Cabin	20	G. T. Brown, operator	100 00		
			W. Ross, lineman	$3 per day		
38	7th Cabin	19	J. A. Armstrong, operator	100 00		
			L. Dubois, lineman	$3 per day		
39	8th Cabin	19	J. Muir, operator	100 00		
			G. Duhamel, lineman	$3 per day		
40	9th Cabin	17	T. E. Harkin, operator	100 00		
			G. Hill, lineman	$3 per day		
41	Echo Lake	32	J. Patterson, operator	100 00	150 and 10	
			F. N. Jackson, lineman	$3 per day		
42	25-Mile Cabin	25	Jas. Murie, operator	100 00		
			J. W. Hovey, lineman	$3 per day		
43	Iskoot	16	J. W. Watts, operator	100 00	150 „ 10	
			J. Lonery, lineman	$3 per day		
44	Telegraph Creek	61	A. S. Gillespie, operator	100 00	175 „ 10	
			W. S. Simpson, lineman	75 00		
			A. J. Charleson, storekeeper	150 00		
45	Shesley	45	A. Johnson, operator	82 50	175 „ 10	
			J. Craig, lineman	75 00		
46	Nahlin	61	S. G. Lawrence	82 50	185 „ 10	
			R. Mckay, lineman	75 00		
47	Nakına	49	R. P. Hall, operator	82 50	185 „ 10	
			J. Huston, lineman	75 00		
48	Pike River	40	Geo. Coutts, operator	82 50	200 „ 15	
			J. A. Thorne, lineman	$3 per day		
(49)	Graveyard Point		S. W. Dobie, operator	75 00		
			J. D. Wells, lineman	70 00		
			A. E. Johnston, lineman	70 00		
50	Atlin	23	F. W. Dowling, day operator	116 66	200 „ 15	
			A. B. Taylor, night operator	100 00		
			H. D. Gagné, foreman	125 00		
51	Center Cabin	35	J. Stromach	82 50		
52	Tagish	40	M. R. Grimes, operator	82 50	225 „ 15	
53	Cariboo Crossing	18	Adam Dickson, lineman	75 00	225 „ 15	
54	Whitehorse	65	A. B. Clegg, dist. supt	175 00	250 „ 15	
			H. Gilchen, store-keeper	150 00		
			J. P. Champagne, clerk	112 50		
			G. S. Flemming, operator	115 00		
			G. W. Marshall, lineman	75 00		
			Mrs. Jefferies, house kpr & cook	75 00		
			Bruce Watson, messenger	35 00		
55	Lower Leberge	59	D. Potts, operator	82 50	250 „ 15	
			J. H. Brown, lineman	75 00		
56	Hootalinqua	30	J. W. Graham, operator	82 50	250 „ 15	
57	Big Salmon	34	H. O. Lakkin, lineman	75 00	250 „ 15	
58	Five Fingers	96	W. S. Langtree, operator	82 50	275 „ 15	
59	Yukon Crossing	8	J. Hope	82 50		
60	Fort Silkirk	50	E. K. Waller, operator	82 50	275 „ 15	
61	Selwyn	30	J. W. Wilson, operator	82 50	275 „ 15	
62	Stewart River	75	Chas. N. Graham, operator	82 50	300 „ 20	

Work's Channel to its head and crossing to the Skeena River over a 10 1/2 mile portage, as I reported to the Minister yesterday in a "private and confidential" report, a copy of which I sent you . . .

In the discussion of the routes I pointed out to you that we would come out upon the north side of the Skeena River at a point about 4 1/2 miles above Aberdeen Cannery and about 4 miles on the opposite side of the river from Port Essington.

Now several parties have been agitating the use of a cable to connect some point of the wire on the north side of the Skeena River with Port Essington. I have always said and I have always maintained that a cable on the Skeena River would not resist the spring freshets, any time, as snags come down, not such snags as we have in the east, but some of them five feet above the stump, with a tremendous root, at every flood, the Skeena and Stikine Rivers, small end first, while the butt or root always trails on the bottom. They would pick up our cable during the freshets and would keep us continually replacing it with another cable. I think you and I discussed this matter and you agreed, and quite properly so, that the north side of the Skeena River would be the side I ought to follow. This decision is quite in keeping with my instructions of the 6th February and quite in accordance with all instructions issued by you to me and which were followed out as the only possible and feasible way of building telegraph lines in this country.

Of course you will understand that people in the east, Members of Parliament particularly, are very apt to represent to the Minister or yourself that it will only cost a bagatelle, trusting to you to find the ways and means.

Now what we will have to do to get back to Port Essington will be to start from the Canyon, which is 124 miles from Port Simpson and 90 miles from Port Essington, to the Ecstall River, go up the Ecstall 5 miles to an Island in that river where we may cross and 5 miles back to the main shore and down to Port Essington, as I wired you and the Minister, 100 miles in all and $250.00 per mile, which means $25,000.00.

We are still stuck here as poor as Job's turkey, have no information as to when Mr. Hardy is coming out, can make no engagements for going north and will not face the men before I have money to pay them.

Now do take pity upon us and hustle money forward.

Yours truly,
J.B. Charleson
Superintendent of Public Works, Yukon Dist.

Note: A letter was received in answer to the foregoing from the deputy minister. It informed Mr. Charleson that the matter of the Port Essington construction had been settled, inasmuch as the honourable minister had telegraphed that he did not propose going on with it as he had not the funds required.

NORTH FROM KITSUMKALUM

Robert Ross, son of Mrs. Annie Ross, for whom Rosswood was named, kept a diary of his experiences when he worked on the Dominion Government Telegraph in 1910. Excerpts from that diary have been made available to us.

The Diary of Robert Ross

October 31, 1910
We went to work for the Canadian Government today on a crew who were constructing a telegraph line into the Nass River Valley. You want to see the country through this section of BC! We will visit the Nass River Valley and return to Kitsumkalum Lake about Christmas time.
Subtitle:November 8, 1910
We have been working for one week now and like it very much. We had some snow several days ago and it is still on the ground. It is very pretty country through here and today we came across two beaver houses. We are travelling through a beaver meadow too.

November 29, 1910
We are camped on Cedar River just now with the temperature down to above zero. We are putting two bridges across the river, one on each branch. Most of the timber throughout this part of the country is comparatively small but there are some nice patches of cedar and spruce along the Cedar River. The cottonwood trees are very large and numerous throughout this entire area. This would be a good place for a pulp mill. There is also plenty of the finest water that can be found anywhere. The land is a glacial deposit and consequently very rocky. The lakes also bear out this fact. The whole coast seems to be, geologically speaking, only a few moments old. Jack pine trees are present all around; occasionally one comes upon some balsam trees. It has been snowing and freezing off and on for three weeks now. We are thinking of returning to Kitsumkalum Lake for the winter.

December 7, 1910
We quit work on the Government Telegraph line last Wednesday; we came down to the lake on Thursday and arrived at the foot of the lake on Friday. Saturday morning we left the Siwash shack, which is at the foot of Mud Lake, and rode to Kitsumkalum. That night we stayed in Kalum and until noon on Sunday. Then we hit the trail again back to the lake arriving here on Monday afternoon . . .

Tomorrow we start for Prince Rupert to spend Christmas.

December 13, 1910
We arrived in Prince Rupert on Sunday after beating our way on the train from Mile 83. We left the lake on Thursday and arrived in Kalum Friday noon. Saturday morning we started to walk to Rupert through the snow but at Mile 83 we came across a train doing some work, and finding out that it was going to Rupert, we boarded it and defied the train crew to put us off. We got to Mile 46 on Saturday night and left the following noon . . .

May 21, 1911
We left Rupert for Kitsumkalum on May 3 and got to the lake two days later.

I went to work Friday for Thorn of the Dominion Telegraph and today, Sunday, we moved to Cedar River. The snow is not all gone from the ground yet but it is nearly so. The water in the river is not very high as yet but they expect a rise almost any time now. Although we are forty miles from town, we are not isolated by any means, as even now I can hear the tic-tic-tic of the telegraph instrument in the tent next to ours. What a grand life this life of the North is!

May 22, 1911
Second day at Cedar River and we are comfortably settled in our camping grounds with a big campfire roaring in front of the tent. I was cutting punching all day and after supper I helped the cook with his dishes. The first span of the bridge is complete and the approaches made. I expect the second span will be completed tomorrow. It is bedtime and for me, the Goddess of Slumber.

May 24, 1911
I am still at Cedar River and will be for a few days yet. I was to the cabin and back today—twenty-four miles—and I had quite a nice trip. I got three letters and half a dozen postcards—some mail! The first bridge is built across one fork of the river and the other fork will be bridged in a couple of days. The telegraph cabin is nearly finished so I guess I will be moving on soon. The weather is pretty warm now except in the early morning when we have a little frost. I saw a couple of grouse today and threw about fifty rocks at one of them before she finally flew away. Well, it is bedtime and I am going to turn in.

June 1, 1911

We moved camp yesterday and are now camped on a little creek about two-and-a-half miles from Cedar River . . . Today we saw a caribou in a little meadow—he was in pretty good shape and he stayed about twenty minutes after we first sighted him. Then he ran off.

There is a mine a few hundred yards from here. The timber through here is fairly good, especially the cedar and hemlock. There is one grand feature about this country—the water! It is excellent and there is plenty of it. Every few hundred yards one comes across a little stream and it is always fresh and cold. One never suffers from thirst in this section of BC!

We expect to strike Sand Lake in about a week, which is over the divide that separates the Nass Valley from the Kitsumkalum Valley. We will soon be in the Nass Valley.

June 5, 1911

Another move today. We are camped within a couple of miles of Sand Lake . . . One more move and we will be there. Two bears have been seen lately by fellows in the crew. The mosquitoes, the pest of the northern woods, are beginning to make their presence known. Tomorrow the teams go down after the canoe, which they will bring up to the lake. It is a big forty-foot canoe of Indian make—that is, it is a dugout. Pen running out of ink so will have to close for this time. Good night.

June 14, 1911

A few more days have rolled past and we are encamped on the banks of Lava Lake. It is a very picturesque lake, quite long but narrow. High bluffs surround it on all sides with here and there a few precipitous bluffs. Timber covers the sides down to the water's edge except where a rock slide has caused the timber to disappear. And in such places it leaves an ugly scar in the timber belt. In some places fire has visited the timber, leaving nothing but dead trees in its wake. Jack pine is the most predominant variety in this section and is of rather a scrubby kind.

Last Saturday we took a cruise from Sand Lake to the foot of Lava Lake to inspect the route of the telegraph line. We had a grand time even though it was a bit stringy paddling the thirty miles. In several places along the water's edge little streams came into the lake and some of these had pretty falls, one of which was particularly attractive. When we arrived at the foot of Lava Lake we had lunch and then looked over the large lava bed there. And also the Siwash cabin we found there. It contained some tools, a few traps and a prospector's outfit. We got back to camp about five o'clock. We were then camped on Gainor Lake. It was not a very large lake and had several rocky islands in it, on one of which was a Siwash lean-to and a small totem pole. There are quite a number of loons on the lake and every evening they used to raise quite a hubbub. There is an Indian notice up there warning white settlers to stay out of the Nass Valley.

June 20, 1911
It is raining but this is the first real rain we have had in a long time. So far we have had excellent weather with only an occasional shower to break the monotony. We are now camped at the foot of Lava Lake and it is a beautiful spot too. All up to the right is a high bluff with a creek emptying into the lake with a rush of white water churned so by the rocks in the creek bed. To the left across the lake is another high bluff with the timber partially burned off by some forest fire. Away up the lake can be seen several points of land jutting out for some distance into the lake. There is a large lava bed only a short distance from here. It is not very old and it is a rugged stretch of country with not a tree on it and only a little moss here and there. Every few feet huge piles of melted rock have been thrown up leaving a big mound. The length of the bed is about two miles.

We built a little log cabin on the lakeside today which is to be used as a refuge cabin for the linemen on this beat. There are several Nass Indians in camp now and a pretty good bunch of fellows they are. There are several more coming to work packing for the telegraph outfit. They are real interesting for describing different things around and in their Native villages, and explaining different things about their life. They seem to be able to talk fair English but of course their "l's" and their "r's" are not very plain. They all have very strong Asiatic features, even to the slant eyes.

June 27, 1911
Once more we have moved our camp and are now encamped about seven miles from Lava Lake near an old Siwash cabin. It has not rained any yet and we are suffering from an overdose of mosquitoes and black flies. Oh, this mosquito-bitten country would near drive a man crazy! There are a bunch of Indian women gathering cedar bark near here and they are great workers. They use the inside of the bark for making baskets and such things, also mats. There is an old Indian up here from Aiyansh with salmon which he sold to the outfit today. We are moving in the morning and we built a cabin this afternoon.

I got a telegram yesterday telling me about Ed Maughlin and Cecil Gaynor being on a survey party which was coming through to the Nass about August 1. I got three letters and a postcard the other day. I must write some letters tonight and send them to Aiyansh for mailing.

July 1, 1911
This is Dominion Day but in place of celebration we worked all day. We have moved since I last wrote and are now camped on a creek about nine miles from Aiyansh. We are passing through a most beautiful country—luxurious vegetation on every hand. In some places it is as high as a man's head and ranges from wild roses to wild strawberries . . . we had a few of these ripe strawberries . . . thimble berry blossoms, pigeon berry blossoms, pea vine blossoms, high bush cranberries and every other kind that one can think of, honeysuckles and Indian heads, twin berry blos-

soms. There are lots of poplar trees and white birch and alder grow on every hand. It is the beginning of the Nass Valley—one of the nicest valleys of the North. (I forgot to say that we were also eating wild onions. Hope they will not smell!)

Today we worked through a patch of heavy timber and then a patch of poplar and Jack pine. All at once we came out upon a bare place that was the edge of a high embankment overlooking the valley. What a sight met our gaze! Opened up before us was the entire Aiyansh Valley with the source of the Nass River away off in the distance. A low-lying ridge of mountains arose on one side of the valley with a higher ridge on the other. To the right of the scene is a high mountain peak with a smaller one on one side and a high hill on the other. A sea of green trees lies between where we were standing and these mountain peaks, with here and there the dry skeleton of a cedar or hemlock to mark the place where heavy timber once stood. The high peak occupies the centre of the picture and a white streak marks the course of a little rivulet down its side. The timber is a dark green with a lighter shade on one side. Away up near the summit is a bare burnt spot with windfalls scattered in piles, thrown in every which way, helter-skelter, regardless of order. White clouds hang low over the mountain tops shutting off the view of the higher peaks. Some snow still clings to the mountainsides and feeds the creeks as it melts, finally finding its way into the rivers and on to the ocean.

Tomorrow night we will reach the Nass River and the Indian village of Aiyansh, then fifteen miles beyond there, and the job will be finished and we will be returning to the Kitsumkalum Valley.

July 5, 1911
Rained today—in fact, it spilled down. Yesterday was the glorious Fourth of July. We did not work yesterday afternoon and as it was a beautiful day, we enjoyed ourselves immensely. I was wrestling with a young fellow named Duncan McGibbon and we sure did have some wrestling match!

We are now camped in Aiyansh, which is a little Indian village on the Nass River. The words "Indian village" may bring to one's mind a bunch of shacks, a dirty, ill-smelling place. Imagine our surprise then, when on coming into Aiyansh, we found a little village of well-built houses, some with cupolas and bay windows, most of them painted . . . also, sidewalks in good repair and a fine, big church. There is also a little sawmill.

There is another village, the Old Town, about a mile upriver. It has a nicer location than Aiyansh and is called Gitlakdamiks, which means "people of the damp ground." In Old Town there are about twenty totem poles, some of them very artistic. Some of these poles cost as much as $2,000. They are carved out of trees and painted each with a different motif. They are put up with great ceremony, which they call "Potlatch." The Indians have a story for each pole, one of which they told us today.

These poles, so they say, are used to push up Heaven. I really don't understand what they mean by this. Each tribe has a symbol, which no other tribe can use. One is a Wolf, one is a Bear, another the Crow and still another the Eagle. These Indians are chopping down their totem poles on account of becoming Christians. The rising generation do not take much stock in the old superstitions of their sires nor pay much attention to their legends and customs. They are remodelling Old Town, building a park and playgrounds, building sidewalks, tearing down old houses and putting up new ones in their places. The Nass River flows by both towns, affording a ready mode of transportation to the outside world.

The telegraph line now being put through to Stewart from Kitsumkalum touches Aiyansh in its route, thus forming another tie to the outside civilization. As soon as the trouble is settled between the Provincial Government and the Nass Indians, the valley, no doubt, will be flooded with settlers as it has a fine soil and climate and ought to make one of the finest farming valleys in the North.

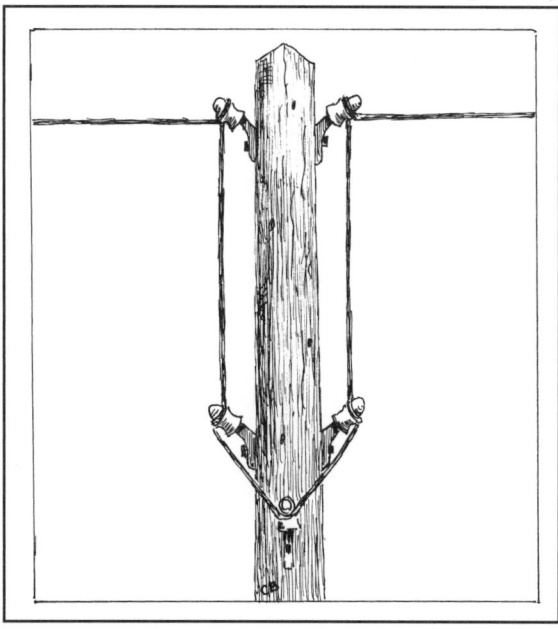

Test Pole (sketch by C. Braam).

July 11, 1911

It has been nearly a week since I wrote in this book. We have moved two or three times since then. We are now camped on a little lake about ten miles north of Aiyansh. We are moving nearly every day now. In a few more days the job will be finished. We have about eight miles yet to go . . .

July 19, 1911

Another week gone and with it comes the closing of this job. We have reached Blackstock's wire and tomorrow we will connect up with it. We will also move toward Aiyansh tomorrow. We have one little refuge cabin to build and we are through on this end of the line. We have been on a spite camp for four days and just got back this evening. We built one little cabin and a footbridge. The bridge was across Glacier Creek, a mountain stream, very swift and milky. I have no more to write tonight as the mosquitoes keep me too busy.

August 21, 1911

Over a month since I wrote anything, proving that the warm weather has enervated me, making me too lazy to write. A lot has happened since I last wrote . . .

We left Aiyansh on the twenty-first day of July, journeying down the Nass River in a large canoe of three ton's capacity. There were nineteen white men and six Indians in the canoe, a total of twenty-five, and each one had about forty pounds of baggage. So that would make in all, about two hundred pounds per man, average. The canoe was pretty heavily loaded and it was a top load at that.

Eight miles down the river from Aiyansh is a very dangerous canyon, caused by the lava which changed the entire course of the river, about three miles from its former bed. This canyon is the most dangerous place in the entire river and it is no wonder there have been several crafts wrecked in this canyon. There are two large blocks of lava at the mouth of the canyon and the water rushes against them with terrific force, causing the water to be thrown back again in a high wave or horsetail, as it is called, which is turned white by the impact. Between these two rocks is a narrow passage through which the canoes must pass in going up or down the river. And in this passage I got one of the most thrilling experiences of my life, although I was pretty scared at the time.

We dashed into this awful place of water with as much speed as it was possible to give the canoe with oars and paddles, everyone working. Our own force, helped along by the current, caused the canoe to fairly fly toward the rocks. Then when we were just opposite one of them, the water suddenly sank away from the canoe, leaving a large hole in the water alongside the canoe. Then is when I received the scare of my life. The canoe slammed into the hole and the next instant a large wave fell across the canoe, fully wetting most of us. But this was practically the end of the hazardous passage and we were once more out on the calm stretch of river below the canyon.

Just opposite the canyon were the remains of an old Indian village with its totem poles and old houses intact. I just had time to take a fleeting glance at this as we passed. The rain poured steadily down all day as we paddled down the long stretch of seventy-five miles of Nass River from Aiyansh, twisting and turning as it snakes its way through the pass between the mountains that tower on both sides of the river. We passed several Indian villages, old ones and new ones. Totem poles were numerous . . .

About 6:00 p.m. we arrived at a cannery at Mill Bay near the mouth of the river. Later we rowed down to Port Simpson, where we caught a steamer, the *Camosun*, to Prince Rupert, arriving on Sunday morning. After staying around Rupert for three days I finally caught a train going upriver and arrived at Kalum on Thursday, after a trip of 360 miles.

Since I got home I've been hunting a good deal and fishing more. Also I have been fighting fire, mushing and rowing, canoeing and sailing on the lake. I shot a big bald eagle, for which I apologize. I'm sorry. Lots of ducks and snipe and plover. Well, that's all for now . . .

September 9, 1911

I've been chasing trouble for the Dominion Government Telegraph since August 23. We are on the march every day; sometimes it is only a few miles and other times it is all the way from twenty to thirty miles. I just got back to Cedar River, the telegraph station today. It is the first time we have been in it for over a week. The wire has been broken a couple of times so we had to find and repair the breaks. Only a few more days and I will be leaving for the States. On our way home today we shot three pheasants and a porcupine. It is very easy to get fresh meat here in the late summer and fall . . .

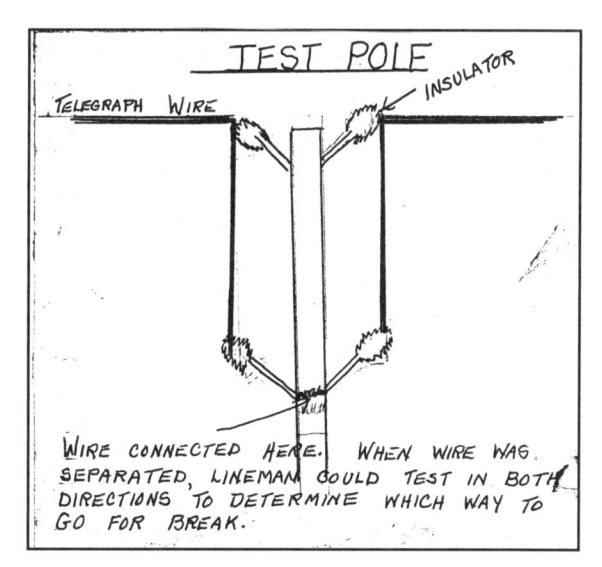

Test Pole (sketch by R. Ross).

Further Notes by Robert Ross

The so-called refuge cabins were small log cabins probably about ten by fourteen feet. We built them to be seven to ten miles apart. Sometimes there was already a small cabin—an Indian or a prospector's cabin—that we could use instead of building another, as it was located in the right spot.

The telegraph cabin at Cedar River was a much larger one than the refuge cabins as it would be a permanent telegraph office. It would be completely furnished with cooking utensils, etc., whereas the refuge cabins had no furniture or things to cook with. Of course the refuge cabins were for saving life in case someone was caught out in a severe storm. There was wood in the cabins at all times, and although one might have to swallow a little smoke, it would be better than being outdoors to freeze to death. I figure we built half a dozen refuge cabins, and the Siwash cabins and other small buildings were used in addition to that.

A lineman's duty, principally, was to keep the line open. If the line was broken in some place he had to find the break and repair it. He had something to help him locate the break. Every mile or two, during the building of the telegraph lines, they put in what was called a testing pole. They ran the wire down from the top of the pole in two layers and connected them at the bottom, so when the lineman came along to locate a break, he unfastened the bottom and checked in with the office in either Kalum or Stewart. If he checked through and couldn't get Kalum, he knew he would have to go farther south in order to find the break. He would go to the next test pole and perform the same operation again—separate the wires and check them. If this time he could get Kalum but couldn't get Stewart, he knew that between those two poles was the break, which he could now find and repair.

He travelled on foot—he didn't have any other means of transportation than Shank's Mare. Sometimes he had to go many miles before he finally found the break. In fact, during the time I was there, some prospector went through and failed to put out the fire he was cooking with and we had five fires along the forty-mile stretch we had to cover. In places there would be forty or fifty trees that had fallen across the line and the only way we could repair that was to cut the line and pull the loose ends out from underneath the trees and fasten them together again. This way it saved a lot of time and then when we did have time, we could remove the fallen trees. Of course in the winter the lineman travelled on snowshoes, but the snow didn't last too long so he was fortunate in that respect.

One of the refuge cabins, I remember, was on the south end of our line at the foot of Kitsumkalum Lake where there was a large government cabin that had been built some years before. At Aiyansh we didn't need a refuge cabin because there were plenty of Indian cabins there to house anyone who got caught out in a storm.

One of the peculiarities we noticed in Aiyansh was that the houses, though most of them were painted and were really so-called modern in design, always seemed to have something lacking—a few boards missed here or there, a porch not completely finished, a window not in, or something of that sort. I don't know whether it was a superstition or whether it was a minor oversight. Anyway, that is the way I remember it and how I particularly noted it.

The little sawmill, I think, was a kind of co-operative affair. The Indians cut their lumber and whoever wanted lumber helped themselves to it. I don't think it was ever sold to outsiders and most of it was for building houses.

I will tell a little story about one of the totem poles at Gitlakdamiks, as the Indians told it to me. They said that one of their tribe had started out for Hazelton, across the river and over the mountain. It was to be a three or four-day journey. While he was on the trail through the woods—not a trail really, but marked so the Indians would know where to go—about the second night out he lay down to sleep. Something woke him up in the early morning and he saw a white man coming toward him, very carefully picking his way so as not to make any noise. The Native was frightened at such a thing and got his rifle and shot the man. He buried him, then instead of going on to Hazelton he went back to Gitlakdamiks. He was so remorseful about shooting a man without ever inquiring what his purpose was, that he erected a short totem pole about ten feet high to atone for the killing. I don't know how true that was, but it is the way it was told to me.

Henry Percival Rutter, a native of Cornwall, England, born December 1886, was an early surveyor of the interior of British Columbia (1910–1914). Although Rutter and Robert Ross knew each other, they did not work together (Ross was a lineman). Strangely, Rutter's pictures in many instances parallel Ross's narrative—place names, etc. They work well separately, and together.

A Pictorial Diary by Henry Percival Rutter

♦ submitted by Margaret Bartlett, Terrace, BC

Entering Prince Rupert.

♦ The Talking Wire ♦

View of Hazelton.

Steamer Hazelton at the head of Kitselas Canyon.

Left: Camp opposite Hazelton.

Right: Steamer Hazelton in Kitselas Canyon.

♦ 115 ♦

Left: Breaking up camp.

Right: Sunday in camp.

Moving camp.

One-and-a-half tons of grub.

♦ The Talking Wire ♦

The survey party, Kitsumkalum, June 1911.

Left: Kitsumkalum Lake.

Right: Coming home from work, Sand Lake.

♦ 117 ♦

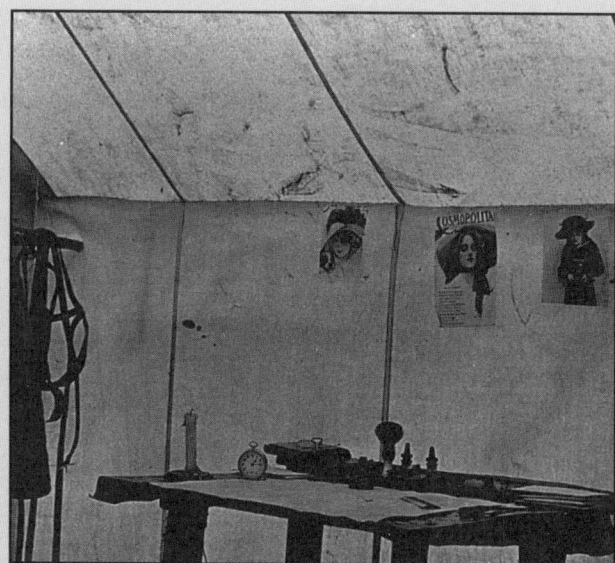

Left: Henry Percival Rutter, early surveyor of the interior of British Columbia.

Right: The survey office, 1911.

Indian protest document.

INDIAN PROTEST

AGAINST WHITE SETTLERS COMING INTO THE AIYANSH VALLEY, NAAS RIVER, BRITISH COLUMBIA.

WHEREAS, we, the Indian people of the above mentioned valley, being the lawful and original inhabitants and possessors of all the lands contained therein from time immemorial; and being assured in our possession of the same by the proclamation of His Majesty, King George III, under date of 7th October, 1763, which proclamation we hold as our Charter of Rights under the British Crown;

AND WHEREAS, it is provided in the said proclamation that no private person do presume to make any purchase from us of any lands so reserved to us until we shall have ceded the same to the representatives of the Crown in public meeting between us and them;

AND WHEREAS, up to the present time our lands have not been ceded by us to the Crown, nor in any way alienated from us by any agreement or settlement between the representatives of the Crown and ourselves;

AND WHEREAS, our case is now before the Privy Council in England and we are expecting a settlement of the difficulty at present existing between ourselves and the Government of this Province at an early date;

WE DO THEREFORE, standing well within our constitutional rights, forbid you to stake off land in this valley, and do hereby protest against your proceeding further into our country with that end in view—until such time as a satisfactory settlement be made between the representatives of the Crown and ourselves.

ISSUED by the members of the Indian Land Committee elected by the Indians of the Upper Naas.

Signed: J. K. FLYAWAY, J. R. BADWEATHHR, Git-lak-damiks.
S. A. ZEEDAWIT, A. M. NAHNEIGH, J. NAKMAUZ, Aiyansh.
AMOS G. NEESGWAKSAW, SAMUEL WEESHAKES, JOHNNY O'YEA, Gwinoha.
Dated at Aiyansh, British Columbia, this 17th day of May, 1910.

♦ The Talking Wire ♦

Left: Gitlacdamix on the Naas River.

Right: Naas River camp.

Party on the Naas River, October 1911.

Left: Looking toward the Naas Valley from camp on Cedar River.

Right: View of the Naas Valley.

♦ 119 ♦

♦ Pioneer Legacy ♦ Volume II ♦

Aiyansh, Naas River, 1911

Caught in the ice at mouth of the Naas River.

Mill Bay Cannery at mouth of the Naas River.

Left: Crew on lava beds, Naas Valley.

Right: November 18, 1911, newspaper story, "Missing Party Arrives by SS Venture."

PRINCE RUPERT, B.C., SATURDAY, NOVEMBER 18, 1911.

MISSING PARTY ARRIVES BY S.S. VENTURE

Thirty-five Surveyors and Timber Cruisers Many Days Overdue on Naas—Had an Adventurous Trip by Trail and Canoe.

By the Venture today arrived the survey party of thirty-five sent out in the early summer by Messrs. Gore & McGregor of Victoria, which has been anxiously awaited at various points on the Naas for ten days or more.

During the long wait on the Naas River, owing to the impossibility of getting boat communicatiok with Mill Bay, the party ate out their grub supplies and were reduced to Indian fare of hard tack and dried salmon. The whole party came down the Naas with Indian pilots in three large dugouts, but when the flow of ice grew thicker the Indians refused to go farther than Greenville, and here the party had to wait.

Against the advice of the Indians H. P. Rutter, Chief of the party, with B. Stirling, A. Fraser, A. Stormerson and E. Mauchline took canoe and endeavored to make Mill Bay. This party was five days missing from the rest of the party and was almost given up for lost. They experienced icy weather in the open dugout and had a perilous passage down the Naas.

The others were brought to Mill Bay by the launch Shrimp which managed to make the trip, and got aboard the Venture none the worse of their experience.

♦ 120 ♦

♦ The Talking Wire ♦

Totem pole at Gitlacdamix.

Lava Bed at north end of Lava Lake.

Christmas Day on the Government Telegraph Line

♦ Walter Warner (from the Terrace *Omineca Herald*)

It snowed the day before Christmas. I had gone to bed after saying the "Lineman's Prayer." In case you don't know it, it asks the Lord for a calm night—not to let the wind blow the timber down.

Christmas morning—line OK to Terrace but gone out north between Rosswood and Aiyansh. That settled it. I was on my way as soon as I made my pack up. Joe Belway's brother was here so I went to see if he could go with me. OK, but he had never mushed with snowshoes.

Cobb had been down with the beam the day before, so there was a fine trail broken for about three miles north and that helped some. As soon as we passed that part of the road, we had not gone but a few hundred yards when my companion gave up and said he could not make it. So I wished him a Merry Christmas and told him to go back as the snow was deep and hard going. I would have gone back too, but could not as the

Winter on the telegraph line. (65-C)

show had to go on. All those north of the break were cut off on Christmas, too, and no Christmas messages could get through. I made for a cabin thirteen miles north and camped there for the night. This was not a telegraph cabin, it was a mining cabin. The claims were closed but, oh boy, I think all the mice in the country had gathered there for Christmas! I had a candle, found one of those jump traps, baited it, then stayed awake the rest of the night taking them out of the trap and setting it again. It sure was good trapping.

I had my dog, Tarzan, along, and crossing the Cedar River a grouse flew up. I had a small six-gun and knocked its head off. There was my Christmas dinner, that is, if I got there on time. Tarzan was not a bird dog so there was a race to run. He liked to eat them, feathers and all, but I was lucky—I got it. I fried it for supper. Tarzan got the bones.

I got out as soon as it was light enough to travel and found the break about three miles north. I hooked the field phone on between the loose ends and got Aiyansh. Oh boy, was I tickled to hear his voice! I put in a splice and started back as I had only thirteen miles to go. As I had broken the trail one way, it was not so bad. I reached home after dark. The snowshoe strings were dragging and I was some tired, as the tools, etc., I had to pack weighed fifty pounds. I had a bath and a glorious supper, then a good hot Christmas drink, something like they used to give out in the navy — that stuff that would make a rabbit spit in a bulldog's face.

After a day's rest, I was ready to go again. Some months I made three hundred miles. No wonder my legs are worn out. Next job I get will be with a wireless outfit!

Note on the author: His stories of the early days when he traversed the old telegraph trail to the Nass River will long be remembered . . . In 1920 he was telegraph operator, travelling by foot, in all kinds of weather, from Rosswood to the Nass River . . .

—*Omineca Herald*

ON HIS MAJESTY'S SERVICE – THE MAIL SERVICE

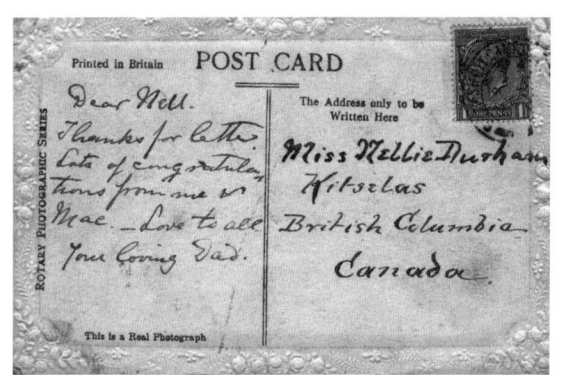

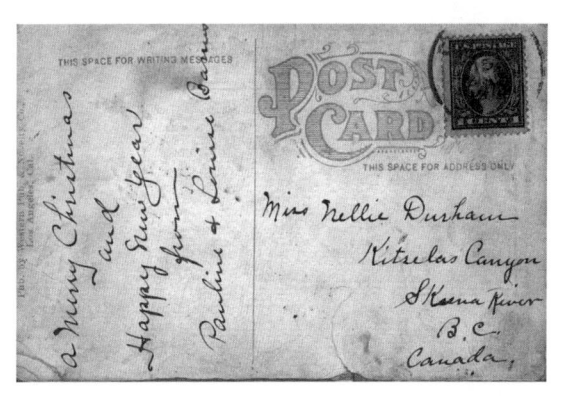

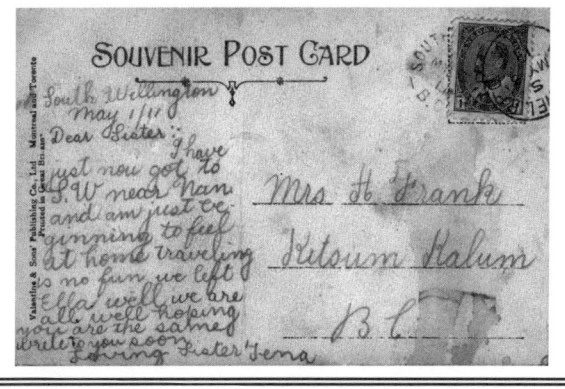

♦ On His Majesty's Service–The Mail Service ♦

The need for communication amongst humans is a very basic one. Whether the method be smoke signals, drumbeats, runners or pony express depends on the time in history and the means available. Once the knowledge of writing became widespread, the need increased, with speed and volume becoming important factors.

Anyone who has ever lived in a remote area for any length of time will recall the excitement and eager anticipation with which whole communities awaited the arrival of The Mail. These few stories from the past recount some of the difficulties encountered in the delivery of mail in our own area and highlight the attitudes of the old-time mail carriers in a way that can only redound to their credit.

Pulling a heavy load of mail ashore near Hazelton. (72)

Date Capsule 7

1891—Sternwheelers speeded up river service, in season. Dog teams could not always operate on the lower Skeena due to ice and heavy snow.
1898—Henry Frank commissioned to open up a trail between Kitimat and the Skeena, at a point near the present site of Terrace, to facilitate mail delivery by dog team in winter.
1906—Post office established in Kitselas; J.W. Patterson first postmaster.

Sternwheelers carried mail in the summer. Pictured is SS Inlander *in Kitselas Canyon. (12-C)*

1908—Post office established at Eby's Store in Kitsumkalum; Ed Eby, postmaster.

1909—Post office opened at Copper River (first called Dobbie's Landing); this was closed in February 1956.

1910—Post office opened at Meanskinisht under the new name "Cedarvale." Mrs. J.W. Graham appointed postmistress.

1912—Post office opened in Terrace; George Little, postmaster.

1912—Post office opened at Rosswood. Mail sorted in Terrace and packed to Rosswood in sealed sacks. Closed 1917. Named after family of first postmistress, Annie Ross.

1913—Post office opened at Lakelse Lake; closed 1917. Reopened 1934; closed 1935. This was the first post office on the Dogteam Trail. It is believed that the mail was originally left at Mailbox Point, across the lake. That destined for distribution from the Lodge Post Office was then taken over there.

SS Port Simpson *arriving at Hazelton. (25A)/BCARS 4943*

Oldest Mail Carrier Blazed Trail in 1900

♦ Stan Rough (from the Terrace *Omineca Herald*)

Eighty-three-year-old Philip Sutton of Cedarvale vividly remembers carrying the mail from Hazelton on the upper Skeena to the village of Kitimat, 140 miles southwest on the Kitimat Arm of the Douglas Channel, from 1900 to 1903.

During the navigation season on the Skeena, the mail was carried from Hazelton to Port Essington—then a flourishing town near the river's mouth—by two-ton freight canoes manned by a crew of five, and by sternwheeler riverboats.

When the river froze over and navigation ceased, the Dominion government awarded Robert Tomlinson Sr. of Meanskinisht (or the Holy City, as Cedarvale was then called) the contract to carry the mail down the Skeena to Kitselas by dog team and then overland to Kitimat Mission, where it was picked up by coastal steamer.

Dog mushers on the Skeena. (71)

Mail leaving Kitselas. (41-C)

Robert Tomlinson was the son of the famous Reverend Robert Tomlinson, a medical missionary who broke with the Church of England and in 1887, with a number of followers from Kitwanga, founded a village twelve miles downriver, under the shadows of the Seven Sisters mountain peaks.

Tomlinson and Sutton blazed an overland trail from Copper City to Kitimat and used the frozen Skeena whenever possible from Kitselas to Hazelton. They made one trip a month from November to April and were paid fifty dollars a trip.

They carried fifty pounds of mail on a toboggan pulled by two or more dogs. Under ideal conditions the trip took four days. The men stopped overnight at Lorne Creek, Kitselas, the north end of Lakelse and at William Brown's cabin on the flats beside the Kitimat River.

They borrowed Brown's boat and took the mail over to the Kitimat Post Office, which was operated by the trader and storekeeper, George Robinson, grandfather of Gordon Robinson, chief councillor of Kitimat Village.

From there they picked up the return mail and returned to Hazelton, distributing it at villages and mining camps on the way back.

Using snowshoes in the snow areas, they at times took ten or more days to make the trip. They carried a revolver to shoot small game to supplement their rations of bacon, beans, rice, smoked salmon and bannock.

They also carried a tent and a pole to test ice conditions on the trail. If they could not make their regular night stops, they camped by the side of the trail, spread their blankets on boughs inside the tent, banked it with snow outside and lit their fire nearby.

For clothing they wore heavy woollens and carried a slicker for wet weather.

Other Cedarvale men who were on the mail run with Tomlinson while he had the contract were J. Mulwain and S. Morgan.

Sperry (Dutch) Cline

♦ Wiggs O'Neill (thanks to Katie O'Neill)

I first met Dutch Cline about the winter of 1907 when he was engaged in carrying the mail from Hazelton to tidewater on the Skeena River by dog team for the firm of Beirnes and Mulvaney. He and another man were in charge of one outfit each week while George Beirnes was in charge himself of the alternate week's mail.

I had heard of Cline a few years before, but I had never met him personally. I used to meet the mail teams at the head of tidewater and take the mail down the rest of the way to Port Essington to connect with R. Cunningham & Son's tugboat, *Chieftain*, which delivered the mail to the post office at Prince Rupert.

One of the mail carriers always accompanied the mail en route, both ways on the trip from and to the post office, between Hazelton and Rupert. This was Dutch Cline's job during the winter for three or four years, but he was employed during the summer months in the Hazelton district on various other jobs. He was very efficient at his work owing to his good savvy and know-how and was never stuck at making things go. Efficiency was his strong point.

Arriving at Eby's Landing with the mail. (1-B)

The Mail Went Through

♦ Sperry Cline (from the Terrace *Omineca Herald*)

After the Kitimat, Hazelton & Omineca Railway was bonded in the early 1900s and the Grand Trunk Pacific from Prince Rupert was accepted, a great change took place along the Skeena River.

With the start of construction work, facilities for travel were established at the mouth of the river. Our old friend, Wiggs O'Neill of Smithers, started a gas-boat service between Port Essington and Telegraph Point, thus enabling travellers to negotiate that part of the river, which had been impassable during the winter months. Many tales could be told of his struggles with tides, gales, ice floes and snowstorms, but the redoubtable Wiggs always got through and maintained a reliable service. Consequently, our mail route was now from Hazelton to Telegraph Point by dog team, then to Port Essington by O'Neill's boat service, then on to Prince Rupert by a daily boat between these points.

With construction work starting again, workmen were brought in by the hundreds. They were mostly from the Balkan countries, while office staff and foremen were mostly Highland Scottish, with a sprinkling of other nationalities.

Together with this influx of railway workers came hundreds of others, forming a cross-section of humanity. There were men with a set purpose and grimly determined to establish themselves in a new land. Such men as the late George Little of Terrace and Frank Dockrill of Telkwa, who clung to their constructive ideas through wars and depressions and finally realized their dreams. Settlers, some with families, willing to face years of austerity and toil to make a home, took up homesteads.

Rugged prospectors flocked in, in search of the end of the rainbow. Some of them succeeded. There were boomers looking for an opportunity to make quick money in any business venture that might present itself. Tinhorn gamblers and denizens of the underworld, who located temporarily wherever there was a congestion of population and were always ready to move on to new locations, followed in good numbers. Also a number of that type of old country man coming to the West about the turn of the century had more than a passing interest in the arrival of mail from overseas.

We of the mail service knew them all. After the close of river navigation, we were their only connection with the outside during the long winter months.

The amount of mail being handled increased rapidly. Besides the government contract there was the Grand Trunk Pacific mail service, which the company was responsible for. This service they let to Beirnes and Mulvaney on a per capita basis, which increased our work considerably.

We soon realized that we were being looked to, to perform other

Skeena River mail team, 1910. In the picture are Barney Mulvaney, George Beirnes, "Smithy" and Dunc McGibbon. (22-B)

duties. Persons in urgent need of some article that they could not purchase locally would commission us to make a purchase at the coast and deliver to same. This increased until the contractors found it necessary to organize an express service. This not only put additional responsibility onto the drivers but also led to certain incidents that I will try to describe later.

Our efforts to oblige were usually appreciated, but as I have said, there was a great variety of people to be considered, and sometimes misunderstandings occurred. A spool of thread not the exact shade of material shown at the time of placing their order was evidence of carelessness. A rise in the price of an article since a former purchase proved dishonesty, and a failure to obtain a desired article after an exhaustive search of all the stores at the coast was incompetence.

As the population increased, more frequent deliveries were demanded until we were delivering two mails per week at Hazelton. The amount of mail had also increased until it required several teams per trip. At peak there were at least seven dog teams engaged on the river, and as the need was felt for an increase in service, Ottawa would be requested to make the increase, and usually responded promptly.

One incident in this connection now seems to be rather amusing but at the time caused considerable trouble. As there was no official body such as the board of trade in the country, a town meeting was called. A chairman and secretary were duly appointed and the object of the meeting put before the assembly in the proper parliamentary manner. A resolution was passed asking the postal officials for a biweekly mail, and we soon received a reply that such service was granted. When the new schedule arrived there was considerable consternation among the village Solons, and it took several exchanges of telegrams between Hazelton and Ottawa to convince the postal department that what had been requested was a semi-weekly mail.

To look after all these activities, Beirnes, staying at Hazelton, would attend to such matters as purchasing of dogs and equipment, hiring drivers, etc. One driver would be in charge of each outfit, which would consist of from two to four teams, and it was in this capacity that I was engaged. On the downriver runs the teams would go on to Prince Rupert while the other drivers would remain in charge of the dogs.

Sacks of registered mail were supposed to receive particular attention but there was really very little that we could do in that respect. I usually took the registered sack from the toboggan at night and when stopping at construction camps, would simply throw it into the bunk that I was assigned to for the night.

There was never any attempt to meddle with these registered sacks and now I often think it strange that such was the case as everyone knew that they contained valuables. On one occasion, after delivery at the Foley, Welch & Stewart head office at Sealy, I learned that the sack had contained over twenty thousand dollars in currency. I think now that we must have either been very lucky, or the people on the Skeena River at that time were a mighty fine lot.

> CORRECTION ON MAIL ITEM JANUARY 16, 1909
>
> Letter to the Editor:
>
> Messrs. Beirnes and Curran who had the contract for the winter of 1906–07, left Kitimat March 24, 1907, and made the trip from there to Little Canyon in 2½ days, and made the trip from Little Canyon to Hazelton in another 2½ days, or the total distance from Kitimat to Hazelton in 5 days, including all stops. As the distance between Hazelton and Little Canyon is about 10 miles greater than from Hazelton to Kitselas, and as the present sleigh road between Kitimat and the Skeena was not then built, you will probably agree that the record established in 1907 has not yet been endangered.
>
> —A Subscriber

RMS Dog Team–Kitimat to Hazelton

♦ from *Northwest Digest*, July 1956

It is interesting to note that the small settlement of Kitimat was years ago slated as the terminus of a railroad.

In 1890 C.W.D. Clifford, who was at that time manager of the Hudson's Bay Company at Fort Simpson, promoted a company to build a railway from Kitimat to the Omineca country. This was called the "Kitimat & Omineca Railway." They obtained a charter from the government and promoted a townsite at Kitimat and sold lots.

The members of the company were mostly old-timers in the country and included J.M.L. Alexander; John Flewin, government agent; Patsy Callaghan, Omineca placer miner; Charles Kendall, Kitselas prospector; and many others.

Later on, when the Grand Trunk Pacific Railway built west, the company took an option on the Kitimat company and did some grading on the south bank of the Skeena near Copper River to enable them to hold the charter. They were also considering the "Outlet" at Kitimat as a possible terminus when word came through from the authorities to push on downriver to the coast and Kaien Island, and what is now the seaport of Prince Rupert.

So, although Kitimat's railway did not materialize in either case, the boom caused at the time resulted in that post becoming an important headquarters for the Omineca winter mail service. Of course, during the summer schedule the sternwheelers handled all the mail between Port Simpson and Hazelton.

Also, there were two short seasons—early spring and late fall—when Indian canoes and crack pilots took over. These trips were dangerous because those men had to contend with spring freshets and later, ice floes—and most of the upstream trip was done by lining and poling. For a number of years Samuel Bright, father of Mrs. Philip Sutton of Meanskinisht, was considered the finest Native pilot in the mail service and long will be remembered as such.

Then during the long winter months the old coastal steamers *Boscowitz*, *Danube* and *Tees* called in at Kitimat on their bimonthly trips and dropped the interior mail. There the bags were loaded onto usually three different dog teams for the long trek to Hazelton.

The teams mushed up through the Lakelse Valley over an old Indian trail and headed for the Skeena, a distance of thirty-seven miles. Camp was pitched at Copper River before they took to the frozen river to travel the hundred miles to their destination. The entire trip usually took from fourteen to twenty days, depending on weather and ice conditions.

The points of call included Skinners and Stuart landings, Kitselas Canyon, Lorne Creek and the Indian missions of Kitwanga (meaning "home of the rabbit"), Meanskinisht (meaning "at the foot of the pitch pine") and Andimaul before reaching Hazelton. There the mail was received by R.S. Sargent, veteran postmaster and fur trader.

The dogs of the RMS teams were mostly of the malamute and husky breed and it required strict and experienced drivers to handle those ferocious mongrels. Their rations consisted mainly of a half a dried salmon daily, fed at the end of the day's travel.

The Tomlinson brothers, Robert and Richard of Meanskinisht, were expert drivers and often had the Kitimat contract. The fellows were brought up in the "wild and woolly North" and were familiar with its primitive mode of life. Consequently they could tackle anything in the way of hard work.

Government mail teams leaving Kitsumkalum. (65-C)

They were experts at handling Indians and dogs, knew how to rough it and could speak several Indian dialects. Their trips were so timed that the telegraph operators along the way could almost set their clocks by their arrival.

It was on one of these trips with the dog teams camped for the night at Kitselas Canyon that H.N. (Hank) Boss, telegraph operator, learned of one of the largest hot springs in North America situated at Lakelse Lake, along the mail route. Later a party of surveyors from Kitimat reported how they had caught fish through the ice in the lake and had boiled them in a large sugar sack for supper. That was in 1906. Hank became interested and staked the property surrounding the hot pool. The hot water proved to be of valuable mineral content so three years later, he and his partner, J. Bruce Johnstone, erected a rustic tourist and hunting lodge. They piped hot water into baths and for twenty years accommodated the public, until fire destroyed the lodge in 1929.

The lodge was the first post office on the Dogteam Trail, seventeen miles out of Kitimat. Mail day was a great event. Prospectors, trappers, settlers and the staff of the old Dominion Fish Hatchery (across the lake) congregated at the lodge for letters, news and the latest word from "outside."

Finally, with the increased activity along the "Skeena right-of-way," the mail became so heavy that Kitimat service was suspended and the dog teams routed through to the edge of the ice at the Skeena's mouth, which was then the nearest approach to Prince Rupert.

Lyster B. (Barney) Mulvaney (now judge at Burns Lake) had the mail contract. He was a strapping and fiery young Irishman of untiring energy and his ready wit made him popular all along the way. His assistants were such men as Pete Curran, George Beirnes and Patsy Burns—all worthy pioneers. At the peak of their activities they maintained a reserve of 125 dogs. The upriver teams met the downriver teams, loads were exchanged and each turned back over his respective run. Skinner Landing was a most important distribution headquarters for dogs, supplies and equipment.

The launch *Strongheart*, owned by Capt. W.J. (Wiggs) O'Neill, now of Smithers, contacted the dog teams near tidewater and rushed the mail into Prince Rupert, a distance of forty-odd miles. There, the mail was signed for by the postmaster, the late R.L. McIntosh of Prince Rupert.

The veteran postmaster had been for several years handling the Omineca mail through Port Essington during the period of navigation on the Skeena River. He landed at Prince Rupert, his new post, in the fall of 1906, shortly after J.H. Bacon and his engineers took up their quarters in tents and shacks. The mail was then light. But three years later when the dog teams went into action, all hands, including the bishop, turned out to assist with the sorting.

Mr. McIntosh held the position of Prince Rupert's first postmaster until his official retirement, and still he and Mrs. McIntosh continued to make their home there, with a summer home at Kitsumkalum. There they were happy in meeting old friends and reminiscing about pioneer days when dog teams and boats figured so prominently in those "good old days."

The *Omineca Herald* Reports

August 29, 1908
Postmaster Sargent (Hazelton) has been authorized by the postal authorities to have the mail now lying at Kitselas brought to Hazelton by canoe. This will be done as soon as arrangements can be made. Until some means are secured to have the mail taken from the Canyon to Essington, the mail will not be sent from Hazelton as it is considered to be just as well off here as it would be lying in the post office at Kitselas.

September 5, 1908
Posters are up calling for bids for carrying the mail between Hazelton and Kitimat during the time navigation is closed. Tenders asked for semi-monthly service, 200 pounds of mail to be delivered at Hazelton each trip. Mail for waypoints is limited to 75 pounds. This is just about the same service as last year's. Assurances were received that we would have an improved service the coming winter. Letters from department officials stated that a weekly service was to be granted, quantity unlimited except that fourth-class matter would not be carried. If the contract is let according to the proposed terms, outside papers with a November date will be received next May and the first boat up the river in the spring will measure cargo in tons.

November 7, 1908
The winter mail contract between Hazelton and Kitimat has been let to Charles Sterrett, who has been with J.H. Gray, the surveyor, at Ootsa Lake. Until he can reach here and assume charge, arrangements are being made for others to handle the mail at his expense. The last mail to reach Hazelton from the coast left Vancouver about October 10, so that quite a stack is now at Port Essington. The Tomlinson brothers of Meanskinisht left for Port Essington the middle of the week and expect to arrive in Hazelton about November 14 with 1,000 pounds of mail.

November 14, 1908
Herb Hankin is making one trip down the river after the mail and left Hazelton this morning. With the present trip Kitimat becomes the port at which mail for the interior will be left by the coast steamers instead of Port Essington.

Robert Tomlinson of Meanskinisht arrived with mail about noon today, after making a remarkably quick trip from Port Essington, considering the time of year. Mr. Tomlinson and two Indians started from Port Essington at 10:30, November 7, with 25 sacks of mail for Hazelton and waypoints. Hole-in-the-Wall was passed the first day, and camp was made the second night at Bateman's Landing. Andimaul, 20 miles down the river from Hazelton, was passed at 9:00 a.m. Friday. Fourteen sacks of mail were left at waypoints and with the eleven brought through, nearly cleared the pile that has been accumulating at Port Essington for the past month.

FROM THE TERRACE OMINECA HERALD

Helen Durham (Adams) acted as postmistress during the time her father, Charles Durham, was postmaster at Kitselas. She laughingly recalls how impressed she was at her own "swearing in"—she was only fourteen years old! She remembers, too, the hassle to get the mail sack down to the track on time so she could place it on the hook suspended from the stanchion-like contrivance provided for that purpose. A metal "arm" from the mail coach could then snaffle it off the hook as the train went by without even coming to a full stop. The incoming mail for Kitselas was thrown off the mail car in a sealed bag. It was small enough for Helen to handle by herself.

November 28, 1908
The mail canoe with Herb Hankin in charge arrived at Kitselas on Wednesday.

January 2, 1909
Word has just been received that a contract has been let for the carrying of a fortnightly mail between Kitimat and points en route to Kitselas, including Lake Lakelse, Copper City, Little Canyon, Kitsumkalum and Kitselas. The installing of this service will greatly increase the amount of mails arriving at this point from the coast, as previous to this, the couriers carrying mail between here and the outside included the mail for the above-mentioned points covered by the new contract in the stipulated weight to be carried each trip between here and Kitimat.

January 16, 1909
The incoming mail arrived Sunday evening after the quickest trip from Kitselas that has been made in the history of the river. The carriers left the Canyon Saturday morning, and covered the distance to Hazelton, 80 miles, in 36 hours, including all stops.

January 1910
On the average, 6,000 letters are received at the PO here each month from outside points, while the number of letters mailed in the same time is nearly 4,000. During the last half of 1909 the money orders issued and paid in the office totalled $42,075. The first steamboat up the river last spring carried over 50 sacks of mail for this office. This large amount had accumulated during the winter, being the excess over the maximum weight of 400 pounds a month which the mail contract provides for. This winter even a larger amount is accumulating at Prince Rupert and if no relief is granted, there will be an enormous amount of overdue mail to come up when navigation opens.

Beirnes and Mulvaney, in addition to the government mail contract, have undertaken to carry mail between Prince Rupert and the various construction camps along the Skeena.

January 22, 1910
WHO IS TO BLAME?
Another week is gone and still no answer has been received to the demands for an adequate mail service. Whether this is so because departmental officials and our representative in the Commons intentionally ignore the telegrams or whether they are answering by mail, the new result is the same; there will be no increase, either in amount or frequency of our present service.

It has been pointed out before now that our present service is actually less in amount than that received in 1908–09, as then two special trips were allowed of 400 pounds each, double the contracted quantity. This year we have only 200 pounds twice a month, with the first trip omitted entirely.

Population and mount of business are increasing at a rapid rate and out of all proportion to the facilities provided by our post office depart-

---

The Omineca Herald, September 3, 1910, reports:

The post office rightly prefers Native to the usual "umshewa" names for new post offices, but from the fact that Meanskinisht is become Cedarvale and Kitsumkalum is to be known as Hemlock, it is a pretty good bet that our old friend Kitseguecla is going to get the axe, when the time comes. Those are surely three mouth-filling names, good ones too, but the department will never be criticized for not retaining any of them.

ment. The entire winter mail service last year, between Kitimat and Hazelton, cost the country less than $4,000. The cost of the summer service is not known but should be slight.

January 29, 1910
Arrivals from Prince Rupert say that the post office there recently notified Vancouver not to send any more excess mail for Hazelton there unless a warehouse were built to receive it, as they have 200 sacks already and no room for more.

William Templeman, cabinet minister and member for Comox-Atlin, tells us the postmaster-general has ordered a weekly mail service to Hazelton. Just when it is to commence the people are not informed, but it is hoped that the service will be installed soon enough to be of some benefit this winter.

February 5, 1910
The first trip of the new weekly mail service, outside the regular trips George Beirnes has been making every two weeks, will arrive in Hazelton about next Thursday. Next downriver mail will close Tuesday evening.

February 26, 1910
George Beirnes announces a regular schedule from now until the boats start running. Mail will leave Hazelton every Wednesday morning and arrive on Thursdays.

April 9, 1910
In spite of storms, thaws and overflows our mail has been delivered by Beirnes and Mulvaney with a regularity not considered possible. Many people have remarked lately that our winter mail service, except for the quantity delivered and for which the mail contractors are not responsible, is better than the service rendered during the summer months with the steamers running. People advocating an alternative route for winter mail have claimed the Skeena is impassable for a time in spring when the ice is breaking up. If it is, the carriers have achieved the impossible in delivering a mail at Hazelton every week.

May 14, 1910
Eighty-two sacks of belated mail, mostly newspapers, arrived by the first two boats up the river.

August 27, 1910
At the start of the navigation season the department gave a contract for carrying mail on the Skeena to the Hudson's Bay Company with the understanding that deliveries were to be made at Hazelton twice a week. That is, they had two boats on the river and each one would make a trip weekly. They were not tied down to any particular day. Their remuneration was to be $150 a week. Things went well until one of the boats was diverted to the Stikine, leaving only the *Hazelton* as the mail carrier. Some weeks go

---

At the time when letter carrier service was inaugurated in Terrace, the speaker representing the Honourable Eric Kierans, postmaster general, expounded on the early beginnings of the postal system in this town: "In 1912 George Little opened his sawmill. Indeed George Little must be conceded a large share of the credit for laying the foundation of Terrace's first industrial boom. One of his important contributions—and it has a direct bearing on our purpose here today—was the building of a lean-to on the north side of his general store to provide space for the first Terrace post office. According to departmental records in Ottawa, George Little was your first postmaster. He was appointed on the first of January, 1912, and served until the twenty-second of April, 1931. I was amused to learn that the revenue of the office for the first year of operation was $55.00. Mr. Little's salary, based on revenue was $8.75—a handsome sum indeed."

It is interesting to note that starting before the First World War, quite a settlement grew up around Kitsumkalum Lake, with possibly twenty-five homesteads being occupied. A Mrs. Annie Ross, widow, brought her family of three boys and a girl and took up land by Hall Creek and the area became known as Rosswood. A sub-post office was opened there, and the mail for the lake residents was sorted in Terrace and put in a locked sack that a government mailman packed out to this sub-office for distribution. As the road at that time was a dirt road winding among the trees and was only used occasionally for hauling in supplies, the residents of the lake walked in when coming to Terrace. On one occasion a certain Joe Belway of Rosswood was walking into town when he met the mailman about halfway and wanted his mail. The postman showed him that the bag was locked and it was against regulations for him to open it. However, Joe insisted and when the mailman refused, Joe pulled out his knife and ripped open the bag, sorting over the mail and taking out his. This is a serious offense and Joe was hauled into court where he was let off with a good talking-to.

by with no mail at all. A deal was made whereby the *Inlander* could carry mail at the Hudson's Bay Company's price, when the Hudson's Bay Company did not get in the two contracted trips per week. Ottawa vetoed this. The result is that there are eight boats now running on the Skeena, one of them carrying mail, and that the oldest one.

October 22, 1910

Since navigation commenced last spring the population of Hazelton has doubled and the population of the whole district has more than doubled. People in this district are no longer counted by the hundreds; there are three or four thousand receiving mail sent up the Skeena from Prince Rupert. Why should the CPR have a monopoly on carrying mail on the Pacific Coast for years? Why should the Hudson's Bay Company have a monopoly on carrying mail on the Skeena? The only possible answer is that department officials are so firmly welded to the old ways that they can see no virtue in anything new.

December 10, 1910

The winter mail schedule, as presently arranged, provides for the departure of the downriver mail every Thursday at noon. This week's left on time, in charge of Bert Schooling and Charlie Monroe (three dog teams). Middle section—Thomas Brewer in charge. The Prince Rupert end is attended to by Barney Mulvaney. George Beirnes, with the help of Dutch Cline, has the Hazelton end. From 40 to 50 dogs will be used in George's outfit and an extra 100 pounds of mail will be brought in each week.

Sam Kirkaldy as Postmaster

To many old-timers in Terrace the name "Kirkaldy" is synonymous with "post office." Since both Sam and his wife, Onnalee, served this community for years in this line of work, and as both are of pioneer stock in Terrace, their story has a place here despite the fact that Sam became postmaster in 1931.

This is a reprint of an article that appeared in the official postal magazine *Postmark*, June–July issue, 1952, relating some of the highlights of Mr. Kirkaldy's career as postmaster:

Nobody in Canada can tell Sam Kirkaldy much—if anything—about the trials of the mail courier. This genial official who has just turned over the mail carrying contract to Don Hull of Terrace, BC, has put in over twenty years on the job—the mail going through day in and day out despite floods and washouts, and the other challenges which only a mail courier knows.

During his entire service he had only one break, and that was in 1948 when he had temporarily to curtail his activities because of his health.

The highlight of Sam's mail-carrying career, which reads like an epic, came during the flood of 1936 when the Skeena River and some of its tributaries went on the rampage and put the railway out of commission in the locality for about six weeks.

Sam decided that if Terrace was to have any mail service, he would have to take matters on his own shoulders. So, after Terrace had received no mail nor dispatched any for some three weeks, he gathered together two sacks of outgoing letters and with his assistant, Jack Sparkes, sallied forth for Prince Rupert.

At Remo River they left their auto and were ferried across in a rowboat to the railway line. From that point to Kwinitsa, travel was mainly by courtesy of the Canadian National Railway's section crews, via speeders and push cars.

Occasionally Sam and Jack had to tote the sacks on their backs. At Shames River they were ferried across on a raft made of shiplap.

At Mile 43 they were taken aboard a gas-boat to Kwinitsa, where they caught the train for Prince Rupert. Their visit was a surprise to Postmaster Morison of Prince Rupert, but after Sam explained the system of transportation, plans were worked out for the return trip and a dozen bags were selected from the large accumulation destined for Terrace and vicinity.

Until the railway lines were finally repaired, mail from Terrace, Usk and Pacific traversed the route pioneered by Sam.

He recalls that in early days Dan MacGregor, the mail conductor, hauled the sacks to and from the trains by wheelbarrow. Next, Tom Young took on the job using a horse and two-wheeled cart. The first auto used was a Model T Ford.

In 1927 he married Miss Onnalee Greig, daughter of the postmistress. His wife boasts that she has actually spent more time in the post office than her husband, having thirty years of service, but being only officially credited with the last year. She adds that she married Sam to get out of the post office, but except for the time off to raise her family she has worked there almost continuously ever since.

Note: Mrs. Kirkaldy's mother, Mrs. M. Greig, for whom Greig Avenue is named, was assistant postmistress under George Little, and her daughter Onnalee received her training in post-office work at an early age.

Early Terrace Post Office—an addition to Little's General Store on Kalum Street. (26-A)/BCARS 82724

The Mailman

♦ Sperry Cline

(with apologies to the author of the original and to no one else)

The soft wet snow was falling fast
As up the Skeena River passed
A youth, with six dogs on the trail,
Mush, you Malamutes, MUSH!

His head was bare, his whiskers long;
He cussed in many a different tongue;
His snowshoes bagged, his back was bent,
Plumb tired out, but on he went.

He reached a house, new-built of logs,
A woman cried, "Get out, you dogs,
And hurry now, give me my mail
If you haven't lost it on the trail."

"What! None from Mother in the lot?
Oh! You've been drunk as like as not
And never told them my first name."
But soft and low his answer came.

He cracked his whip and onward sped,
"And those parcels ordered from below—
I s'pose they're soaked with rain and snow.
And my dress pattern, can you tell?"
The youth replied, "Aw . . ."

Fresh snow comes down—trails to break;
All other travellers in his wake.
"We've waited hours for you to come,
Our snowshoe filling is on the bum."

The ice gives way; he plunges through
In currents strong beneath the snow;
Rights like mad and gains the shore
And hikes along the trail once more.

His clothes are wet, his face is froze,
No feeling in his hands or toes.
He gains a Mission dark and drear,
The preacher cries: "You can't stop here."

Next morn they found him on the road,
Lying dead beside his load,
With glassy stare fixed on the trail,
As if to say: "I dare not fail."

There in the twilight cold and grey,
Lifeless but beautiful he lay,
'Twas not the hardships of the trail,
But folks ungrateful for their mail.
Mush, you Malamutes, MUSH!

RAILS WEST

Engine and train crew of HRH Duke of Connaught's Special, Prince Rupert, September 23, 1912. Fred Durham from Kitselas, a member of the crew, is on the left. (65-C)

History of the Railway

from *Canadian National Railways' History in BC*[8]

Shortly after the turn of the century, Charles M. Hays, newly appointed general manager of the Grand Trunk Railway, made a hurried trip to the company's headquarters at London, England. He met with the directors and spoke of a proposal for a new railway to the Pacific coast, running through entirely new country, north of the CPR, and capable of being conveniently linked to the existing Grand Trunk network. He also pointed out the desirability of establishing a new port on the BC coast, offering unlimited scope for future development and "securing to this enlarged system an unassailably dominating position."

Hays's proposal drew avid interest in London and on July 29, 1903, the Canadian government entered into a contract with the Grand Trunk for the construction of a second transcontinental railway, much along the lines as proposed by Hays.

The Grand Trunk Railway had expanded in eastern Canada by building and purchase until by 1900 it owned a network of lines covering Ontario and Quebec. It also owned and operated the Grand Trunk Western, providing a connection with Chicago, and a line from Montreal to the seaboard at Portland, Maine. The directors looked enviously at the long-haul traffic that was developing in the West and came to the conclusion that to protect their interests they should have a line to and through the Canadian West.

Their traffic to the West was interchanged with the Canadian Pacific at North Bay, that railway securing the long haul. They did not share in the haul of traffic from the West as the Canadian Pacific utilized its own lines for distribution. The Grand Trunk proposed to the government that the railway should build a line from North Bay to Winnipeg and should have a charter to expand in the West between Winnipeg and the Pacific coast. This proposal was not looked upon favourably by the government as there was fear that if such a line was constructed, the Grand Trunk would divert the through traffic to Portland, Maine, instead of to the Canadian ports of Saint John and Halifax.

The outcome was an agreement between the government and the Grand Trunk Railway to build the National Transcontinental and the Grand Trunk Pacific. The National Transcontinental was to be built by the government between Moncton and Winnipeg, and the Grand Trunk Pacific agreed to construct and operate a line of railway, with feeder branches, from Winnipeg to the Pacific coast. The purpose of this railway was to provide an outlet to the Pacific and enable the parent company to share in the very profitable traffic that was expected to develop in western Canada.

The Grand Trunk Pacific Railway (GTP) was incorporated on October 24, 1903, and surveyors were already at work throughout the West locat-

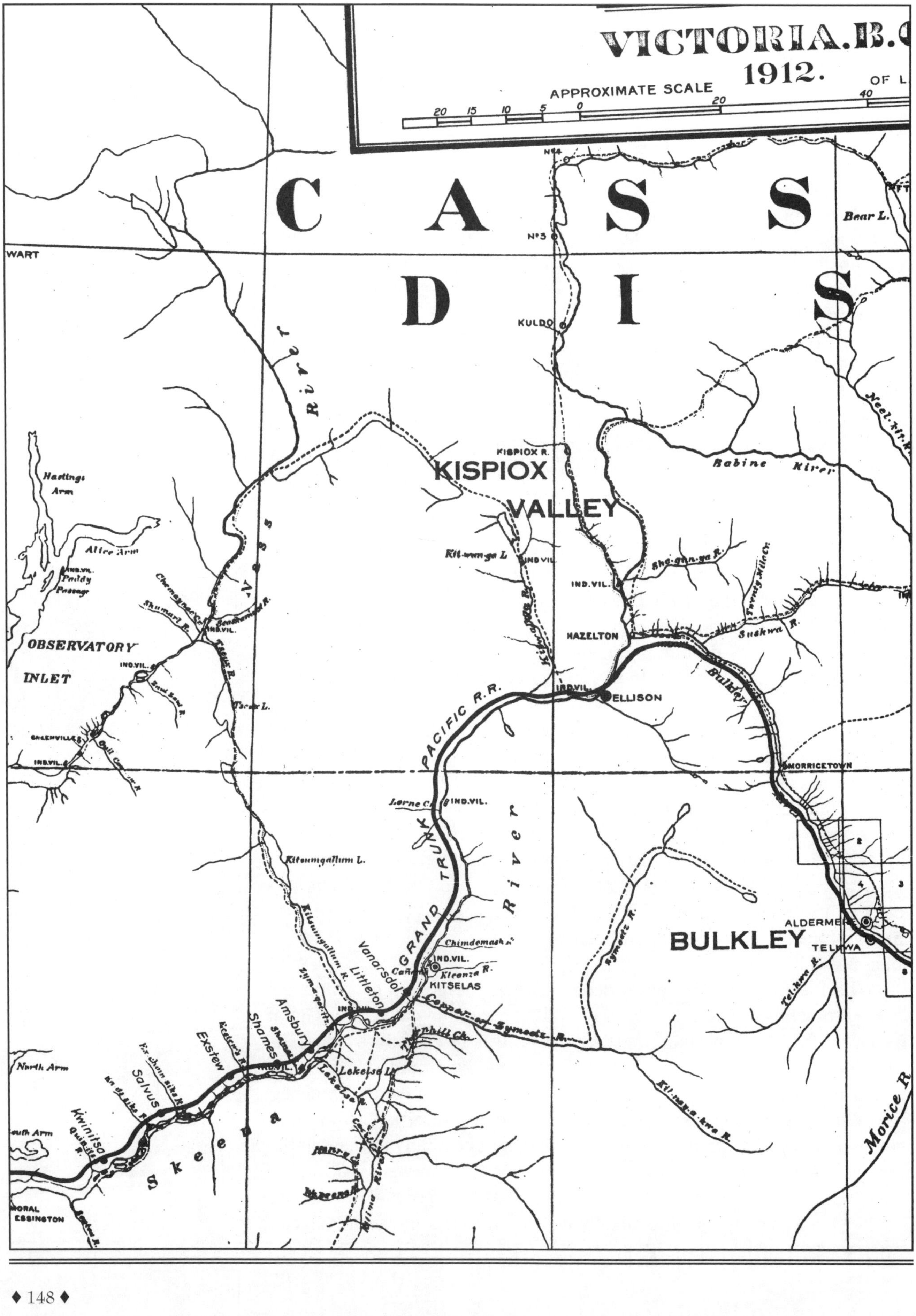
VICTORIA.B.C
1912.
APPROXIMATE SCALE
OF L
20 15 10 5 0 20 40
CASS
DIS
WART
Bear L.
KULDO
KISPIOX R.
KISPIOX
VALLEY
Babine River
Hastings Arm
Alice Arm
Paddy Passage
OBSERVATORY
INLET
IND. VIL.
HAZELTON
ELLISON
Suskwa R.
Bulkley
MORRICETOWN
GRAND TRUNK PACIFIC R.R.
Lorne Cr.
Kitsumgallum L.
Chimdemash
Kleanza R.
KITSELAS
Littleton
Vanarsdol
Amsbury
Shames
Exstew
Salvus
Kwinitsa
Lakelse L.
Skeena
North Arm
South Arm
ESSINGTON
BULKLEY
TELKWA
ALDERMERE
Morice R.
Kit-wan-ga L
Sho-gun-ga R.
Copper or Zymoetz R.
Tsaux L.

ing a right-of-way and attempting to determine a new port on the Pacific coast —one that would cut the shipping distance to the Orient by some five hundred miles.

Several routes in BC were considered. The GTP routes were all projected through the Yellowhead Pass as far as Prince George. This pass had been surveyed by William MacKenzie and Donald Mann in the spring of 1908. By utilizing the Yellowhead Pass, the lowest crossing of the Rockies would be secured, as would the best gradients on the North American continent, the grade against westbound traffic being 0.4 percent and against eastbound traffic, 0.5 percent. Terminal sites were suggested at Port Essington, Kitimat, Kaien Island (at the mouth of the Skeena River) and Port Simpson (close to the Alaskan boundary).

Finally, in 1906, Hays met with his engineers and decided that the terminus would be at Kaien Island. Seven months earlier, following a nation-wide contest, the name "Prince Rupert" had been chosen for the Pacific terminal.

By 1907 the GTP surveys were completed and on May 7, 1908, the first sod was turned at Prince Rupert to begin eastward construction. It was not until 1910 that westward construction of the Grand Trunk Pacific

Historic GTP Loco 123 on construction east of Prince Rupert, BC, summer of 1910. Courtesy Canadian National Railways

reached the Alberta-BC boundary. It had been decided originally that instead of the usual procedure of building cheaply in the first instance and improving out of earnings, the railway should be built to a high standard of grade, curvature, structures, etc., and, in general, to conform to the standards of the Grand Trunk Railway.

The last spike was driven at Fort Fraser on April 5, 1914, by Edson J. Chamberlin, president. There was a great flurry of excitement the day Chamberlin pounded home the last spike. Standing beside him for the momentous occasion was A.W. Smithers, chairman of the board, London. Charles M. Hays, unfortunately, could not witness the fulfillment of his dream, as he was one of the passengers who perished aboard the ill-fated *Titanic*.

The first through train reached Prince Rupert three days later and regular passenger service was inaugurated September 6.

By the fall of 1915, the GTP was beginning to feel the pinch of World War I. The government took receivership of the Grand Trunk Pacific on March 7, 1916. On August 23, 1920, the GTP was turned over to the Canadian Northern Board for operation and on January 30, 1923, became a part of the growing Canadian National Railways system.

The GTP had a good chance of survival, had it not been for the impact of the First World War. This shut off the flow of risk capital from Great Britain and Europe, led to a cessation of immigration and raised operational expenses to such a peak that it was impossible to compensate them by substantial rate increases. Thus the company went into receivership.

Locomotive 112, first through train to Prince Rupert, April 9, 1914. (70)

♦ Rails West ♦

Railroading, 1921. Pictured (left to right) are B.J. Walkland, Roy Lawcett, Tom Cullen and George Raymond. (73)

Date Capsule[9]

1903—July 29—Canadian government contracted with the Grand Trunk for the construction of a second transcontinental railway.
1907—autumn—GTP surveys in BC completed.
1908—May—First sod turned at Prince Rupert to begin eastward construction of Grand Trunk Pacific.
1910—spring—Westward construction of GTP began in BC.
1910—December—Eastward construction had reached six miles east of Terrace.
1914—April 7—GTP construction in BC completed. Last spike driven at Fort Fraser by GTP President Edson J. Chamberlin.
1914—April 8—First train arrived at Prince Rupert from Winnipeg.
1914—Sept. 6—Regular passenger service between eastern points and Prince Rupert inaugurated.

The Construction of the Grand Trunk Pacific Railway in British Columbia

♦ J.W. Lower (from *BC Historical Quarterly*, Vol. IV, 1940)[10]

No single factor had a greater influence upon the opening up and development of central British Columbia than the Grand Trunk Pacific Railway. In 1900, before its construction, this vast area could be reached only by way of the Cariboo Road from Ashcroft. This led to Quesnel and Fort George (now Prince George), from which points local roads and trails extended into the surrounding hills and valleys. Except in the immediate vicinity of these two towns, travel conditions had changed little since the days of the fur trade. But within fifteen years this section of British Columbia was to be traversed from east to west by a first-class railroad; communication was to be opened to the south by means of regular coastal steamship service from Prince Rupert, as well as by railways from Quesnel and Tête Jaune Cache; settlement was to be greatly increased; hitherto undiscovered resources were to be developed; and central @Body Text:British Columbia was to enter upon a boom period.

Although in 1900 there was no east-to-west communication system through central British Columbia, there was, as Sandford Fleming had pointed out thirty years before in his Canadian Pacific Railway exploration surveys, a natural route for the construction of a railway. At the eastern boundary an excellent pass, the Yellowhead, opens a way through the Rocky Mountains to the headwaters of the Fraser River, which flows northwest through a region of plateaus, low mountains and river valleys. >From Prince George, where the Fraser River turns southward, this railway route follows its tributaries, the Nechako and Endako rivers, which flow from the northwest. From Decker Lake, near the source of the Endako River, it is possible to cross the Bulkley Mountains by a short pass to the headwaters of the Bulkley River. This river flows northwest until it empties into the Skeena River, which flows southwest through the Coast Range into the Pacific Ocean. This is the route followed by the Grand Trunk Pacific Railway. Along it lies the chief belt of settlement in central British Columbia.

The construction of the Grand Trunk Pacific Railway was a natural outcome of conditions in Canada at the beginning of this century. Whereas the decade before 1896 had been one of depression, the years 1896–1913 were years of unprecedented prosperity. Capital, both from Great Britain and other countries, was ample and credit was cheap. Of even more significance was the spectacular increase in immigration to Canada, both from the United States and from Europe. This great influx may be attributed to the strong imperialistic sentiment in Great Britain at that time, to the aggressive propaganda of Clifford Sifton and to the shortage of free land in the United States that resulted from the end of the "frontier" movement. Whereas the number of immigrants to Canada in 1898 was only 31,900, in 1903 it had reached 128,364 and the following years were to show still larger figures.

Thus boom times, cheap money and unprecedented immigration resulted in a veritable flood of newcomers to the Canadian Prairies, and with their coming there arose an increasing need for more railway facilities to the West. A new railway to serve the Prairies north of the Canadian Pacific main line was a necessity; but, unfortunately, this expansion was carried beyond all rational limits and, probably as a result of the blind optimism of the times, not one, but two, new transcontinental railways were concurrently constructed through this section.

In 1902 the railways west of the Great Lakes proved inadequate to handle the greatly increased grain trade. At that time western Canada was served by two railways of importance—the Canadian Pacific, extending to the Pacific, and the youthful Canadian Northern, which in 1902 had twelve hundred scattered miles of line extending between Port Arthur, Ontario, and Erwood, near the eastern boundary of Saskatchewan. But early in that year two more transcontinentals were planned. The Canadian Northern announced its intention to build from coast-to-coast, and in Quebec a group of promoters was planning a railway to pass through the northern latitudes to be called the Trans-Canada Railway. This latter line was actually begun and sixteen miles were constructed in Quebec. It died a sudden death when the Grand Trunk made its unexpected announcement that it planned to support another transcontinental line to the Pacific coast.

This line was first conceived by the officials of the Grand Trunk as an independent railway, to be called the Grand Trunk Pacific, which was to be a subsidiary of the older company and was to serve as an extension into the West. The project undoubtedly sprang from the vigorous mind of Charles M. Hays, who had served as general manager of the Grand Trunk from 1896 to 1900 and had just returned to the road after a single year with the Southern Pacific. Hays realized that the financial difficulties of the Grand Trunk were caused not only by its inefficient methods, but also by the fact that it was not gaining the amount of new business from the West that it should. The increased settlement on the Prairies had resulted in an enormous increase in the export of wheat, but this traffic was controlled by the Canadian Pacific Railway. The Grand Trunk, traditionally concentrating on Ontario, was in the humiliating and unprofitable position of depending on its rival for any of this trade that it might handle.

Furthermore, the Canadian Pacific threatened not only to encircle the Grand Trunk lines with its track across northern Ontario, but it was actually building branch lines into the south and destroying the monopoly that the other railway had consistently sought to maintain. In Hays's opinion the solution of these difficulties was the building of a feeder line to the Prairies that would be subsidiary to the Grand Trunk. Such a railway was first planned as a projection of the line through Chicago to Winnipeg and the West, but Hays realized that the Canadian government would not approve this route, both for political reasons and because of tariff difficul-

As early as 1909, the GTP had considered a line from Terrace to Kitimat. This did not, however, come into being until much later. In 1952 Canadian National Railways (CNR) surveyed the forty-one-mile line, construction began at once and it was in operation during the winter of 1954–55.

ties. The Grand Trunk therefore proposed to build the extension westward from North Bay, the existing terminus of its lines in northern Ontario.

Hays's first steps in the development of this new railway were a general survey of the territory and the submission of a proposal to the Canadian government on November 2, 1902, for the building of a line from North Bay to Port Simpson, on the Pacific coast. The terms implied a subsidy of $6,400 and five thousand acres of land per mile of line, as well as certain other concessions related to mail subsidies, free importation of construction material and taxation exemptions. The government turned the proposition down.

In spite of this, on November 24, 1902, Hays made a bare announcement that a transcontinental railway would be built that would be entirely independent of the Grand Trunk Railway, but which would have exclusive traffic arrangements with it.

Meanwhile the government was trying to bring the Grand Trunk and Canadian Northern railways together in an attempt to have each build lines that would be complementary, rather than opposed, to each other. After several meetings the two lines could not agree, and for some reason the government did not exert the pressure that it could have used to force such an agreement. Instead it permitted the railroads to plan separate transcontinentals that at times paralleled each other at a distance of less than thirty miles. Probable reasons for the failure of the two companies to come to an agreement were the excessive demands of the Canadian Northern and the belief of the Grand Trunk that it could easily crush its younger rival.

Early in 1903 the officials of the Grand Trunk and the government discussed possibilities of construction and terms. Judging from the fact that Mr. Blair, the minister of railways, resigned from his position on July 10, it must be supposed that these talks were mainly between the railway officials and Prime Minister Wilfrid Laurier, who was becoming very enthusiastic about the plan. As a result of his attitude it is only right to accept the Grand Trunk Pacific Railway as a Liberal project, just as the Canadian Pacific Railway has been accepted as the work of the Conservatives under Sir John A. Macdonald. The chief result of these discussions was that, for political reasons, the project was extended still farther and the railway was planned as a transcontinental stretching all the way from Moncton, New Brunswick, to the Pacific Ocean.

On June 4, 1903, the bill providing for its construction passed the Railway Committee after being discussed for seven days. On July 9 it was accepted by the Liberal caucus. This was followed immediately by the resignation of Mr. Blair. On July 29 Laurier signed an agreement with the company, and on the following day personally presented the bill to the House.

The acts that ultimately resulted in the construction of the Grand Trunk Pacific Railway provided for a transcontinental line that was to be built in two divisions. The first of these, to be known as the National Transcontinental, extending from Winnipeg to Moncton, was to be constructed by the government. The other, to be built by the Grand Trunk Pacific Railway, was to extend from Winnipeg to Port Simpson "or some

Residents along the CNR's "north line" will probably recall the odd-looking train that was used for a time during the early part of World War II in the vicinity of Prince Rupert. It was Canada's first and only armored train. One unique thing about it was the engine—a pioneer diesel-electric locomotive built by the CNR in 1928.

other port on the Pacific coast." When the National Transcontinental was completed it was to be leased to the Grand Trunk Pacific for fifty years, with the privilege of renewing the option at the end of the period. By way of rental the Grand Trunk Pacific was to meet "working expenditures" during the first seven years and to pay three percent of the "cost of construction" for the remaining time. As it turned out the National Transcontinental was not taken over by the Grand Trunk Pacific as agreed, and ultimately the line became part of the Canadian National Railways.

The Grand Trunk Pacific was an independent company with a capital of $45 million, consisting of $20 million in preferred stock and $25 million in common stock. The new railway was to be divided into two sections— the prairie section, extending from Winnipeg to Wolf Creek, Alberta, and the mountain section, from Wolf Creek to the Pacific. Except for a thousand shares held by the directors, the Grand Trunk Railway held all the common stock. The Dominion government guaranteed principal and interest on the bonds issued by the company up to seventy-five percent of the cost of construction in each division, but it was stipulated at first that the principal so guaranteed was not to exceed thirteen thousand dollars per mile on the Prairies and thirty thousand dollars per mile in the mountains. In 1904 this restriction was removed from the mountain section and no definite limit was set. The company was to pay interest on the bonds for the prairie section from the date of issue and the government was to pay the interest on the bonds of the mountain section for seven years, at not over three percent. This meant that the company was to have the use of seventy-five percent of the capital expended on the mountain section free for seven years. The remaining twenty-five percent of the bonds on both sections was to be guaranteed by the Grand Trunk Railway.

The Grand Trunk Pacific Railway had two motives for building through British Columbia. In the first place, it aimed to be a colonization road, which would open new land to settlement, exploitation and the discovery of new natural resources. More important, the line in British Columbia would form a link between the Prairies and eastern lines, which were expected to pay, and a Pacific port. Through traffic from the coast to points across the continent had proven highly lucrative to the Canadian Pacific Railway, and the Grand Trunk Pacific clearly wished to reach the Pacific and secure a share of the Oriental traffic. Because its route was two hundred miles shorter, the Grand Trunk Pacific expected to have a very definite advantage over the other transcontinentals in competing for this trade.

Reconnaissance surveys for the new railway began soon after the bills passed the House of Commons. The first sod was turned at Sand Hill, Manitoba, on August 28, 1906. By July 1909, the line had been built from Winnipeg to Edmonton, and in the following year the prairie section was completed to Wolf Creek.

Of the 840 miles in the so-called mountain section, approximately 71 miles were in British Columbia. Building of this section began from both the eastern and western ends. When the prairie section was completed from Winnipeg to Wolf Creek, construction continued progressively west-

Variations in dates, even from reliable sources, are both interesting to note and inevitable. Two CNR sources provide us with two dates for the driving of the last spike—April 5, 1914, and April 7, 1914.

The Prince George Herald *gives the exact time as Monday, April 6 at 12:30 p.m.*

It seems to be generally accepted that April 7 was the official date.

ward into the mountain section until it met the tracks from the west, which had been begun at Prince Rupert. The contractors for the entire section were Foley, Welch & Stewart, but the work was almost entirely sublet to contractors in sections that were usually shorter than 5 miles each.

Edmonton was the base of operations for the construction gangs building from Wolf Creek westward. Supplies were carried from there to the different bases either by construction trail or by wagon. The construction train was able to run over the tracks as soon as they were laid, and because it could not average over eight miles per hour, it was nicknamed the "flier." Wagons were used to carry supplies to those camps that were beyond the "end of steel." The customary price for hauling was five cents a pound, regardless of distance. There were about six hundred teams working along the line through the Rocky Mountains, about two-thirds of which were privately owned.

Another common method of obtaining supplies after steel had crossed the Yellowhead Pass and reached the Fraser River was by steamer from Soda Creek, up the river to the end of steel. F.W. Stewart of Foley, Welch & Stewart Construction Company had two steamers in operation, the *Operator* and the *Conveyor*. Each had a capacity of 175 tons and was powerful enough to push a scow carrying a 90-ton load against the current. Steamboats were not as satisfactory as teams, however, as they could only be operated when the water was high. In 1912, because of the light snowfall, they were only used for three weeks.

The summit of the Rocky Mountains, which marks the British Columbia boundary, was reached by steel about November 15, 1911. From this point the road followed the Tête Jaune gorge for about ten miles to the headwaters of the Fraser, at Yellowhead Lake. Steel reached Moose Lake, twenty miles farther, in March 1912, and a triweekly service from Moose Lake to Edmonton was inaugurated in August. From this point construction was much easier, as supplies could be obtained by the riverboats and the country was much less rugged than in the Rockies. The greatest problem in this section was the "gumbo," or clayey mud, which is the common terrain.

In April 1913, steel reached Raushuswap River, where a bridge 850 feet long was built. Two months later trains were running from that point to Tête Jaune Cache. Late in November the railroad crossed the Fraser for the third time near the present site of Hansard, and by the end of the year the line was at Willow River, less than twenty miles east of Prince George. By January 12, 1914, steel had reached the Fraser River opposite Prince George, and on January 27 the tracklayer crossed on a temporary bridge that was destroyed by ice the same day. Fortunately the construction of the

---

MARINE TRANSPORTATION

The marine aspect of the transportation history must not be forgotten and although Terrace itself is not a port, it is greatly affected by marine traffic both at Prince Rupert and at Kitimat.

Canadian National first appeared afloat in BC in 1908, when the Grand Trunk Pacific (GTP) acquired MacKenzie Brothers Steamships, Vancouver—a tug and barge operation. The GTP used the vessels to transport men, machinery and equipment from Vancouver to Prince Rupert.

In November 1909 the GTP received a Dominion government contract to provide steamship service between Prince Rupert and the Queen Charlotte Islands.

The Grand Trunk Pacific Coast Steamships was incorporated on May 26, 1910, and within months, the first two passenger ships, the SS Prince Rupert and the SS Prince George, arrived to begin service between Vancouver, Victoria, Seattle and Prince Rupert.

Construction of the Prince Rupert dry dock began in 1913 and was completed four years later.

Service to Skagway, Alaska, commenced in June 1916 and was discontinued in 1918.

permanent steel bridge required at this point had been begun on August 31, 1912, and the structure was completed on March 7, 1914. The laying of tracks across this bridge linked Prince George to the east by rail. Progress from that time was rapid. By the end of March 1914, the present site of Finmoore, which is fifty miles west of Prince George, was reached, and on April 5, 1914, the rails met those from the west at a point two miles west of Nechako Crossing, just east of Fraser Lake. The meeting place is a solitary spot today, being marked only by a sign that states that the Grand Trunk Pacific was completed there.

The Pacific coast end of the railway presented many difficulties. The first of these was the problem of a suitable terminus. The original contract had mentioned Port Simpson, which is located on the Tsimpsean Peninsula, about twenty miles north of the mouth of the Skeena River, but it was understood at the time that this would not necessarily be used if a better place could be found. Surveys showed that the best location would be on Kaien Island, which was in a small inlet known as Tuck's Inlet. An old Admiralty chart showed a rock in the harbour that would be a serious obstruction to navigation, but a new survey failed to locate this impediment and, as a result, the island was selected as the western terminus of the Grand Trunk Pacific. The name "Prince Rupert" was given to it as a result of a competition sponsored by the railway. Five thousand answers were received, the winner being Miss Eleanor MacDonald of Winnipeg, who received a prize of $250.

On May 4, 1904, by an Order-in-Council, the government of British Columbia entered into an agreement with E.V. Bodwell, who was acting for an American financier, Peter Larsen, to dispose of ten thousand acres of land on and near Kaien Island, provided that the latter sold it to no one but the Grand Trunk Pacific, and provided further that the terminus of the road was placed upon it. Larsen duly sold this land to the Grand Trunk Pacific at no profit, and Bodwell became the representative of the railway on the Pacific coast. For some unrevealed reason this agreement was not made public for two years, and the result was a crop of unproved charges of graft that gave rise to the notorious Kaien Island investigation. This inquiry was conducted by a select committee of the legislative assembly and completely exonerated the government from any charges of improper practice.

On July 12, 1904, Charles M. Hays, president of the Grand Trunk Pacific, had stated: "So soon as the progress of the surveys in British Columbia will permit, construction will be commenced from the Pacific coast to the end of the road and be carried on continuously in an easterly direction until the road is completed." However, much to the dismay of British Columbia, it was discovered that there was no clause in the contract that forced the railway to build from the western end. The Grand Trunk Pacific sought to use this fact to force concessions from the government in the form of either a cash subsidy or a land grant.

In 1905, while the legislature was in session, F.W. Morse, vice-president of the company, spent five weeks in Victoria. Apparently his demand was a land grant of twenty thousand acres per mile to abut on the railway, which the company agreed to sell at prices set by the government. As it was estimated at that time that there would be about four hundred miles of line built in British Columbia, the grant under these terms would be over eight million acres. The government, evidently considering that in view of Hays's earlier statement that such a demand was a breach of faith, told Morse definitely that he would receive no subsidy. Morse thereupon left British Columbia, determined not to build from the west.

Premier McBride now found himself in a difficult position. Apparently he had saved the land grant but had lost the agreement of the railway to build from Kaien Island eastward. However, a weapon soon appeared by which he was able to force the railway to build from the Pacific end. The railway was trying to obtain possession of certain Indian reserves, particularly those near Kaien Island, but to do this it was essential to have the consent of the provincial government. McBride used this lever not only to withstand the pressure of the Liberal government at Ottawa, but also to force several concessions from the railway. Not the least of these stated that construction was to begin at Prince Rupert by June 1, 1908, and was to continue steadily eastward.

The first sod on the western end was turned at Prince Rupert on May 7, 1908, a month after the first subcontracts were let. Construction began at Copper River, (first called Newtown, and now called Copper City), on the Skeena River, about one hundred miles east of Prince Rupert. The beginning of the work is described as follows in the Prince Rupert *Empire* of August 24, 1908:

"Construction work has been started on the Kitimat branch of the Grand Trunk Pacific at the mouth of Copper River . . . the Kitimat branch is being built under a charter granted by the provincial legislature several years ago . . . The company that obtained this charter also received a promise of a cash subsidy of $5,000 a mile provided $100,000 in construction work was expended before a specified date this year. The Grand Trunk Pacific purchased the charter in 1905, and in order to get the cash subsidy have let a contract to "Jack" Stewart and his associates. Ninety men with horses and supplies were unloaded at Port Essington on August 1, and went by the steamer *Northwest* up the Skeena to the mouth of the Copper River."

One of the serious problems that faced the railway surveyors was the selection of the best route between Aldermere, near the present town of Telkwa, and Copper River. Two alternatives were carefully considered. One of these was via the Telkwa and Zymoetz rivers to the Skeena River; the other followed the Bulkley River to its junction with the Skeena at Hazelton. The former route was about eighty miles shorter and was favoured by the engineer in charge of the district, but pressure from the provincial government resulted in the latter being chosen. It was shown that this route would serve both the agricultural district near Hazelton and the northern mines, especially those in the Babine Range; would afford an outlet to the Babine and Kispiox valleys; and, finally, would afford a satisfactory junction point for a railroad to Dawson in the Yukon. Such a railroad, which was contemplated in the original Grand Trunk Pacific plans, would find a natural route to the north through the Kispiox and Nass river valleys.

♦ Rails West ♦

Ross Camp on the GTP, 1911. (32-A)/BCARS 80818

Bulkley Valley survey crew with pack train. (12-A)/ BCARS 76176

Construction camp, Mile 79 on the GTP. (25-A)/BCARS 59853

♦ Pioneer Legacy ♦ Volume II ♦

Dining room, Bostrom & Green's Camp, Fort Fraser, BC. (32-A)/BCARS 80816

Construction days on the GTP. (32-A)/BCARS 80817

Ties and dense timber, Mile 38 on the GTP. (25-A)/BCARS 6326l

♦ 160 ♦

Construction of bridge over the Skeena River at Skeena Crossing. (17-A)

Bridge construction at Skeena Crossing. (32-A)/BCARS 80807

Skeena Crossing bridge, was completed July 7, 1912. (32-A)/BCARS 80806

The 180 miles from Hazelton to Prince Rupert offered the most difficult engineering problems on the entire railroad. In 120 miles the Skeena River drops 1,000 feet, which makes this one of the most rapidly running waterways on the coast. The last 60 miles are tidal, which further complicated the problems of construction. The railway follows the banks of the river through almost solid rock for these 60 miles. Moreover, on these mountains, avalanches and snow slides were so frequent that a tunnel almost 1,600 feet long had to be driven near Kwinitsa in an attempt to reduce the hazards of operation.

Farther up the river is Kitselas Canyon, where great rock barriers made three tunnels measuring some 400, 700 and 1,100 feet respectively necessary. In the first 211 miles of railway there were no less than thirteen tunnels, totalling 8,886 feet, or well over 1 1/2 miles length. When the railway crossed the Skeena at Skeena Crossing, about 13 miles west of Hazelton, a bridge of six spans with a total length of 930 feet was needed. One cut in this section of the road was 6,600 feet long and took almost twenty-six months to complete. So difficult was the route that over 12,000 miles of trial lines and surveys had to be run in order to locate 186 miles of track.

Construction of the first two sections—the first of 100 miles to Copper River and the second of 140 miles to Aldermere—was carried on simultaneously in many places. The arrival of steel was delayed by the Zanardi Rapids, which lie between Kaien Island and the mainland. The problem of bridging them was accentuated by the tide, which not only runs at a speed of from twelve to fourteen miles an hour, but rises at times as high as 26 feet. The bridge across this channel was not completed until July 1910 and consisted of six spans totalling 645 feet.

Steam shovel at Mile 22. (25-A)/BCARS 55621

This delayed the completion of the line from Prince Rupert eastward, and materials for construction were therefore carried to the camps up the Skeena River by means of shallow-draft, sternwheeled steamers. They were used in the summer but were of little use in the winter. Their speed was estimated at fifteen miles per hour. Because of the strong current in the river, in actual operation this speed varied greatly, and whereas it took five to eight days to travel upstream to Hazelton, the return journey could be made in fourteen hours. Sometimes the current was so strong that it was necessary to haul the boats through the canyons by cables attached to donkey engines.

By March 31, 1910, grading and culverts were completed for almost one hundred miles east of Prince Rupert and the wharf had been completed in that city, but only about seven miles of track had been laid and no stations or buildings of any kind had been built along the road.

On July 31, 1910, the first construction train from Prince Rupert crossed the newly completed Zanardi Rapids bridge, and from this time the

♦ Rails West ♦

GTP passenger train at Skeena Crossing, July 7, 1912. (32-A)/BCARS 80805

Sealy, BC, 1910–1912. This was taken during construction of the GTP along the Skeena River west of Hazelton. (65-C)W.W.W. 95065

Residence of Dr. Stewart, Sealy, BC, 1910. (65-C)/W.W.W. C1289

trains greatly assisted the work. By September, steel was laid for seventy miles and C.C. Van Arsdoll, the chief engineer of the mountain section, had moved his headquarters to New Hazelton. At the same time lots were offered for sale in Ellison, the first townsite to be sold east of Prince Rupert. Steel went little farther that year because of Kitselas Canyon, where the tunnels were not completed until January 20, 1912.

By March 1912 the rails had reached Skeena Crossing, where they were again forced to wait for the building of a bridge. Meanwhile, trains were run from Prince Rupert to this point and passengers took a boat across the Skeena to the remainder of the track. In September 1911 arrangements had been made with the Hudson's Bay Company by Foley, Welch & Stewart by which boats met the trains and made it possible to buy a through ticket to Hazelton.

In the spring of 1912 track-laying was pushed ahead rapidly and, in spite of the fact that there was snow on the ground, thirty miles were laid in six weeks. On March 31 the Skeena bridge was completed. In August the tracks reached Sealy, where a huge gulch necessitated the building of one of the longest bridges on the line, measuring nine hundred feet.

It should be noted that Ellison was also called Sealy. It was three miles west of New Hazelton. The land thereabouts lacked a sufficiently level grade, and later the station was built a short distance to the east, at South Hazelton. Price Ellison was minister of lands in 1910. J.C.K. Sealy was proprietor of the Omineca Hotel in Hazelton.

The choice of Sealy (or Ellison) as the temporary terminus of the railway for some months was the result of an attempt by the railway to exploit this route. Hazelton, which is on the north bank of the Bulkley River, could not be made a station since the railway ran along the southern bank. It was therefore planned to build a station on the opposite side of the river to the town, in the section known as New Hazelton. But the land adjoining this site was owned by the Northern Interior Land Company, which was determined not to agree to the terms offered by the railway. Finding itself unable to exploit more than a small section of New Hazelton, the Grand Trunk Pacific attempted to erect its station first at Sealy and later at South Hazelton. An appeal to the Railway Commission resulted in a decision that the station must be built at New Hazelton. Thus balked, the railway for some time unloaded its passengers at Sealy, ran empty trains to the "Y" at New Hazelton and returned empty. This practice continued for almost a year before a station was built at the latter place.

From this time the work progressed steadily. On February 28, 1913, trains were running to Porphyry Creek, about eighteen miles east of New Hazelton and near the site of the present station of Beament. On May 23 steel reached the Telkwa River; in September it was at Decker Lake; and by the end of the year it was at Burns Lake, 316 miles east of Prince Rupert and 136 miles from New Hazelton. By March 15, 1914, steel was laid to Fraser Lake, and on April 5 it met the rails from the east. The last spike was driven by H.B. Kelliher, the chief engineer, and although no official ceremony was held at the time, a crowd of fifteen hundred people was present.

The first train from the east reached Prince Rupert on April 8, 1914, but it was not until September 6 that regular passenger service was inaugurated from Prince Rupert to Winnipeg.

With the beginning of the regular train service the actual construction of the Grand Trunk Pacific Railway may be said to have been completed, although there was still much to be done, such as the improvements to the roadbed, the construction of sidings and the replacement of temporary bridges. When this was finished the Grand Trunk Pacific was recognized as one of the best built of the colonizing lines in North America. The vision of Charles M. Hays had been realized.

One of the fundamental reasons for the construction of the Grand Trunk Pacific Railway through British Columbia had been the development of trade with the Orient. In connection with this, the promoters of the company hoped to establish a trans-Pacific steamship service. The British Columbia Coast Service was expected to be the beginning of this great steamship system, for in 1909 Captain C.H. Nicholson was appointed manager and organizer of the Pacific fleet, and its extension to China and Japan.

The Grand Trunk Pacific Coast Steamship Company operated a regular service for many years. The *Prince Albert* was the first of its fleet to reach the coast and arrived from England at William Head near Victoria on May 30, 1910. From there it went to Seattle for docking before entering service.

Two fine new steamers, the *Prince Rupert* and the *Prince George*, arrived at Esquimalt on June 4 and July 12, 1910, respectively, from England, where they had been built by Swan, Hunter & Wigham Richardson at Newcastle. The *Prince Rupert* sailed on her first voyage from Seattle on June 12 and from Victoria and Vancouver on June 13, 1910. She reached Prince Rupert on June 16. The *Prince George* joined her on the run late in July. Each steamer made a round trip each week from Seattle, Victoria and Vancouver to Prince Rupert and Stewart. In 1916, 1917 and 1918 a summer service was operated to Skagway. For many years they maintained the fastest service to the northern coast.

In 1911 a fourth vessel, the *Prince John*, was the last ship to be added to the Grand Trunk Pacific Steamship Company's fleet. When the railway became a part of the Canadian National Railways system, the steamship service on the Pacific coast was maintained.

The Grand Trunk Pacific Railway did two things for British Columbia that earn it a permanent place in the history of the province. It opened the area between Prince Rupert and the Yellowhead Pass, supplying it with transportation and telegraph facilities. Furthermore, it afforded an outlet from this area to the remainder of Canada so that the agricultural lands, mines and fisheries of central British Columbia could be developed. Whatever condemnations may be heaped upon this great project, the indubitable fact remains that the years that saw its construction were clearly one of the vital periods in the development of British Columbia.

The Building of the Grand Trunk Pacific

♦ Phylis Bowman

The 184 miles of track between Prince Rupert and Hazelton has been described as the most difficult section of railway ever to be built in North America.

The line took more than five years to complete, with the route being changed numerous times as more than twelve hundred surveys were made over the dense mountains and through the fertile valleys and swift-flowing rivers.

Work on this section began in the rainy, cold autumn of 1908 and ended when the short western line and the longer eastern line met at Finmoore on April 7, 1914, to complete Canada's second transcontinental railroad.

It was a gigantic task, for not only was the company faced with problems from the weather and the rugged and rocky terrain, but also from political representatives of the Dominion and provincial governments, who haggled and wrangled over various details and costs, which resulted in serious delays in this tremendous undertaking.

The building of this railway was the brainchild of the president and director of the Grand Trunk Railway, Charles Melville Hays, who saw a wonderful opportunity to extend his company's eastern system to the Pacific and thus secure a large share of the lucrative traffic to and from Asia and the Orient.

His idea was to build a first-class railway across Canada north of the Canadian Pacific line through the Yellowhead Pass and along the rivers of central British Columbia—all at low elevations—to the coast. Here a seaport would be built, five hundred miles closer to Asia than any other rail terminal on the Pacific coast, a full day's travel in those days and an important factor to consider in national trade.

His was no idle dream, for he knew the results of the original reconnaissance surveys of the CPR, one of which had covered this same route, following the mighty Skeena River, but turning north ten miles before it reached the sea (probably near Tyee or Haysport—hence the name, Hays' Port). From there the line followed the narrow Work Channel to reach the ocean at Port Simpson, an Indian village where the Hudson's Bay Company had established a fort in 1834 to catch the Canadian and Alaskan fur and mineral trade.

However, there was at that time a fierce dispute over the exact location of the Alaska boundary, and President Roosevelt had threatened to send troops to that territory to quell any uprisings. Canada's prime minister, Sir Wilfrid Laurier, who had taken a great personal interest in the proposed railway, requested that a site further south be chosen as a terminal city.

After extensive surveys along hundreds of miles of coast, railway engineers chose the northwestern shores of Kaien Island as a likely spot. A nation-wide contest was held to pick a name for this new city and the name Prince Rupert was chosen from more than twelve thousand entries.

Another change in the original route was made at the request of Sir Richard McBride, premier of the province, who wanted the line to pass through the rich agricultural lands around Hazelton instead of following the Telkwa River and crossing to the headwaters of the Copper River. This change increased the line by eighty miles and mounted its cost by several millions of dollars.

Altogether it took more than five years to obtain official permission for the route from Winnipeg to the west coast of Canada. The Grand Trunk Pacific Railway (GTP) was formed as a subsidiary of the Grand Trunk Railway, and the westbound line was started on the open Prairies fifteen miles north of Carberry on August 29, 1905.

In all the negotiations for the transcontinental railway, countless disputes arose and tempers were aroused as leaders of the government and the railway companies argued out their rights and demands.

The outcome of some of these differences was an agreement that the two sections of the railway be built in British Columbia: one portion starting eastward from Prince Rupert, and the other— thirty-five miles of track—running from Copper River to Kitimat. Work on the second project was dropped as soon as subsidy requirements had been fulfilled and it was not until the early 1950s that this line was actually completed, but on the opposite side of the river from its intended location.

The railway company started development of its terminal city in April 1906, when Assistant Harbour Engineer J.H. Pillsbury arrived with a crew of thirty men to survey and build a wharf on Kaien Island.

Scowloads of equipment and supplies arrived from Vancouver and contract companies levelled the townsite of huge trees and underbrush. Docks were built to accommodate the growing fleet of coastal steamers and freighters, and hotels, rooming houses, business offices, cafes and railway buildings sprang up on rocky, muddy shores amidst an assortment of shacks, tents and other living quarters.

Great hillsides were blasted out to make room for the growing community, with the rock being used to line the harbour's edge for a roadbed for tracks and railway repair shops.

Much of the work was done with great difficulty by hand, as work crews laboured to carve a roadbed out of sheer canyon walls, through dense forests and on the shifting sandbars of the Skeena River.

Although the shores of the river were extremely hazardous to follow, it was deemed advantageous to use this route, for sternwheeled vessels with shallow drafts could be used to carry supplies up the river as far as Hazelton, which had been established as a trading centre.

A fleet of five sternwheelers was bought by the contractors, Foley, Welch & Stewart, who were in charge of construction of the line from the coast to Hazelton. The ships *Distributor, Skeena, Omineca, Operator* and *Conveyor* hauled tens of thousands of tons of railway construction materials, groceries, meat, passengers and supplies to the work camps as the line crept eastward.

Although many difficulties were experienced along the way and lives were lost in accidents and treacherous waters, two spots proved to provide more than the usual amount of problems and headaches for the engineers.

These were at Zenardi Rapids, where a bridge had to be constructed to link Kaien Island with the mainland; and at Kitselas Canyon, where the railhead remained for sixteen months while crews sought to tunnel through the sheer rock walls of the canyon.

At Zenardi, too, work fell far behind schedule, as more than one hundred men were employed to place four cement towers fifty-five feet apart across the swift-flowing rapids. The bridge was forty-nine feet high and steel cables had to be swung from tower to tower across the boiling waters so crews could be lowered to work on the piers. Divers and boats laboured against great odds, bucking the tides, wind, weather and darkness.

The rapids had been named after one of the most colourful workers on the GTP crews, Count Carlos Zenardi-Landi. He sometimes spelled his name "Zanardi" and insisted on being called "Mr. Zenardi." A short, vivacious fellow of only five feet, with a great red mustache, he arrived from Smyrna in 1906 without any funds, but with a large selection of sporting guns. Hired as an axeman on a survey party, he was later promoted to levelman and provided plenty of life and humour to many a party. He had married a niece of the empress of Austro-Hungary and had fled from Europe with her as he could find no work there and his life was in danger.

He had left his family in Vancouver while he worked in the North, and later moved there to rejoin them. One of his daughters was Elissa Landi, the well-known movie actress. The count went into the real estate business in Vancouver and after the First World War worked with a large Italian salvage company to raise ships that had been torpedoed during the war.

After the bridge was completed in July 1910, one of the first people to travel over it was Prime Minister Sir Wilfrid Laurier, who was touring the west coast. His special train stopped at the bridge so dignitaries could inspect the splendid structure, and then he and his party went on to watch the processing of fish at Inverness, one of the first canneries established in the North. Sir Wilfrid and his party visited the school at Metlakatla before returning to Prince Rupert, where he attended meetings, banquets and parades and met with civic leaders and Indian chiefs.

Once Zenardi Rapids was bridged, the line grew quickly past the mouth of the Skeena and crept along its north bank. In fact seventy miles of track went down in two months.

On this estuary section it has been estimated that it took two million dynamite blasts, requiring more than ten million pounds of high explosives, to clear the way. One rock cut was 6,600 feet in length and took twenty-six months to complete.

At Mile 44, a tunnel 1,600 feet long was driven into the rock to protect the tracks from avalanches and rock slides, and at Kitselas, the gap in the mountain wall, it took 2,200 feet of tunnelling to pierce a granite casement.

In all, there were 8,886 feet of tunnels made on the Skeena section. On the estuary most of the breaks in the rock work consisted of cribbing and heavy piling behind which dikes were built to dam the sloughs and backwaters.

In some places the drillers had to work on a scaffolding of logs or planks suspended in the cliffside by chains attached to iron dogs driven into the rock wall. When they had chiselled out standing room, they worked with ropes attached to their belts. After drilling the holes and tamping home the charges, they lit the fuses and were quickly yanked upwards out of harm's way before the blasts went off.

In all this fierce struggle of construction, the "station" was the work unit. It usually consisted of a hundred feet of roadbed that was sublet to an individual or a group. The station men were paid on yardage, and many of them lived and slaved like animals, for their profits depended on the speed with which they could complete one job and move on to the next.

One of the hardest-working station men was "Swansie, the Tireless Swede," who worked his crew from two or three in the morning to nine or ten at night, scarcely stopping for food or rest. But on the completion of the project each man received twenty-four hundred dollars cash for his efforts at that particular section.

Historians have recorded that the most successful of all station men were a number of young Scots who stuck together throughout the whole construction and accumulated modest fortunes by using their heads as well as their muscles.

In charge of the whole project was C.C. Van Arsdol, divisional engineer for the mountain section of the GTP. He was better known as "Four-tenths Van," for he had discovered the GTP's easy grade to the Pacific, which does not exceed 0.4 percent at any point of the three to four thousand miles of track from coast to coast. The maximum grade over the entire line meant only twenty-one feet to the mile.

Tunnel at Kitselas Canyon, looking to the west. (41-A)/BCARS 88172

Two tunnels on the GTP near Usk (looking to the east), about 1915. (41-A)

Kitselas tunnel, 1911. (32-A)/BCARS 80804

Newspaper reports blared out accounts of the railway's progress with vivid write-ups of "the laying of steel" and of the many losses of lives that occurred in construction accidents. Widespread advertisement drew people from all over the world to this section of Canada, for the magic words "Grand Trunk Pacific" brought visions of rich farmlands, vast rolling prairie lands, rushing waters well stocked with all kinds of fish, and fertile valleys and riverbanks promising rich crops of fruits and vegetables.

Many settlers gathered in a valley on the banks of the Skeena called Kitsumkalum. A new townsite had been laid out on property owned by an early pioneer, George Little, who planted shade trees of maple and birch along the main street. This booming settlement was first called "Littleton" in his honour, but the name was later changed to "Terrace" when it was found that there was another Littleton in Canada. Incorporated in 1927, this community has rapidly expanded as the hub of industry in BC's prolific interior lands.

It has been estimated that between Terrace and Prince Rupert, twelve million tons of material had been blasted out and four million cubic yards of solid rock had been excavated. And the cost was more than $80,000 for each mile.

The first excursion train from the coastal city to Terrace was on the May 24 holiday in 1912, with a return fare of $3.20. A Prince Rupert baseball team defeated a Terrace team three to one in a seven-inning game and newspaper accounts record that several boxing bouts were featured in the evening, followed by a huge dance. The excursion train waited until the festivities were over before the return trip home.

Graves of Russians killed in blast during construction of Kitselas tunnel. (22-B)

When the Kitselas tunnel was finally completed, sixty-four miles of track was laid in sixty-three days. At Skeena Crossing, Mile 174, the big bridge was ready to link up the tracks, but at Sealey Gulch, eleven miles eastward, an unusual delay occurred at this nine-hundred-foot-long trestle. When the bridge was assembled it proved to be five feet too short for the bridge seats and this meant another costly delay and new equipment and construction pieces were brought in.

By the end of 1912 the roadbed had been built through the Bulkley Canyon. Many difficulties had been experienced on this portion, too, but it had proven to be not quite as arduous as the Skeena section. Three hundred and sixty miles of roadbed had been completed, and by May 1912, regular trains were running between Rupert and Sealey Gulch, the return trip taking eleven hours.

Camps had been set up every two miles along the construction route, and divisional points had been selected at intervals of approximately 125 miles apart. The first one, Pacific, 120 miles east of Prince Rupert, has long passed into oblivion, but it was a bustling little community in its day. Headquarters for that divisional point are now at Terrace.

Telkwa would have liked to have been the next point, but it was on the wrong side of the river. Settlers and speculators had anticipated the next site for a divisional town and had started a settlement called Hubert. But railway officials decreed otherwise and started a new townsite along a great stretch of straight track just west of Telkwa. They called it Smithers, after A.W. Smithers, chairman of the GTP. The little settlement of Hubert faded out as trade and population grew around the new community.

The next large settlement was in Pleasant Valley, where a contest had been held in 1910 to choose a name for the little town. The winning entry chosen was Houston, after John Houston, the vociferous editor who had started the first newspaper in Prince Rupert in its early days. Houston freely wrote his opinions and criticisms of railway and political figures and policies and got into hot water more than once over his frank statements and challenges.

And so these isolated communities were linked together by that important line of tracks winding eastward, with parties travelling back and forth to join in social activities or vie with each other in sports and exhibitions.

As a point of interest, the Trans-Canada Highway was not completed through this territory until September of 1944 when the dusty, gravelled, winding portion of road was finally finished between Prince Rupert and Terrace.

British Columbia was linked with the rest of Canada by railroad at Finmoore on April 7, 1914, after seven years of negotiations, quarrels, contracts, much hard work and millions of dollars.

At this point midway between Prince Rupert and Wolf Creek, many excited pioneers and railway workers gathered in the snow and mud to watch the track-laying crews race toward each other, with the east line beating

Tracklayer laying steel from Kitselas to Hazelton, 1912. (25-A)/BCARS 68319

Charles Durham on "Jigger," checking the line near Usk. (65-C)

Skeena Subdivision, 1912. Pictured (left to right) are Pete Ron, section foreman; Bill McGinnis, brakeman; Fred Bostrom, conductor; Pete Gibson, conductor; George Raymond, brakeman; Andy Abbot, brakeman; and Walter Star, brakeman. (41-A)/BCARS 88154

GTP railway station at Pacific. (25-A)/BCARS 66200

Sid Cooper hauling ties for the GTP at Telkwa. (38-C)

♦ Pioneer Legacy ♦ Volume II ♦

"Pioneer" laying railway track on the GTP, 1913. (22-B)

GTP construction near Smithers. (25-A)/BCARS 52227

Near Telkwa. (32-A)/BCARS 80808

♦ 174 ♦

♦ Rails West ♦

Laying track on the GTP near Telkwa, July 20, 1913. (32-A)/BCARS 80811

"Passengers' First-Class, Open-Air Express—Ride now, pay later." Possibly in front of Siems-Carey (subcontractors) office, Mile 53, 1913. (25-A)/BCARS 59852

Typical GTP railway station under construction, about 1913. (25-A)/BCARS 79483

♦ 175 ♦

the west by twenty minutes. And so the nation's second transcontinental railway was completed with no fanfare or speeches, but with great expectations and plans to open up a great country to thousands of new settlers and immigrants.

But Charles Hays did not live to see the completion of his dream, for he was one of the 1,503 passengers who drowned when the steamship *Titanic* struck an iceberg on her maiden voyage on April 14, 1912, and sank before the dawn of the next day. He had been in England on a business trip and had been promoting his new railway, claiming it passed through lands of wealthy mines, inexhaustible timber tracts, the world's finest fishing waters and the most fertile valleys and farmlands.

His grandiose plans for a $2 million GTP hotel in Prince Rupert have never materialized, nor have the elevator or docks. As a matter of fact, the Grand Trunk Railway got into financial difficulties soon after its coast-to-coast completion and had to be subsidized by the Dominion government.

Besides these difficulties, the First World War, followed by a deadly nationwide influenza epidemic, took their toll of personnel and finances of this and other subsidiary railways in Canada. They struggled along as best they could with government subsidies but were unable to survive the enormous costs of operation and the mounting debts.

On October 4, 1922, the government granted an Order-in-Council creating the Canadian National Railways. The Grand Trunk and the Grand Trunk Pacific were absorbed into it, along with several other railways. Sir Henry Worth Thornton was named first general manager.

And so the colourful history of this line has passed through many phases, with its importance diminishing rapidly in these days of road and air travel. At one time, the echoing whistle and rumbling wheels of the old steam

Railway station at Usk. (65-C)

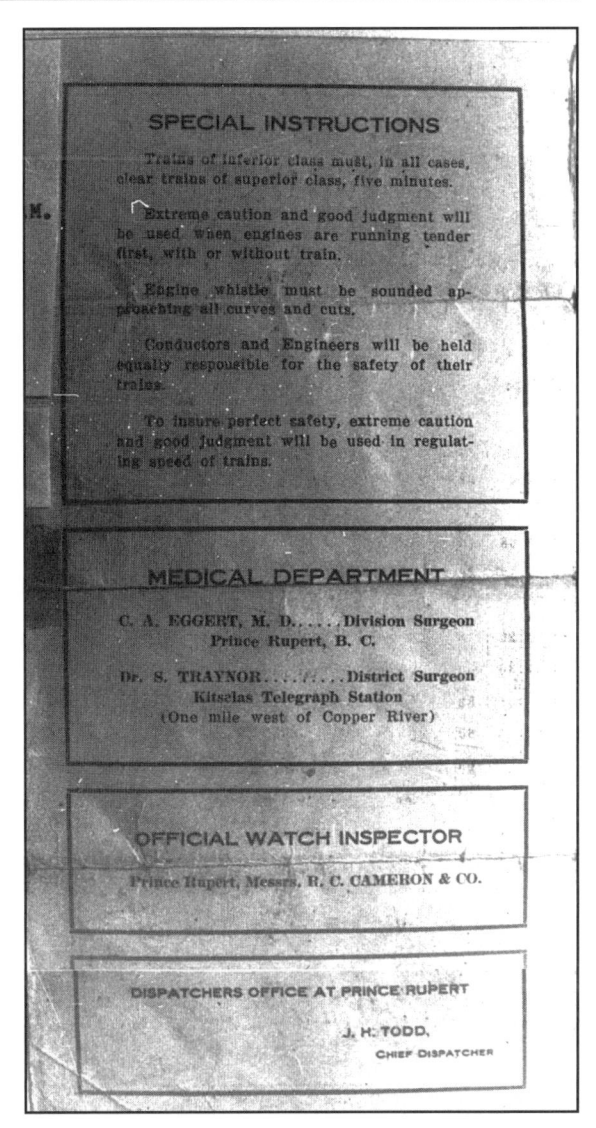

engines meant mail, supplies, visitors—the bright spot in the otherwise humdrum existence of the people in the isolated communities of the province's interior. The quieter diesel engines took over the route in March of 1958, causing many an old-time railroader a moment of sadness and reminiscing.

But some things remained unchanged—the roaring, rushing rivers, the magnificent snow-capped mountains, the miles and miles of forest and stream. They remain the same as when they were listed in magazine advertisements in 1914 to entice immigrants to settle in this great new country: "Trains of the Grand Trunk Pacific will traverse some of the finest scenery to be found on the American continent, across wild and fertile fields, by the banks of the mighty rivers of the North, through deep, dark canyons where in midsummer from beneath the north windows of westbound trains will come the sweet fragrance of wild roses, while from the south windows the traveller can look out on a glittering glacier whose cold shroud trails to the margin of the mountains—this is the trail the railroad follows on its shortcut across Canada."

And it still remains that way today along "the most difficult section of railway ever to be built in North America."

Left: Train schedule posted in GTP railway stations.

Right: Notice posted in GTP stations. (22-B)

The Coming of the Steel

♦ Blaine Boyd (from *BC Digest*, May–June, 1963)

It was spring 1906. The big land boom was on in central British Columbia with construction underway on the Grand Trunk Pacific Railway that would provide a direct link with Winnipeg, Edmonton and the new port of Prince Rupert on BC's north coast. Every town was plastered with posters urging people to make themselves rich by investing in new townsites and farms, and if a person as much as stopped to read a poster, the salesmen descended. They just happened to know about a town lot that would make you wealthy in a few years. Or if you liked country life, they would sell you 160 acres of the world's finest farmland.

My brother, Pat, and I decided that country life was for us and headed for Prince Rupert to take advantage of the new frontier. We were young, enthusiastic, confident—and, of course, inexperienced. Prince Rupert proved to be a city being carved from rock and overflowing with hundreds of people from all over the world attracted by the brash advertising of the townsite speculators and the prospect of land that would make them wealthy.

We soon learned that there was no farmland around Prince Rupert, but were told that Hazelton, some two hundred miles up the Skeena River, was the place to go. Here we would find miles of the finest land on earth just for the filing. So Hazelton became our destination. The Grand Trunk Railway was completed about one hundred miles east from Prince Rupert to a point on the Skeena called Kitselas Rapids. Above the rapids a sternwheeler connected to Hazelton. We took the train to Kitselas but on our arrival discovered that from the end of steel to the start of sternwheeler service was a five-mile stretch over which we had to walk, carrying our hundred pounds of luggage.

The Indians would carry it for five dollars apiece, but money was scarce with us and we decided that what an Indian could do, we could do. Ever since then I have had a great respect for the Indians. With a huge brass-bound trunk on their back and a big suitcase in each hand, they took off up the trail as casually as if they were pushing a baby buggy in the park. We struggled and sweated with our hundred pounds that appeared light in comparison and finally made it.

On the way we got acquainted with a couple of men who were going to take the boat. Since they had no heavy luggage, they offered to take ours if we wanted to walk to Hazelton. Well, Hazelton was about sixty miles away, two days walk we figured, and since the boat fare was about thirty dollars, we could make good wages by walking.

When we reached the boat landing we left our bundles with the two men and started up the railroad track to Hazelton. We soon learned that walking railway ties is a real art. The ties are too close to be a comfortable step apart, but then two ties are too much for a single step. Usually it comes down to taking two or three extra short steps and then one extra long one. The result is a somewhat comic "hoppity-hop" gait.

Pat's shoes proved a little too big for him, consequently his feet sort of slid around in them. By the time we had walked twenty miles his feet were a mass of blisters. He took his shoes off and slung them around his neck and wrapped his feet up in a couple of burlap sacks that we picked up along the track. My one regret about the trip is that I did not get a picture of Pat hiking along with his gunny-sack shoes.

While we were clumping along a big, husky foreigner caught up with us. He had an employment ticket to Hazelton but his job was ten miles down the river from the town. For some reason he decided to walk the fifty miles up the river to his job rather than ride to Hazelton and walk the ten miles back. He gave us his ticket and we decided that Pat would use it because of his sore feet and I would buy a ticket on the next boat. When we reached the landing we found several people waiting for the sternwheeler that had been at Kitselas when we left. We had apparently walked faster than she had sailed, and all wondered what the problem was. In about an hour we could see her coming upriver and we suddenly realized the difficulties of river navigation.

The Skeena River was in full flood. Just below the landing was a turbulent stretch that in normal times would have been a riffle. The steamer snorted up and hit the riffle at full speed. About halfway up, her progress slowed to nil and puffing in protest, she slowly drifted back downstream. Below the riffle she halted and black smoke rolled from her funnel as a new head of steam was built up. With the paddles churning furiously and flames shooting from her smokestack, the old girl tore into the riffle again. At first it seemed she would make it, but progress became slower and she was washed downstream again. But the pilot learned something about the current and he hung a monkey wrench or something on the safety valve. The next time he tore triumphantly to the top of the riffle, teetered a moment and plopped into the slower water and to our landing.

Pat presented his ticket and for $2.50 I got a ride the rest of the way to Hazelton. The trip on the sternwheeler was interesting. All along the river there were cords of dry wood and, as needed, the boat stopped and all hands loaded fuel. The engines had a tremendous appetite. The fireman, who worked a two-hour shift, stripped to the waist and stood in a pit in front of the firebox. He picked up a stick of four-foot cordwood, opened the fire door with the end of the stick, threw it in and banged shut the door. He reached for another stick and repeated the operation. Probably during a normal flow of water he had a breathing spell, but that day there was no rest until he went off shift. The heat from the furnace made his body a pinkish red and the sweat literally ran off his naked torso. I have never seen what I considered a hotter or more monotonous job.

But persistence won and we reached Hazelton without trouble. We got our bundles and soon had our tent pitched on the edge of town. We stayed in Hazelton a week but learned that the good land had been corralled by the big land companies for speculation and they were not as yet willing to sell it. Later on, a wild land tax helped to turn the land over to the bona fide settlers, but for quite a while, most of the good land was tied up by speculators. There is no doubt this action held back development of the country for quite a while.

At Hazelton we also learned why laws are made and how they are evaded. A class of society known as the "B" girls—and no frontier town is without them— either became too thick or too bold and were banished from the town. Thereafter no "B" girl could operate within a three-mile limit of Hazelton. Well, the girls went the three miles out of town and set up their own place and called it "Three Mile." Since their trade was largely from the construction men who craved companionship, they managed to part a lot of them from a payroll that had previously been spent in Hazelton. As a result, Three Mile flourished. I understand that it is now known by the more dignified name of New Hazelton.

Hazelton, like so many northern towns at that time, was infested with dogs. In winter, dogs were at a premium for sled animals, but in the summer a greater number of them that were not used for pack dogs were turned loose on the town to shift for themselves. Half starved and half wild, they looked to be a menace and were. Luckily they were well grounded in the belief that man was a superior animal who must be obeyed, or I think that in their starving state they would actually have attacked people.

We heard that at Telkwa, seventy-eight miles up the Bulkley River from Hazelton, there was lots of good farmland so we headed in that direction. There was a wagon road of sorts along the railway right-of-way on which supplies for construction crews came by freight teams. There were four and six-horse teams and they went in groups of five teams under a foreman. This train was called a "swing." When the frost went out of the ground in the spring, the road became a dark muddy streak and sometimes ten or twelve miles travel was a good day's work.

There was a horse-drawn stage at Telkwa but rumour had it that the stage was rougher than a wild bronco. The news gave us a good excuse to save some more money by walking to our destination. Three days later we reached Telkwa and set up our tent just across the river from the town.

In our search for land we encountered the same problem as at Hazelton. It was all tied up by promoters. There was, however, plenty of it up the line at Decker Lake. The song was now growing stale and we could see that it would be expensive to get started with transportation so high and the cost of supplies so great. We sat down to count our money, time and enthusiasm. The supply of each was growing smaller day by day.

Construction of the railway itself was at times spread over a hundred miles of right-of-way, with most of the work done by horses and hand. In a few places where steam machinery could be used, the machines were taken apart and hauled in over the winter snow. The work was so slow that the line was nicknamed the "overall and tobacco road," because old-timers said the company made more off the sale of those items than they did from the contract.

A problem that caused much trouble—and sometimes laughs—was the liquor situation. In the beginning only a few of the roadhouses or hotels along the right-of-way had licenses to sell. When construction started, a ten-mile-wide strip along the line was proclaimed a dry area. Since it was no crime for the licensed houses to sell liquor, or for a person to have it in his possession, this loophole opened up quite a field for the bootlegger.

Construction men are notoriously thirsty and soon there were many roadhouses along the right-of-way with illegal stocks of liquor. At first there was a three hundred-dollar fine for bootlegging, but some of the places were making so much money that they paid the fine and never even closed. Then the penalty was increased from three hundred dollars for the first offense to six months in jail for the second. Traffic still didn't stop so the fine became six months for the first offense. Then liquor became hard to find.

Note: According to another person's memory, the "girlie" place out of Hazelton was at Two Mile and to this day is still referred to as "Two Mile."

A Note on the Yellowhead Pass
♦ F.A. Talbot (from *The New Garden of Canada*)

The Yellowhead measures about one thousand feet from side to side. Indeed, you would never know that you were at the "pass" if you failed to observe that the Miette on your right hand when you face the north is running east to swell the Atlantic, while on your left the streams turn westward to the Pacific . . . except, indeed, for that insignificant four-foot post, merely a squared, slender tree-stump. Even if it caught your eye, you would be somewhat perplexed probably by the hieroglyphics inscribed on one of its faces thus:

LBM 3720
GTP

They indicate the surveying engineers crowning triumph, and show where the Rocky Mountains will be threaded by the iron road at a lower altitude than has ever been achieved before. Interpreted, it means: "Location Branch Mark, 3,720 feet above sea level. Grand Trunk Pacific." One cannot help contrasting the engineer's achievement in this latitude with that many hundred miles to the south, in Colorado, where in order to carry the railway over the same formidable range, the metals had to be lifted to an altitude of some 10,000 feet above the ocean level . . .

The Yellowhead Pass was so christened by the Indians because a famous trapper in the service of Jasper Hawes, at the Hudson's Bay outpost in Jasper Park, flitted to and fro through this breach in the mountain wall between the post and the Fraser River, whereby he reached Fort George, some four hundred miles distant to the west. He was an Iroquois of huge stature and physique, blessed with flowing locks of bright auburn hair, and the Indians, with their quaint aptitude, promptly dubbed him "Tête Jaune," while the path he followed through the mountains became known as the "Pass of Tête Jaune." Afterwards this was turned into its briefer English equivalent, "Yellowhead Pass."

The Resident Engineer's Camp

♦ F.A. Talbot (from *The New Garden of Canada*)

It had been arranged that the first night out should be spent in one of the Grand Trunk Pacific resident engineer's camps, the day's ride being made short purposely to get things into shipshape. We had come up as far as Wolf Creek with the young engineer, and he had cordially invited us to partake of the camp's hospitality. We were not a bit sorry when at last the strains of a phonograph, grinding out, "Put on your old grey bonnet," struck our ears, for we had been in the saddle a matter of four hours and our anatomy, unaccustomed to maintaining its equilibrium on the saw-edge of a pack horse's backbone, bore painful testimony to the ordeal.

These camps are distributed along the grade at intervals of about twelve miles, the duties of the engineer being to supervise construction and to check the work as it is carried out. Each camp numbers about half a dozen young fellows all told, comprising chainmen, a rodman, a transit man, cook and possibly one or two other supernumeraries. It is a somewhat lonely life, since the camps are ahead of construction so that the little colony is entirely dependent upon its own resources for amusement and the profitable utilization of leisure moments. "Canada" music offers a staple form of recreation and keeps the party in touch with the musical world and the latest triumphs of the vaudeville art. The phonograph is started up about six o'clock in the evening and is kept continuously at it until bedtime, only to be resumed directly the gong awakes the sleepers in the morning, and to be kept churning until the party starts off for the day's labours. A musically accompanied shave, toilet and breakfast is somewhat novel, but after we had passed the third camp we all keenly anticipated the time when we should be beyond the strains of this concentrated music hall, orchestra and concert platform.

The little colony at this camp was indeed industrious. In their spare time a lofty tower for experiments in wireless telegraphy had been built up; a stream just below was being dammed, a primitive piledriver having been fashioned for driving logs of wood to form a barrage for securing a sufficient head of water to run a small water turbine whereby the camp could be electrically lighted; while a small cleared patch in the bush testified that horticulture had one or two enterprising exponents.

The members of the camp are for the most part young fellows to whom the lonely life appeals; while, owing to the absence of inducements to spend, they unavoidably save their money. They make their quarters snug and comfortable, and their employers see to it that no complaint can be offered in regard to the commissariat or the cook. I can vouchsafe for this fact from personal experience. In these resident engineer's camps, I secured a far greater variety of more nourishing food, more appetizingly and better prepared, than I had enjoyed in a first-class Canadian hotel. Certainly many of the latter establishments could not point to such a master hand in their kitchens as these camps possessed. The cooks, for the most part, I found to be young fellows from home, who like the life and consider a monthly salary of £12 clear a good wage. And it may be pointed out that this wage is not confined to the railways. Mining in the West pay this figure, and it is not a bit difficult for a young man to save £120 or more a year, for his requirements in the way of clothing are obviously very limited. One young man whom I met in the wilds, presiding over the kitchen of a mining camp, stated that he had left London twelve years before, had been in steady employment ever since he reached the Far West, and had contrived to bank over £1,000 as the reward of his culinary skill. The demand for good cooks in the West is steady, for the employers know that nowadays the skill of the chef has much to do with the contentment of a small community in the wilds, a satisfied "little Mary" more than counteracting innumerable irksome deficiencies.

In the railway camp no complaint on the side of insufficiency of food could be raised. We sat down to an evening meal. There was infinite variety, and everything in plenty. Although extensive resort has necessarily to be made to canned foods, an expert cook can ring the changes pretty frequently thereon, while if he is a good pastry hand and can concoct delectable dainties in the way of pies—well, his comrades will forgive his lack of prowess in the preparation of other dishes, for to the Westerner, pie, whether it be mince, pumpkin, raisin, pineapple, peach or anything else, is the great gustatory delight.

Railway construction was in active progress near the camp, and here the resident engineer introduced me to a phase of life which is not seen outside America, and is depicted to its fullest degree in Canada. This was the "station man"—not the superintendent of an aggregation of buildings and administrative machinery, but what may be perhaps best described as the very bottom rung of the ladder of success.

A railway contract is divided into stretches of one hundred feet each. The basis of the contract is payment by the cubic yard, the survey plans and specifications showing how much earth it is necessary to remove from this point to be dumped at that. Instead of engaging a large staff of navvies working at so much an hour, the contractor encourages the labourer to become his own master. A man can take over a "station," as a length of one hundred feet is called, and is paid so much a yard for excavation; this sum is, of course, less than that which the contractor receives, the latter's profit being represented by the difference between the two amounts. The scale of payment varies according to the nature of the earth worked; so much for ordinary earth, or "common" as it is called, a little more for loose rock, and a higher rate for solid rock. The last, as it involves drilling and blasting, is generally taken over by the most expert hands, but anyone who can wield a pick and shovel is competent to tackle the other classifications.

Now it is perfectly obvious that under this arrangement, the more work a man does, the more he earns; his prosperity is governed entirely by his industry. On this particular station it was mostly "common" and loose rock. The sole tools required were pick, shovel, crowbar, wheelbarrow and one or two planks. The station men I saw here were three burly Galicians, ruggedly clad—for any clothes suffice for this work—and they were toiling like slaves . . . It was now past nine o'clock in the evening and yet there were no signs of cessation.

Working under these conditions is somewhat of a dog's life. The men are out on the job about four in the morning and slog incessantly until seven, when they make a short pause for breakfast. This is gulped down, and they are at it again until the mid-day hour compels another brief respite for a scanty meal. This is quickly digested, and then ensues a straight toil until six in the evening, when supper is disposed of, followed by a fourth spell of work till fading daylight compels abandonment until dawn.

Such is the round, day in and day out, with Sunday as the only break. The men live in little rude shacks, and the day of enforced idleness—from their point of view—is spent in washing what clothes they require and the performance of other domestic duties for the ensuing week. Their food, though wholesome, is reduced to the minimum, pork and beans being the staple diet, for these men have to board themselves, and consequently they reduce living expenses to the minimum. The work is hard but it carries its own reward. They only ply their calling during the summer months, when the days are longest, and put in the other six months on a homestead.

This is one way in which Canada is becoming peopled with a solid backbone, for these men get their land practically free, perform the necessary improvements prescribed by the homestead law, and while the produce on their farms is maturing they are earning from £10 to £12 a week upwards. They carefully husband their wages, and by the time they have secured the patent for their farms are comfortably well off and have the capital in hand for the purchase of agricultural implements and so forth.

Galicians and a few Irishmen form the station men for the most part, especially where work is in "common." Scandinavians and Italians figure on the heavy rock work, for they are born "rock-hogs," as the drillers and blasters are called. The average navvy regards the station man and his work with disdain, preferring to toil for £6 a month, all found, ignoring the fact that the station man is on the way to become his own master. Many railway subcontractors of substance in Canada today numbered a hundred-foot length as their first start, and had not a penny of capital to their name.

Canada offers a great field for the young engineer. Wages are good and promotion is rapid, according to a man's merit. There is many a youth in the Old Country who, when he issues from his apprenticeship in civil engineering, could "make good" in the West. The British engineer is preferred, as he generally has a good all-round knowledge, whereas the native railway engineer is specialized in a single branch of his profession. As a rule he has made his way up the ladder from the humble position of axeman, lopping down trees for the surveying party at £7 a month all found. The young engineer from Britain, if he were given an axe with which to start, would probably throw it down in disgust and march off in high dudgeon, feeling that this was a slur upon his abilities and a poor reward for his apprenticeship. But he has got to learn how to wield an axe, and he might just a well be paid for gaining that knowledge as not. Next he will take the position of rear chainman, walking over the tumbled country with a hundred-foot measuring length. The same wage, £7 a month, will be the reward for this labour, and then he will graduate to front chainman at £8 a month, after which he will receive a slight increase in salary to £9 a month as rodman.

If his brains warrant it, he will then make a big jump, both in position and salary, to instrument man, entrusted with the transit and level, at £15 monthly. This position achieved, and his skill being sufficiently marked, he becomes resident engineer as soon as a vacancy occurs. He will be responsible then for the construction of a section of track varying from one to twelve miles in length, according to its character and situation, at an inclusive monthly wage of £25. His next rise is to assistant divisional engineer, supervising on the spot a whole section of line at £35 a month. As divisional engineer he will command a salary of £60 per mensem, and then his future rests in his own hands.

This may seem a long ladder, but the rungs are not very far apart, and energy and brains enable a capable man to climb from axeman to resident engineer in two or three years or so. The positions above are the plums of the profession, and in view of the tremendous amount of railway construction at present underway in Canada, they are not difficult to pick up.

A Railway Construction Hospital

♦ F.A. Talbot (from *The New Garden of Canada*)

Nestling among the trees was a strange blend of civilization and the wild North-West. Here was a long, rambling building erected in the ordinary log-shack manner. The large door was entered, and there stood out in regular rows a number of cots replete with snowy white linen. This was the railway construction hospital, and it would have done credit to many a town in regard to its equipment. The care of the men in sickness and accident is one of the first thoughts of the contractors. One ward was available for contagious diseases, while its fellow served for housing accident cases. The floor was spotless, as were also the walls and ceiling, though fashioned of rough timber. The cots were equipped with every requirement, and two attendants were retained to tend the patients. At the time of our visit there was only one solitary case—an axeman, while wielding his axe, having lost three toes of one foot through the tool glancing and cutting through his boot. No case, no matter how complicated its character, could baffle the resources of this hospital in the bush. There was an operating theatre, spacious, well-lighted and finished off in white American cloth, to permit easy and rapid washing down, with every requisite for the most serious operation. Alongside was a well-stocked dispensary.

The hospital is presided over by a fully qualified physician and surgeon, as well as a resident doctor, but fortunately their services are seldom required. The worst case that had come into their hands up to the time of my visit, the doctor related, was where a man in working a grading plough had slipped and had his thigh, body and legs torn badly by a hook. Septic poisoning was feared, but he recovered in next to no time, an effect due in a great measure to the healthy physique of the patient and the bracing air.

The rapidity and ease with which men who meet with accidents in the bush recover without skilled medical advice or special treatment is astonishing. A man's axe slips and pulls up in his leg, inflicting a gaping wound or possibly lopping off a toe or two. No antiseptic or other washing is resorted to, but the injury is bound up tightly with the first material that comes handy. These men never give a thought to the possibilities of foreign matter or microbes entering the wound. They know practically nothing about blood poisoning. There is no special dieting, for the simple reason that it cannot be adopted, even if advisable; but in a few days the man is out and about, following his usual occupation.

The Surveyor

♦ Sperry (Dutch) Cline (from the Terrace *Omineca Herald*)

A worthy sort of fellow, he,
The man with the transit and chain,
Wrestling with life where danger was rife,
Whether on mountain or plain.

He fought and conquered our forest,
Left township and farm in its place
With mosquitoes a pest, denying him rest,
And the wrath of the Natives to face.

He threaded a road through the canyon,
Clinging to walls, high and steep,
Hovering there, with a hope and a prayer,
Over waters swirling and deep.

He spanned the Zenardi Narrows,
Dangerous as ever could be;
Hidden from sight, in a caisson tight,
He bluffed the eternal sea.

Undaunted, onward and upward,
The pride of his country and friends
Till a June day bright, on a new townsite,
His life—and this story—ends.

He fell from the peak of that townsite,
Fell from the ice and the snow
At the front of the park, in a crevasse dark,
To Main Street, a mile below.

How we wept for our surveyor,
As we sponged up his remains,
And he is now surveying townsites
On those fair Elysian plains.

George Raymond

◆ Norma Bennett

It is regrettable that I did not meet Mr. Raymond some years earlier as I know he had a fund of knowledge concerning early railroad days that would have been both fascinating and enlightening. However, time waits for no one. Therefore I am thankful to have had even this brief acquaintance with the fine old gentleman and to have sampled even in this small way some of the stories he had to tell.

George Raymond hired out as a brakeman from Prince Rupert in 1911. In 1913 he was promoted to conductor and he carried on in this capacity until his retirement in 1949. There wouldn't have been much that went on in railroad circles from "Prince to Prince" that Mr. Raymond didn't know. In fact, I would consider him the prime source of information concerning this line and can only regret that he has never preserved his experiences in writing.

Many people in the area have cited Mr. Raymond as the first conductor out of Prince Rupert but when I mentioned this to him, he only chuckled and shook his head.

"Oh no", he said, "not me—that was Frank Warren. Yes, Frank Warren was the first conductor out of Prince Rupert." So I guess he should know.

Mr. Raymond recalled a bizarre experience when one of the porters cut his own throat. As the train proceeded west from Edmonton, all appeared normal. The porter was on the job as usual at Prince George. He did mention, though, to one of his fellow workers that he had had his fortune told in Edmonton the previous day. Although he didn't elaborate, it did seem to be on his mind.

In those days the dining car fed the train crew ahead of the passengers, who were wont to linger over their excellent meals, enjoying the conversation of other travellers newly-met, or just in feasting their eyes on the ever-changing scenes of beauty as they sped through this vast, little-known territory.

The porter, this particular morning, did not show up for breakfast so a waiter was dispatched in search of him. He was nowhere to be found. Finally the waiter looked in the men's toilet and there was the porter with his throat cut! Pale and shaken, the waiter made his way back to the dining car to report. It took some ingenuity on the part of the train crew to cover for the unfortunate porter and to keep the passengers from learning of his sad and untimely end.

Another time, Mr. Raymond reminisced, a lady traveller did not sleep well. Feeling sorry for the woman who was obviously distressed, the conductor instructed a porter to give her a compartment where she could rest and relax, away from the other passengers. A couple of hours later the conductor was called again. The woman was in labour and the birth seemed imminent.

Quickly a call was put out for a doctor or nurse aboard the train, but to no avail. No one even volunteered to assist in the emergency. By wiring ahead a nurse was picked up at Topley and she delivered the baby—a fine healthy specimen. So at Burns Lake the baby reached the hospital ahead of the mother.

Many were the times the train was delayed between slides—mud or snow. Once they were caught between two washouts and had they not been able to get food from Mrs. Archie McInnes at Perow, they would have gone hungry. In 1936 it was six weeks to the day from the time the train was brought out of Prince Rupert until Mr. Raymond got back.

Sometimes there were fights aboard and the conductor became the policeman or the peacemaker, as the situation warranted. On occasion a passenger, who continued obstreperous, would be put off at the next stop.

The "Indian trip," on the train, as on the riverboats, was a memorable event. It was truly a hectic time as the Natives, returning to their homes from working at the canneries, had plenty of money to spend on booze before ever boarding the train. They had their families with them in the coaches, and the baggage car was well stocked with dogs.

All seats were taken. It seemed that Natives of all shapes, sizes and ages were everywhere. Some were sleeping, some eating, some sprawling well out into the aisles (perhaps a little the worse for drink), children were crying and as time went on, those who had been imbibing too freely sometimes became noisy, argumentative or downright belligerent.

There was trash strewn everywhere. All in all, it was a relief when the coaches emptied and peace was restored once more.

All sorts of people travelled the line—miners, salesmen, locals, immigrants, tourists, government men, policemen, school teachers. Sometimes a special coach was attached for some prominent railway official. The Prince of Wales and Lord Byng were the two most noteworthy that Mr. Raymond could remember among his passengers.

An age has come and gone during this man's lifetime. Anyone who can remember train travel in the "old days" shudders in comparing it with the same mode of transportation today.

Gone are the friendly coloured sleeping car conductors who took such expert care of you from the moment you claimed your space in the sleeping car until you alighted, shoes ashine and coat freshly whisked, to reclaim your luggage at the platform, and entrust it to the able redcaps, who were everywhere in attendance.

Gone, too, is the gracious atmosphere of the dining car. In those days you dined and there is a great difference between dining and just eating. The elaborate silver service, complete to finger bowls, is now lacking, as are the spotless linens, the obsequious soft-footed waiters and the tantalizing, many-course menus.

Progress? It makes one wonder—and I'm sure Mr. Raymond does too.

Accidents

Accidents were not unknown, even on such a new line, as this report clearly indicates:

> The Hubert *Times* and Bulkley Valley *Advertiser*
> May 13, 1914
> **TRAIN ACCIDENT**
> Mr. Van Arsdol Badly Injured

Last night the first serious accident occurred to the local train from the end of steel. A fill about 10 miles west of Rose Lake gave way beneath the track after the whole train with the exception of the two passenger coaches and the express car, had passed in safety, with the consequence that these cars breaking loose from their couplings fell bottom up some 20 feet into the ditch below in which there was some three feet of water.

Under the able direction of Conductor Abbott, who, with the rest of the crew, were in the forepart of the train when the accident occurred, the bottom of the cars were soon cut out and the passengers amongst whom were several ladies, rescued, and an engine and caboose were rushed to Telkwa for medical aid.

Dr. Wallace answered promptly to the call, taking with him Nurse Peterson, who had kindly volunteered her assistance and to whom many thanks are due.

By the time the doctor and his assistant had arrived on the scene all the passengers had been removed from the upturned cars, and they were soon heroically at work, relieving the injured, who were taken the following morning to Hazelton Hospital.

There were quite a number of passengers on the train at the time of the accident, and it is extremely fortunate that the injuries were not more serious.

Among those hurt was Mr. Van Arsdol, GTP Divisional Engineer, one shoulder blade broken, other shoulder dislocated and a bad cut over the head.

No blame can be attached to anyone over the accident, and it seems quite likely that had the train been going a little quicker, all the cars would have safely cleared the danger point. In all probability trains will not run further than Telkwa or Hubert until the track east of these points is put into better condition, and although this will prove of considerable inconvenience to many, we still have to thank the GTP for the service they have given us up to the present, under trying conditions.

The Man from West Virginia

◆ Wiggs O'Neill

In the early years of the location and building of the Grand Trunk Pacific Railway out of Prince Rupert, there arrived on the scene an engineer by the name of John W. Moore Jr. He was appointed to the position of locating engineer from Prince Rupert east up the Skeena River. He was a likable fellow but, like some Americans, was pretty windy and important, always wanting you to keep in mind that he was John W. Moore Jr. of West Virginia, late chief engineer of the Coal and Coke Railway.

During the time I knew him I heard more about the state of West Virginia than I ever learned at school. About all I remember about Virginia was that there were blue hills there and as for the Coal and Coke Railway, I had never heard of it.

I was an operator on the Government Telegraph line, stationed at Telegraph Point when John Moore's party was working in that vicinity. He used to spend many evenings at our station, very often with Mrs. Moore, who came from West Virginia also—a very nice little woman who was content to let John do all the talking. It was during these little visits, when we would play cards and have a cup of coffee and some Bachelor's Bannock, that I learned so much of their state history. On one occasion I remember well, John was comparing the methods of engineering employed by the Grand Trunk Pacific and the Coal and Coke.

"You see," said John, "this stretch along the Skeena River—the line can go nowhere else but follow the river—as long as you follow it and keep your elevation, that's all there is to it. This outfit requires a complete survey in detail and all projected on detail maps. Why, down on the Coal and Coke all we would do is drive a few pegs in the cracks of the rocks to establish the elevation and go ahead and build her. She can't go any place else anyway. They are wasting a hell of a lot of money."

John had for an instrument man, a Mr. Green from New Westminster, but he and John never seemed to agree on anything. Every time Green made a statement, Moore always had another slant on it. We always remembered this and took note of it.

After they had moved camp farther up the river, we called on them when we were on the line patrol. There was an island six miles long just west of the "Hole in the Wall," across which the telegraph line had been built. It had all grown up into a thicket and the trail was very rough. We were anxious to have a trail cut that we could follow when on patrol. One evening we took Mr. Green up in our canoe and showed him the two choices in locating the railway. They could cross the slough behind the island and build on the island, or stay on the bank of the Skeena.

We took Mr. Green up some of the smaller sloughs and showed him the big spruce trees on the island, where under their lower branches you could see distinctly the river mud sticking to the bark, showing the high-water mark of 1894.

"My God," said Green, "we can't build here. The water mark is six feet above the island—no, we will have to follow the main shore."

The next evening we took John W. Jr. and showed him the two routes available but took good care we did not show him the high-water mark on the trees. To cap it all we mentioned the fact that Green seemed to favour the bank of the river, keeping clear of the island. That did the trick. Moore stuck his chest out and said, "There you are! Just shows how much Green knows about railroad construction. By taking his advice we would have at least two miles more of road to build and that costs money." So John Moore stuck to the island and the survey axemen cut us a fine trail the whole length of it. Walter, my partner, and I always figured we were real diplomats in that case.

Engineer Moore and the Grand Trunk Pacific, and subsequently the Canadian National Railway, have played in great luck ever since, for we have never since had high water comparable to the flood of 1894. We always call this island "Devil's Island" and the railroad station at Salvus is situated on the island today. If we ever have another 1894 flood, they are almost certain of losing six miles of railway and one station thrown in. As the road follows the railway, the Highways Department would also be in for a big headache.

Skeena Trip is Described

Pen Picture of Beauties, Dangers and Progress on Big River–Work on Construction of Transcontinental Makes Stream Busy

♦ from the Big Canyon *Weekly*, published at Kitselas, BC, October 28, 1909

"A trip to the upper waters of the Skeena is one of the rarest treats of travel that is possible to obtain," says a writer in the Prince Rupert *Optimist*.

After leaving Port Essington the interest never flags, but is constantly awakened by fresh and ever-changing scenes. The high, bald mountains and tumbling cataracts, and at this time of year, the many and varied colours of the foliage, furnish constant entertainment to those who enjoy the beauties of nature. Everywhere the banks are covered with the rich yellow of frostbitten leaves, interspersed by patches of deep, deep green.

Along the left bank we see the right-of-way of the Grand Trunk Pacific rapidly nearing completion. The most impressive thing in this work is its appearance of solidity. Whatever else may be said in criticism of the engineers, no one can deny that the rock bed of the GTP has all the qualifications of strength and permanence. As we pass up the river we see the camps of those whose names are familiar to us, and whose faces we sometimes see in Prince Rupert. Every piece of work has its peculiar interest. Freeberg & Stone's has a tunnel, Angus Nicholson's a crib, Staino's has a "shot," etc.

Kitselas Canyon looks every inch a frontier railroad town. It is crowded with railroad men of every kind and description. Below the town is the North West Bar, which was responsible for the *Northwest* wreck and probably other wrecks. At Kitselas there is another bar that will also very likely be responsible for a good many wrecks before the next few years go by.

The navigation of the Big Canyon above Kitselas is attended with extreme peril. Probably no other river in the world is as dangerous and treacherous as the Skeena. At the Canyon the very worst spot is encountered. It is very narrow, and it is necessary to aid the steamers by heaving them up against the raging torrent with a wire cable.

The *Distributor* was taken through on this particular trip by Capt. S.B. Johnson, who is not only one of the most experienced of the Skeena captains, but whose equal for navigation of swift water is probably hard to find. The passenger, with half his wits scared out of him, fails to see how a man can be so cool and collected as he glances up at the captain, quietly smoking his pipe, and taking everything so calmly as the big steamer strains and surges, and gives such nerve-shattering bumps as she swings about in the eddies and whirlpools.

Above the Canyon the river is also a succession of rapids; at Hardscrabble, the steamer apparently climbs four feet. At this point the work is let to the veteran contractor, D.A. Rankin, whose genial face is well known in Prince Rupert.

Then comes the work of Michael Sheady, and Tony McHugh, and Pete Salvus: and Norman McLeod, and John Bostrum—in fact, all of Foley's best-known contractors. Mr. Bostrum's work is opposite Meanskinisht. It is reported that nobody will be allowed to smoke on this contract during the period of construction. Meanskinisht has been the scene of the mission work of Reverend Tomlinson, one of the pioneer missionaries of northern BC. A very imposing church overlooks the Skeena from high ground at the upper end of the village.

The Indian villages of Kitwanga and Kitseguekla are adorned with totem poles and present a very picturesque appearance.

It would be hard to find a more beautiful spot than the village of Hazelton. It is situated on a succession of benches, with low ground in front, where the main business portion is located. This place is one of the oldest of the Hudson's Bay Company posts, and therefore had historic interest.

Duncan Ross has a contract above Hazelton on the second section, and is already getting in supplies.

The work, indeed, of forwarding supplies is proceeding very satisfactorily, being much expedited by the unusually high water at this time of year. Foley, Welch & Stewart, with their characteristic celerity, are establishing camps all along the riverbanks, and it is now assured that several of the large cuts will be started this fall.

Above the Canyon they have constructed a warehouse and if the water in the spring prevents the steamers from going right through, the cargoes will be transshipped to the Canyon, and taken forward by that portion of the fleet which is to be kept on the upper river.

It is a very fortunate thing that the construction of the Grand Trunk Pacific on this section is in the hands of contractors of the financial strength of Foley, Welch & Stewart, and of a group of managers whose skill and experience guarantee that the work will be carried forward with the utmost energy and rapidity. The building of this railroad to the Rockies is an appalling task, and it is good that the contract is in the hands of a firm that is trusted and relied upon by the public.

The *Distributor* is (as are, in fact, all the other boats) an exceedingly comfortable river steamer, sets an excellent table and has most courteous and obliging officers.

Next year will probably see the last of the steamers travel on the Skeena. Anyone who neglects to make this trip will miss one of the most enjoyable bits of travel that can be taken, perhaps anywhere in the world.

Twelve Thousand Head North

♦ Wes Jasper (from the Terrace *Omineca Herald*)

There have been many articles written on the early-day cattle drives from Texas and the southern States, with their hazards of rustlers, quicksand and stampedes. But nothing has ever been printed about one of the biggest and most successful cattle drives in Canada, when P. Burns & Co. contracted to supply beef for all the construction camps of the Grand Trunk Pacific and the Pacific Great Eastern railways through BC. I worked for Burns for four years and took part in the killing and driving of twelve thousand head.

Delivery of meat to the construction camps through the Prairie provinces was fairly easy, but when the work started in BC there was a much more difficult terrain to cope with. When the steel got to the Fraser River in the Rocky Mountain Trench, the beef was transported down the river by boats or scows to the camps along the route; but when the route left the river and started across central BC, supplies—including cattle—had to go overland through rough country.

Construction had started on the west end of the line about 1908, and by 1910 had come to the end of river transportation on the Skeena at

Hazelton. Then all beef had to be driven in overland from the Chilcotin, one of the largest cattle areas of BC, and this is where I entered the picture.

I was a lad in 1910, working at the Douglas Lake Ranch, having come from Washington across the line, when I heard about P. Burns taking an experimental drive of cattle from Chilcotin to Hazelton, which was evidently a success. About this time I received a letter from my brother Bill, who was in Kamloops, telling me to come at once as he had signed us both on for the beef drive to Hazelton. Wonderful news for a young fellow my age who had big ideas on being a top cowhand! We were to leave Ashcroft on April 20 for the Chilcotin to round up beef to start on the drive.

Joe Paine, foreman on the experimental drive, was in ill health now, so Ulysses Campbell took his place, as he had been on the previous drive with Paine. Most of the crew was recruited at Kamloops. They were Campbell, Antoine Allen, Johnny Cannon, Gus McGregor, Ezra Knapp, Abe Spooner, Alva Shaffer, Jack Lidlaw, Pete Duncan, my brother Bill and myself.

At Ashcroft we met Cy Heman, Burns's cattle buyer in the interior of BC, who had bought up a bunch of saddle and pack horses for us, as everything had to go by pack horse after we left the Chilcotin. It was five hundred miles of trail from Quesnel, the end of the wagon road, to Hazelton. Most of the horses Cy had bought were very poor due to the previous hard winter, so we were glad to hit Canoe Creek, where the horses from the first beef drive were wintered. Now we were pretty well mounted for our trip through the Chilcotin to Chezacut. There we started gathering the beef that Heman had contracted for at the price of fifty dollars per head for three-year-olds, sixty dollars for anything older and thirty-five dollars for cows. The cattle were pretty thin this time of the year, so we handled them slow and easy to get all the fat on them we could before they reached the construction camps. Burns received twenty-five cents per pound delivered to the camp.

From Chezacut, on the upper Chilcotin, we started south receiving cattle at the various ranches along the way till, by the time we reached Riske Creek, we had nearly eight hundred head. Riske Creek was to be our main camp and receiving point for the beef that was to go north, as there was plenty of grass on the rolling prairie country and lots of good water. Here Fred Becher operated a hotel and bar with a varied assortment of liquors at reasonable prices, as well as a post office and a very good store. Becher obliged the cowboys if they were broke by charging a bottle of spirits to Burns and putting it on the store bill as a shirt or six pairs of socks.

On our arrival at Riske Creek with the beef, we were pleased to find Archie McLean and Jim McDonald there with sixty head of fresh, fat saddle horses sent over from Alberta. We spent several days shoeing the horses—all the saddle horses and fifteen head of pack horses—and branding a "10" on the left hip of all of them. We also branded all the beef with Burns's "NL" brand for the trail brand. There was no brand inspection in those days, and in all the ten thousand or more head we drove out of the interior, there was never a complaint of P. Burns taking an animal he hadn't paid for.

We were planning on leaving Riske Creek on May 10 when Blake

Wilson, Burns's superintendent from BC, arrived unexpectedly by horse and buggy from Ashcroft. He said the camps were out of meat at Hazelton and we were to pick out five hundred head of steers and make a fast drive to Hazelton. So we loaded enough supplies—mostly bacon, beans, flour, sugar, syrup, dried fruit, coffee, tea, Klondyke vinegar and rice—to last till we got to Quesnel, our last store till we reached the Bulkley Valley. There were seven cowboys, a cook and a packer, who had to act as a horse wrangler as well, and about forty-five head of horses.

The first night out, we night-herded the cattle, as they were restless so soon off their range. We held them on the flats north of Meldrum Creek, which is now Allen Jeffries' ranch. Two riders were on duty, changing one at a time every two hours. One man would go to camp, unsaddle his mount, wake up his relief and usually get a cussing for doing so, and so on till daylight. At daybreak we could count scores of deer coming up from the river, heading for the mountains.

At Riske Creek we left about three hundred head of beef, which was to become the nucleus of another drive; Harry Curtis was to start out with this drive thirty days after us. During this time he was to enlarge the corrals and build a branding chute, as he had to rope and stretch out every head we re-branded.

Our route followed the west side of the Fraser River and the trip was uneventful until we reached what is now known as the China Ranch, owned by Sing Lees. We told the cook that he was a better packer than cook. My brother Bill, who was a first-class cook as well as a top cowhand, became our cook and horse wrangler.

Eight days passed before we reached Quesnel. Here we stayed a couple of days to rest the cattle and stock up on provisions to last the entire trip. Bacon and beans were the staple articles.

At Quesnel we met Jean Cataline, the old packer, who had two pack trains loading up for the trip to Hazelton and north to the Ninth Cabin on the old Telegraph Trail. He had sixty mules and sixty horses in his train. From Cataline we got much information regarding the camping places along the trail, as there were only certain places where there was enough feed and room to night-herd the cattle, and where there was good water. Some of these spots were only three or four miles apart, others twelve to fifteen. We were always on the move by six o'clock in the morning, but sometimes we would be in camp for the day by nine or ten.

As this northern country is all covered with brush, mostly red willow, and the trail narrow, the cattle had to be strung out single file. We counted out the cattle in the morning between two riders, the lead man taking about fifteen head to start out, and a rider swinging in behind every fifty head. That way, they were soon all in single file. You never saw the cowboy in front or behind you all day unless you were in the lead and got stuck at some mudhole or boggy creek and couldn't get the cattle to cross. The foreman always counted out in the morning and the lead man counted in at night. Sometimes it took about two hours before the last ones were in.

When we reached Mud River, we decided to rest the cattle in this big, open, grassy country for a couple of days while the cowboys cleaned up and had a good sleep. A swim and change of clothes sure felt good, as we had only taken off our boots at night since we started.

At Mud River it was the usual routine: count the cattle out in the morning, ride all day, count them in at night—bacon, beans, bannock and coffee, until we came to the Nechako River at Fort Fraser. Here we had to swim the cattle across the river. We let the herd rest and fill up for a couple of days, during which time we built a pole corral and a chute or runway into the water where the stream was about 150 yards wide and very sluggish. We found an old flat-bottom scow at this point, which we used to ferry two cowboys and their horses across to hold the cattle as they came out of the water. The boss had hired two Indians with their canoes to point the leaders across. We had to wait two hours for the sun to get around so it would not shine in the cattle's eyes when they were swimming, as they were apt to turn back if it did.

After getting the first bunch about a quarter of the way across, and seeing they had made up their minds to cross to the other side of the river, we started stringing the rest of the herd in. It was only a half-hour before the whole bunch was on dry ground across the river.

Then came the job of loading all our camp outfit on the scow and ferrying it across. After that we swam the horses, but that took but a short time as horses swim much faster than cattle. It was about two miles to the Hudson's Bay fort from the crossing, and we decided to camp there and do some trading. The factor had not had any fresh beef since the fall before so, as we needed a few essentials, the boss ordered a steer butchered for trade. After all the trading was done we had a balance to our credit, which was adjusted with a gallon of Hudson's Bay rum, much appreciated by all.

Up to this time we had had very good weather; but after we left Fraser Lake, it started to rain, and we had rain and drizzle every day for thirty days. Some of the cattle got mud fever or foot rot—the foot swells to three times the normal size and then breaks between the toes. These animals had to be watched very closely during the day, as they would sneak off the trail into the thick underbrush and lie down. We often passed them by, not missing any until the count was made at night. Next morning, someone had to backtrack to find the lost ones, which were generally following along at a very slow pace.

We were getting into the vicinity of Burns Lake by now and had been warned by packers and Indians to watch for poison weeds in this area. Because there had been so much rain, the wild parsnip, which is deadly to cattle, was easily pulled up by the roots. We were lucky to lose only three head going through this stretch of country.

When we finally came to the Bulkley Valley it looked like the Promised Land to us after fighting the mudholes and underbrush of the last four hundred miles. We travelled down this valley of large open sidehills until we came to what is known as the Government Ranch, about fifty-six miles from Hazelton. Here we decided to hold the cattle for the summer and drive out from the main herd what was needed for the camps every week.

Burns & Co. had built a slaughterhouse at Hazelton by now and wanted meat right away, so we took a hundred head of the best steers there,

Early Hazelton—supply centre for the area. (65-C)/BCARS HP 1101

killing a few along the way at the construction camps that were just getting started east of Hazelton. Two men were left to range-herd the four hundred head left in the Bulkley Valley.

Because there was such a demand for horses, the boss at Hazelton, Bob Grant, decided to sell all the surplus stock and send the outfit around by Prince Rupert and Vancouver to Ashcroft. There he would get a fresh bunch of horses and start out again for Chilcotin to round up another drive for the north.

A butcher and I were sent back to the herd camp for another drive to supply the slaughterhouse and camps for a week. We worked at this job for three summers. We would take the camp orders on the way out and in that way knew how many head to bring each week. If a camp wanted four beef or one, it was killed right at the camp on the ground, and I would continue on to the next camp and wait for the butcher to overtake me. Again he would shoot as many as they required, and I would travel on with the rest of the beef until none was left.

On one of these trips in the vicinity of the 20 Mile House, which was a roadhouse and bootleg joint, I lost one steer. While tracking it around through the underbrush about a quarter mile from the buildings, my horse stepped into a large hole but recovered his footing and got out. It all looked level to me, but on closer scrutiny I removed three feet of moss and found a cache of five cases of liquor—rye and Scotch. As I did not care for Scotch, I left it and gave my partner a surprise party on the road when he overtook me. I never did find that steer and always after when we stopped at the 20 Mile House, they didn't seem too friendly!

During the course of the summer three more drives of five hundred head each arrived at the herd camp, making a total of about two thousand head for the summer. Cattle fatten very quickly in that north country on the lush pea vine and vetch, but they also lose their fat just as fast when the frost hits the pea vine. So about the tenth of September we started making larger drives to the slaughterhouse at Hazelton. There they froze a thousand carcasses to last till fresh beef could arrive from Chilcotin the following year.

The last of the cattle were brought in the first of November. As there was a good demand for horses, we sold all our saddle stock at $150 per head and loaded our camp outfit and gear in a forty-foot Indian canoe and started down the Skeena River to Kitselas, about eighty miles from the end of the steel. Track-laying had been tied up here, waiting for completion of the tunnels at Kitselas Canyon.

At Prince Rupert we took passage on an old coast steamer, the *Camosun II*. It was my first boat ride and I got very sick crossing Queen Charlotte Sound.

The crew split up in Vancouver after a few days. I was sent to Ashcroft by the Burns Co. to drive a meat wagon, delivering beef to the Grand Trunk construction camps along the Thompson River. I worked at this till it was time to start north to Hazelton, about April 20.

Some of the old hands were in the new crew and we had a new bunch of horses from the Okanagan. We started gathering beef from Canoe Creek, Dog Creek and Alkali Lake ranches. We arrived at Chimney Creek Bridge on the Fraser River with 350 head in 1912, just when they were taking out the old wooden towers and putting in the present steel towers. During this construction they allowed only three head on the bridge at one time, so it was a slow job crossing our cattle. The cattle were wild, never having become gentle on the feed ground, as ranchers seldom fed cattle in the winter in those days. It took us three days to cross, and we had to rope the last few and drag them over the bridge.

As the grass had become pretty well eaten out along the old Telegraph Trail north of Quesnel, it was decided to try a new route through the Nazko River, where we found large, open bunch-grass sidehills and splendid fishing in the river. Frank English and I each staked a homestead here, seventy miles from Alexis Creek, on those sidehills. They were the first stakes in the locality —but we never went back.

From the Nazko we followed an old Indian trail crossing the Blackwater River and Mud River, about thirty miles upstream from the Telegraph Trail crossing. We came onto the Telegraph Trail again at what was then known as the Government Meadow, about three days travel from Fraser Lake. After a short rest at the Nechako River, we swam the cattle across and encountered a lot of poison weed between Burns Lake and the North Bulkley River. After a very dry summer, the country was just blue with wild larkspur, which, at a certain time of flower, is very poisonous to cattle. We had to camp one night where the growth was very heavy.

In the morning we found nine of them dead and nearly forty head unable to get off the ground. After more than two hours work, such as bleeding by cutting the tail or ear and keeping them rolled up on their stomachs to prevent bloating, I was left to get the poisoned ones along as best I could. As one recovered a bit, it would get up and follow the trail for a mile or two, then fall down in a fit. After a short rest it would get up and continue. In handling these animals you had to stay well away from them, for when they got excited, they would fall down in a fit and that caused another delay. After three days slow work these animals were all back in the herd, quite a few minus their tails or ears, but we never lost any more than nine head.

By this time the railway contractors had built a good many miles of wagon road from Burns Lake west, and driving cattle was much easier than the previous year through this part of the country. We were told by road gangs that the road would be finished by late fall.

The cattle were herded at the Government Ranch as before and killed at the camps. By now the camps had built corrals and a windlass to hoist the carcasses, which was a great help to the butchers.

After killing off the last of the cattle—and selling the poorer horses to the Indians, who were by now beginning to appreciate a horse for packing but very seldom ever rode one—we loaded twenty-five head of horses on the train at New Hazelton, the end of the steel by now, and travelled to Prince Rupert. From here we took our horses on the SS *Prince Rupert* to Vancouver, encountering some very rough water, which made most of the horses very sick. They were a sorry-looking bunch when we unloaded at Vancouver, but still were not at the end of their journey. They were loaded again on the CPR and shipped to Ashcroft, where they wintered on a ranch in Highland Valley.

Burns & Co. got all their beef in the winter from Calgary, and there were two trainloads a week to be unloaded at Kamloops and fed and watered. I was sent to Kamloops to look after this stock. I stayed till spring, then went to the Perry Ranch at Ashcroft to take care of the saddle horses that had wintered at Highland Valley. The horses were very poor and had to be fed oats as well as hay. As they had tons and tons of potatoes on the ranch for which there was no market, the foreman suggested feeding them to the horses. This was finally successful after mixing the potatoes with cut-up carrots and oats. After thirty days you wouldn't have known they were the same horses. When the time came to start north on the beef drive, three cowboys were bucked off the first morning.

In 1913 the drivers started out earlier than before, as there was a greater demand than ever for beef on the Grand Trunk Railway. We had close to eleven hundred head gathered at Riske Creek to be divided into two drives—one going by the Nazko route and the other by Quesnel and the Telegraph Trail, starting north at the same time. The herds had been sorted and corralled for the night, ready to start the next day. Sometime during the night something gave them a scare and they stampeded. They tore down the fence, and as there was only one wrangle horse in camp, there was nothing we could do until daylight. It took us three days to round them up again. For several days the steers would spook and run at every unusual sound.

I had been working with Harry Curtis's outfit during the beef roundup in the Chilcotin and had gone with his drive via the Nazko route as far as the Blackwater Crossing on the Telegraph Trail. I then joined my brother's drive on north. Curtis's drive went into Prince George, where Burns had built a corral and a slaughterhouse. The main herd was left at Six Mile Flats and a bunch was driven in every week to the slaughterhouse. This was the boom year for Prince George, which had, with all the construction workers and land seekers, an estimated ten thousand people in the area.

When we got to the Nechako River the water was very high, too high for the cattle to land in their usual place. After waiting ten days for the water to recede, we attempted a crossing, but the river was still high and the cattle got to milling around in the middle of the stream and about ten head were trampled under and drowned.

I worked at my job of driving beef to the camp all summer. We killed about the same number of beef on our end of the line and about fifteen hundred head went to Prince George, making thirty-five hundred head of beef for the railway in 1913.

On November 1, I had a wire from my brother at Riske Creek. He was gathering cattle for the last drive to Prince George and he wanted me to meet him in Quesnel as soon as possible as he was short of men and horses. After killing the last of the beef, Ezra Knapp, Kim Pratt and I headed south with a bunch of tired, weary horses and with ten inches of snow on the ground. Our horses were very thin, as there had been a lot of swamp fever that summer, and we lost three on the way to Quesnel. We were pleased to see the boys feeding their horses oats when we met the big drive. There were ten pack horses loaded with oats as well as a four-horse team for the chuckwagon and beds. There were fifteen cowboys to handle 860 head in this drive.

About the fifth of December we arrived at Prince George with the last beef drive for the construction of the Grand Trunk Pacific Railroad. In the course of four years this had been a very profitable market for close to twelve thousand head of Chilcotin cattle.

The First Big Snow Slide at Mile 44

♦ Wiggs O'Neill (from the Terrace *Omineca Herald*)

When the first trains ran out of Prince Rupert, they ran as far as Shames Station, below Terrace, I believe in 1909. That winter a big snow slide occurred at what used to be called Mile 44 and blocked the GTP railway track. The rotary snowplow was up the line when the slide occurred, so they hightailed it down the line to clear things up.

The company had made ample precautions for such an eventuality by building some snowsheds on the mountain above, but when the big slide came, it took all the snowsheds with it and blocked the track and continued on out into the river.

The rotary plow arrived on the scene on the upper side of the slide and dived into it, throwing snow to beat hell. When they got well into the slide, the rotary impeller picked up a lot of the wreckage of the defunct snowsheds, and some rock, which snapped the big steel shaft like matchwood. The rotary plow stood on the track, helpless, unable to move forward or backward until more snow slides came down and covered her up.

An engineer—or fellow who thought he was one—hired a small tugboat from the Georgetown Sawmill Company and some cannery bunkhouses on scows and sent them up the Skeena with about 150 Italians. They were all equipped with shovels to clear the track so they could get the snowplow out and get her back to Rupert to have her repaired. You can imagine this operation was like trying to bail the ocean out with a teaspoon. It was a wonderful scene to behold, 150 men about 10 abreast, shovelling snow and muck, all talking Italian at the same time—and getting nowhere.

The engineer, using precautions, had a man out on the ice on the river with a gun. He was to keep his eye on the mountain above and if he saw another slide coming, he was to shoot as a warning for the workmen to get out of the way fast. Things went well the first day, but not too much progress was made in the clearing operations.

Mile 44 is near the head of tidewater and when the tide is high, there is always a movement of the ice in the frozen river. Suddenly there occurred a big crack in the ice, accompanied by a terrific report. The Italian workmen thought it was a shot fired from the ground out on the ice. They dropped all shovels and beat it down the bank as if the devil himself was after them, all yelling at the same time. There was no new slide, of course, but the men refused to go back on the job.

A tugboat had to take the camp scows and all the men back to Rupert and the Grand Trunk Pacific was tied up for the rest of the winter. The rotary plow was there, too. When spring came and the ice and snow had melted, then the rotary was rescued, but not before.

The company gave a contract to Archie McDougal, one of the Foley, Welch & Stewart contractors, and he constructed a tunnel through the solid rock under the brow of the mountain to make sure such a disaster did not occur again. It was always known as McDougal's Tunnel.

Of late years I have noticed that the railway has been using the old original track along the foot of the mountain, and not going through McDougal's Tunnel. I feel it wouldn't hurt them to look through the old Grand Trunk Pacific logbooks now and again. They would at least have discovered that Archie McDougal's tunnel was built for a purpose and they should find out why. If they had routed the trains back through Archie's tunnel for the winter months, they probably would have saved themselves a few headaches this winter from slides.

I was running my passenger boat *Strongheart* up as far as Mile 44 that winter and saw all this affair myself and did not get it second hand.

Winter on the Skeena... 1910

♦ Syd Cooper (from the Terrace *Omineca Herald*)

My chum, Jim Hatfield, and I were working for the B&B (GTP Bridge and Buildings gang) on the first snowshed they were attempting to build west of Kwinitsa (a slide subsequently took out the shed and a long tunnel was driven in place of it). Two small slides came down while we were working, so it was considered too dangerous to continue and the crew went back to Rupert. A severe blizzard occurred and five feet of snow fell there, a record unequalled since.

The train was held until the storm abated and as there was no work to be had and funds were running low, we tackled Meehan, the super, for a job on the snowplow train. It started out with a wooden Russel plow, two small Standard locies, a car of coal, a boarding car and a lunch, intending to reach the end of steel that night. Instead we found a slide about fifteen feet deep just west of the snowshed. They hammered away at this and finally got through it at nightfall. Next morning we started across the Kwinitsa flat and a strong wind got up with zero temperature, which drifted the snow in behind us as fast as we pushed it out ahead. The crew had to keep shovelling out behind so that the plow train could back up for another push ahead. Most of us got frozen fingers, toes or ears. Finally we reached the through-cut east of the present station and that was the payoff. Springs at the trackside had covered the rails over with solid ice on top of which ten feet of snow had drifted and it was impossible to keep the plow on the track. The engineers drew the fires, drained the boilers and the crew headed back for Rupert on foot.

Jim and I figured there was no percentage in going back, so hiked east up the line to Mile 54, where a bridge gang was putting in cofferdams for the Kasiks River piers. We went to work there until the end of January, when the camp ran out of grub and the bridge gang had to beat it for Rupert. We did not want to turn back, so on the last day of January we again took off up the line. There were seven feet of snow on the ground and it started snowing heavily that afternoon. We reached Mile 56 (Hole in the Wall) and stayed there that night. Next morning there was three feet of new snow, making an even ten feet on the level. It took us three hours, from nine to twelve, to make one mile to the sawmill at Mile 60, which had been cutting timbers for the snowshed. We had lunch at the mill and whittled makeshift skis out of rough boards and started on again. This was the hardest trip that I ever made, as the snow stuck to our rough skis and had to be continually pounded off with a stick. We travelled until ten o'clock that night and reached a section shack at Mile 70, where Exstew station is now.

All that the section crew had to eat was some oatmeal mush. It would have been a grim prospect for us, seventy miles from any food, ten feet of snow and no snowshoes. However, when the trains stopped running, the dog teams operated by Beirnes and Mulvaney (four teams on this run) had made a trip to Rupert for the mail and had cached food at points on the way down. It was our good fortune that they had been delayed by the heavy snowfall and were at Mile 70 when we arrived.

Our troubles were over. We each drove one of the dog teams while their drivers broke trail ahead on their snowshoes. It was my first experience in dog mushing and I still remember the names of the team: Dick, Skookum, Prince and Buster. We reached George Little's tie camp, where Terrace now stands, on a Sunday evening and stayed the night. Rev. Thomas Marsh was then living at Kalum and visited the camp to hold church service. He came up on snowshoes and had a big husky dog packing the hymnbooks.

And that was the end of our cold, bitter hike back in 1910.

Local Newspapers Track the Railway's Progress

The following are from the *Omineca Herald* unless otherwise noted:

July 25, 1908
It is learned on good authority that supplies for the GTP construction work will not be taken through the Canyon. A tramway will be constructed around the Canyon and all goods will be transferred. It has not been decided yet just what form of tramway will be used, although it is thought likely a heavy enough rail will be laid so a donkey engine can be used if considered desirable.

September 12, 1908
Good progress is reported on the grade of the GTP between Prince Rupert and Kitselas. Most of the camps are working full handed and what men are needed at the others have been sent for. Reports from the coast, claiming that only a pretense was being made at grading the line, seem to be without foundation.

September 19, 1908 (Prince Rupert *Empire*)
Reports that an additional 100 miles of the GTP in British Columbia east of Prince Rupert will soon be let should be taken with several grains of salt. Railways cannot be built without supplies and Foley, Welch & Stewart will have all they can do to get enough supplies through to the front this fall to keep the subcontractors on the first 100 miles at work. It is not likely work on another 100 miles can be commenced earlier than mid-summer next year.

September 10, 1908
If Foley, Welch & Stewart get the contract for the second hundred miles, navigation through the Canyon at Kitselas will be done away with at that point. This would be a great help as it would allow almost uninterrupted service along the river during high water.

November 14, 1908
The first chapter in the construction of the Grand Trunk Pacific Railway was closed when the location of the line was completed from Prince Rupert to Edmonton. To do this and do it right was a task in itself, taking four years of time and the best men that could be obtained. At times the difficulties were great and sometimes slight delays became unavoidable, but the work went ahead summer and winter. Every possible route was tested to obtain the best grades with the shortest distances. Lines were run on both sides of the Skeena as far as Hazelton and on both sides of the Bulkley, as well as over the once-discussed cut-off via the Copper River.

Finally the present route was chosen which, crossing from the north to the south bank of the Skeena at Hankin's Riffle, a short distance below Kitselas, follows the south bank of the Skeena as far as the mouth of the Bulkley River and then up the Bulkley, on the south side a distance of something over 100 miles. From Edmonton west there are but two summits to be crossed, Yellowhead Pass and the Divide between the watershed of the Skeena and Fraser rivers, the latter being so low as to be scarcely noticed. No other transcontinental railway will have such easy grades as the GTP and consequently no other railway will haul freight so cheaply.

(*Note:* The "present route" stated above was not the chosen one. Crossing from the north to the south bank took place at Skeena Crossing, BC.)

November 14, 1908
Monday morning the last of the GTP surveyors left Hazelton, going down the river by canoe. In all there were about 40 men in the two parties recently disbanded here. Some of the men are going to Prince Rupert where they will be engaged in the work of surveying the townsite.

November 21, 1908
The latest papers from the coast cities announce that work on the GTP is to be pushed more vigorously. Fifteen hundred to two thousand more men are to be put on the job and four big steam shovels are to be added. It is the supposition that rails will be laid to Copper River in less than a year. The contact for the second hundred miles is to be let soon enough to allow preparations being made to start active work in the spring. From Copper River to the Bulkley the work is light with no heavy rock cuts. The statement has been made by one in a position to know, that allowing the first 100-mile section a year's start, the second hundred miles would be ready for steel as soon as the first. Foley, Welch & Stewart have been building railways for many years and still have their first failure to look back upon. When word is passed from headquarters

that the work must be hurried, it is pretty safe to say they will come through with their part.

February 13, 1909
Rumours of changes of local and higher-up officials of the GTP Railway have been in circulation ever since the visit here by President Hays in October. A practical railroad man may be quoted as saying: "What is wanted on the GTP is a good practical western railway man as manager. There are too many officials, high and low, from down East and from the southern States to build a railway like the GTP on time." (Manager Morse was succeeded by E.J. Chamberlain.)

April 3, 1909
Tenders are being called by the GTP for the construction of six steel bridges along the first hundred miles from Prince Rupert, bridges to be completed by the end of August of the present year.

April 24, 1909
It was announced by J.E. Balrymple, assistant freight traffic manager for the GTP, that a contract for the supply of steel rails for the 100-mile section between Prince Rupert and Copper River has been awarded to the Dominion Iron & Steel Company.

May 8, 1909
Two large steamers loaded with rails for the western end of the GTP have sailed from Nova Scotia on the long voyage around Cape Horn and due to arrive at Prince Rupert in July.

June 5, 1909
Notice has been received that wages were to be reduced on government roadwork from $3.00 per day with board to $3.50 per day without board. (Reaction: Any reduction in wages at this time would not be justifiable due to the high cost of living.)

March 10, 1910
The Grand Trunk Pacific has been completed to a point 122 miles west of Edmonton, making the total mileage completed 1,360 miles from Fort William to Wolf Creek.

April 16, 1910
British Columbia was once described as a "Sea of Mountains." Little or nothing was known of the part of the country through which the Grand Trunk Pacific is being built. Many thought quite seriously that it might be all right if it could be rolled flat.

Mary 28, 1910
William Salvus, a brother of Peter Salvus, a railway contractor, was killed by a blast near Kitwangar last Saturday evening.

The blast had been prepared with the intention of breaking the rock toward the river, and not counting on anything else. Salvus and the foreman of the work went up the grade about 200 yards to a point where they thought they were in a place of safety and were standing on the grade to watch the effect of the explosion. Instead of breaking the direction expected, rocks were thrown with terrific force directly toward the two men. Both endeavoured to dodge the flying missiles, but there were too many of them, or they were coming too fast, and one piece weighing several pounds struck Salvus in the right side, inflicting almost instant death. The foreman had his left arm broken between the shoulder and elbow at the same time.

July 23, 1910
GRAND TRUNK RAILWAY PARALYZED BY CANADA'S MOST GIGANTIC RAILWAY STRIKE
Men quit work simultaneously in all departments throughout the entire system. Company preparing to import strike breakers.

July 30, 1910
A party of photographers in the employ of the GTP and newspapermen are making the trip over the railway line from Edmonton to Prince Rupert and are expected to arrive within the next few weeks.

July 30, 1910
The laying of steel on the GTP out of Prince Rupert is going ahead at a rate calculated to make good the statement by railroad officials that the first hundred miles would be laid before fall. At the beginning of this week the rails were at Mile 40; the close of the week should see them at Mile 45. At Mile 43 there was a trestle to put in which accounts for the small mileage laid this week. As work progresses up the Skeena, rails will be laid faster as the roadbed becomes straighter and the many curves of the tidewater end are passed.

August 6, 1910
The change in immigration regulations permitting the coming in of railway labourers on the same terms as farm labourers must be met with approval. Immigrants other than farm labourers were supposed to have in their possession, at the time of landing, the sum of $25.00 and the price of transportation to their ultimate destination. A number of instances have occurred where large gangs of railroad workers from Seattle have been compelled to turn back from Prince Rupert and return across the line when they were badly needed here. There is so much railroad building going on in Canada and especially on the Pacific slope that there has been more jobs than men. The western end of the GTP, being most remote, has suffered most from lack of labour. Anything that will make it possible to secure full gangs of men in the camps along the Skeena, without letting in undesirables, should be welcomed.

August 6, 1910
The second drive of beef cattle for P. Burns & Co., amounting to 470 head, is at hand and will be turned into the hills until the cold storage plant is ready.

October 1, 1910
WHAT IS REALLY HOLDING RAILWAY WORK BACK
There is considerable discussion among the Western press about what practically amounts to a plea by the GTP for Oriental labour to build their road.

Food and sanitary conditions about the camps are good. It is simply a case of the station men not being able to make any money . . . In our opinion the present backward state of the works is due entirely to one cause, not enough steamboats at the right time . . . They had more men than they could feed and keep working during last winter. With the completion of the first hundred miles being delayed, instead of being able to send supplies halfway to Hazelton by rail, everything has had to be brought up the river to feed the men. There is another shortage in sight. If the camps are supplied, the material for the bridge across the Skeena River cannot be brought up, and this bridge will be delayed.

People in this country would rather see the work held back than the country filled up with Orientals.

There is no hostility to the GTP: without it the population of this district would be what it was ten years ago. However, the fact remains that it is current talk that the whole service would be improved, including the building of the western end of the line, if every matter of importance did not have to be before a board of directors in London, England, causing delay.

October 13, 1910
The application of the Grand Trunk Pacific for permission to employ Orientals on construction work has been turned down by the Provincial executive.

October 29, 1910
THE TRANSPORTATION PROBLEM FOR 1911
In seeking information as to the intention of the GTP regarding the opening of the first hundred miles from Prince Rupert for traffic, the casual inquirer meets two distinct sets of ideas on the subject. In the absence of an expression of opinion from President Hays in any of the interviews given out during his trip to the Pacific coast or since, it may be presumed that no one out west knows very much about it. The interior wants one question answered: Will the Grand Trunk Pacific deliver public freight above the canyon at Kitselas at a rate, say, of one hundred tons a day, commencing on or before June 1, 1911?

It is a matter of concern to everyone living along the Skeena and all those in the interior whose goods are carried on the riverboats. It is more than that; it is the most serious matter that the people of the interior have to face, resolving into the question of whether this part of British Columbia is go ahead or whether it is to be held back.

Notwithstanding the fact that a new and capacious boat was put on the river this year, the steamboat service was overwhelmed. Roughly speaking, there are 200 tons of Hazelton freight lying at Prince Rupert and Port Essington that will never reach here this year. There were another 300 tons ordered but either refused a landing at the transfer point or else left on the docks at Vancouver and Victoria. Still another 250 tons would have been ordered had there been any possible chance to get it up the river. Altogether, this district is about 700 tons of general freight short of what it would have been had there been transportation for the traffic offering. In 1908 little or no freight was left at Prince Rupert and Post Essington and the total received at Hazelton was in round number 1,000 tons.

November 12, 1910
All reports from downriver are enthusiastic about the rapid way in which the grade is being built. Stretches of six and seven miles are all complete and only short gaps are left along the line. Camp No. 21, above Kitselas, where a large number of teams are at work, will close down in about three weeks and teams will be put to hauling freight from Sealey out to the various camps. In all about seventy teams will be worked this winter. Foley, Welch & Stewart have nearly forty heavy teams and the rest will be hired.

Camps are being built at the long tunnel east of town but work will not be started on the tunnel till spring, as it is intended to put in an air compressor.

November 26, 1910
Angus Beaton made a flying trip from Prince Rupert this week arriving here (Hazelton) in four days. Needless to say he made the first hundred miles on the work train. The rest of the way he travelled on foot.

December 10, 1910
With the completion of the second tower, more rapid progress is being made with the Skeena bridge. The cables are now across, and within ten days the structure will be ready for use.

December 17, 1910
From an official source it is learned that the GTP will make an effort to maintain a semi-weekly accommodation service on the first section of the road, from Prince Rupert to Copper River. The absence of snowsheds is likely to give considerable trouble during the winter; but it is hoped a fairly regular train service will be given.

February 11, 1911
The snowplow and two engines are reported stalled at Mile 51 between two snow slides. The rotary plow was sent from Rupert to relieve the situation but was unable to get beyond Mile 40. Powder is being used to clear the slides.

February 11, 1911
Owing to the closing down of camps on the lower end of the line, those travelling to the coast will find no convenient stopping places between Kitselas and Prince Rupert except Kitsumkalum, the sawmill at Mile 60 and the snowshed camp at Mile 45.

February 18, 1911
After travelling the 50-odd miles of the GTP grade from Hazelton to this place (Lorne Creek) the impression is that no obstacle exists to prevent rails being laid to the Skeena Bridge by early fall. Reports on conditions between here and the end of steel indicate that there may be delay, however, on that portion of the line which will prevent any steel laying before August.

There is great activity all along the line, and every camp appears to be working to the full limit of its equipment. Four months more, with plenty of material and supplies, would see the grade complete from here to the bridges, with the exception of one rock cut on Norman McLeod's contract, just below the crossing, which is estimated to take until September 1. The tunnel on Bostrom's work, below Gitwangak, will be completed before steel can possibly be laid that far.

Everything looks very favourable for the stretch of road between the present end of steel and the Skeena Bridge being able to handle a limited amount of traffic next winter without any difficulty.

February 18, 1911
KITSELAS FATALITY
By an explosion which occurred near Kitselas on Sunday, five men were killed and two severely injured. The men were working in a small tunnel when a box of dynamite placed at the mouth of the tunnel, presumably to thaw, became overheated and exploded. Eight men a short distance away had a remarkable escape.

The dead are: M.F. Burgess (foreman); Charles Quornstrom; Eli Ogrezobich; John Otisovich; E.H. Kova.

The following items from 1911 are taken from the Prince Rupert *Daily News* and present that city's viewpoint:

May 17, 1911
REGULAR RAIL SERVICE UP RIVER NOW TO BEGIN
Early next week the first of a regular service of trains will leave for Kitselas with goods chiefly for Foley, Welch & Stewart. This is the beginning of the real rivalry between the rail and river services, which will, of course, result in a win for the railway.

May 18, 1911
Kitselas: A sad accident has happened near here, by which it is feared Mr. W.H. Tully, port engineer for Foley, Welch & Stewart, and William Grant, fireman of the steamer *Skeena*, have lost their lives.

Tully, who had come up the Skeena from Prince Rupert, left Kitselas at noon yesterday to go to Kitsumkalum in a small rowboat. As the Str. *Port Simpson* was entering Little Canyon, the captain and passengers discovered their boat turned over and the oars floating down the river. The boat had evidently been capsized, losing Tully and Grant in the Canyon, which, on account of the high water, is now a fierce raging torrent at that point.

June 14, 1911
The recent action of the GTP in ordering eight million feet of lumber from the US instead of giving the order to firms in BC is much discussed (and criticized).

June 21, 1911
This morning a tugboat arrived with barges in tow bringing 400 tons of steel for the Skeena River bridge, which, after the Kitselas tunnels, is the next great undertaking.

June 21, 1911
Pictures of first passenger train pulling out appear in Canadian and American press. Live member of the *Daily News* saw to it.

First Passenger Train Left Rupert Today
♦ from the Prince Rupert *Daily News*, June 14, 1911

In business-like style but with an enthusiastic send-off, the first passenger train pulled out for Copper River 100 miles east.

Today the first passenger train eastbound from the Pacific Coast terminal pulled out with clang of bell and hissing blast of steam at 1 p.m. A crowd of the live citizens of Prince Rupert gave the train a send-off at the wharf depot, where before long will be built a permanent railway station. Tickets were on sale aboard the train as well as at the GTP booking office.

Engine 103 had the honour of hauling the first trainload of booked passengers, with E. Nehring as engineer and E. Chesley as conductor.

Today's train took for the first 100 miles upriver about 200 passengers, made up of two passenger cars, brake van, Gen. Supt. Mehan's private car and several freight cars. It pulled out at 1:00 p.m., scheduled to reach Copper River shortly after 9:00 tonight.

Arthur C. Little, newsstand proprietor, bought the first ticket, #25538—a return ticket to Copper River for $4.05 one way.

June 16, 1911
The first train to come in through from Copper City arrived yesterday afternoon. It had some 80 or 90 passengers aboard.

Life is Made Pleasant for Railroad Workers

Railroad YMCA Doing a Noble Work Along the Grand Trunk Pacific Right-of-Way–How Men are Helped

♦ from the *Omineca Herald*, October 27, 1911

Along the banks of the Skeena River for the past three or four years have been employed several thousand men by Messrs. Foley, Welch & Stewart, contractors for the Grand Trunk Pacific right-of-way. A large portion of these men are hundreds, if not thousands of miles from their homes and their friends, and if not born with an English-speaking tongue have, since coming to Canada, acquired it. Day in and day out, month after month, in all kinds of weather the work has proceeded and the men see or hear little but their work by day and sleep by night. The magnificent scenery, of which so much has already been written, but to which no writer or artist can do justice, is nothing to those whose ceaseless toil brings them into contact with it continually. They are hundreds of miles from the business and social circles or the home fireplace. But they have not been forgotten and a great deal of work has been, and is being, carried on among them.

The Young Men's Christian Association, with branches all over the world in every town of any size, has also a railroad department, and that great institution has been working among the men affording them pleasure and enlightenment.

On the Foley, Welch & Stewart contract Mr. W.H. Morrison is Secretary and the man in charge, and had the country been searched, a better and more capable fellow could not have been found. Early and late, Sundays and weekdays, Mr. Morrison is on the go carrying with him that which enables men to live better, work better and feel that there is more in life than work and three meals a day with a bed at night. The weary, sick, discouraged and discontented all go to Mr. Morrison who is the mental and spiritual physician of the camps.

The work of the YMCA among the railway workers is far reaching and beyond the conception of the average man. Not only are gospel meetings held on Sundays and the men taught those things which help them see beyond the present life, but through Mr. Morrison is distributed newspapers, magazines, books and literature in all forms. Most of the periodicals are late and out-of-date for a city man, but they are eagerly sought and earnestly read on the railway right-of-way and thus these men keep abreast of the times.

Phonographs or gramophones are now in every camp and thousands of records are in use and passed from one camp to another, keeping the men up to date in the musical world. In these railway camps one hears the latest songs and the newest music sung and whistled in unison with the pick, shovel and hammer and by the teamsters plodding along behind their horses.

This fall Mr. Morrison has established his headquarters at Skeena Crossing bridge where from 200 to 300 men will be employed throughout the winter. Here the Secretary has erected a building 22 by 40 feet in which are found many comforts of civilization. He has provided a large reading room in which are found the leading papers and magazines. There are writing tables with stationary and writing materials. In connection are two bathrooms with hot and cold water; two pool tables; checkers, chess and other games; and a small loaning library.

All these things which do so much to make life pleasant and profitable are furnished the men free of charge, although they are privileged to make contributions and a movement is now on foot among the men themselves to contribute regularly to the institution. By such they are able to enjoy even more of those necessary luxuries.

Mr. Morrison has an assistant at Skeena Crossing, Mr. Ed Kenney, who has charge of that camp while Mr. Morrison is visiting the many other camps along the road between Prince Rupert and Aldermere and ever beyond.

In all the work undertaken by the YMCA the contractors, Messrs. Foley, Welch & Stewart, and all their official staff have given noble and

First passenger train leaves Prince Rupert for 100 Mile near Kitselas June 14, 1911. (4-B)

First GTP passenger train from Prince Rupert to Copper River, June 14, 1911. The general superintendent's car is at the rear of train. (42-A)/BCARS 8271

hearty assistance. They work hand in hand with Mr. Morrison and his requirements in the way of material, land, transportation, etc., are given first consideration. Foley, Welch & Stewart are expert employers. They know their men and their needs and they do everything possible for their convenience and comfort and the same policy is followed by the subcontractors.

Toward Completion

♦ Norma Bennett (from material gathered from the *Omenica Herald* files)

The drama of railroad building as it affected people along the Skeena was well documented in the newspapers of the day. Chronicles of progress, frustrations and tragedies were headlined in every issue.

A terrible accident occurred in February 1911 during the construction of the Kitselas tunnels. Five workers were killed and another two severely injured when a box of dynamite at the mouth of the tunnel exploded. Killed were M.F. Burgess (foreman), Charles Quornstrom, Eli Ogrezobich, John Otisovich and E.H. Kova.

In July 1911 it was made public that the Grand Trunk Pacific (GTP) had awarded a contract to Foley, Welch & Stewart to drive a fifteen-hundred-foot tunnel near Mile 44, where the big snow slides had occurred in 1910. This was not without its problems. In September two men, Charles Ericson and Henry Hansen, were injured by a shot in the tunnel. Ericson was hospitalized but Hansen could not be moved. Early in the following month another workman was injured by a premature powder blast. His eyesight was feared to be in jeopardy as a result.

Later, on McDougall's contract, two workmen were the victims of another horrendous accident at the Kitselas tunnels. During the early morning shift, D. Collati and A. Cerci were buried alive by a slide of mountain mud that entombed them in the tunnel. It was estimated that it would take three days to extricate the bodies.

On October 25, 1911, the Prince Rupert *Daily News* gave a target date of November 30 for the completion of the Kitselas tunnel. It also painted a rosy picture of GTP plans for the future of that area. The Grand Trunk Pacific was said to have acquired a long lease of the Indian reserve at Kitselas for the sum of one hundred dollars per year. The company hoped to erect a sumptuous twenty-five-thousand-dollar hotel and to build bridges to the "picturesque islands" lying in the Skeena as an attraction to prospective tourists.

After the tunnel was finished all supplies would be carried as far as possible by rail and thence onward to interior points by pack train. Hundreds of horses were being employed at this time, hauling out of the old town of Hazelton to the new townsite from which Foley, Welch & Stewart would operate in order to complete the last big grading contract for the GTP.

Freighting by horse team became an important project. In January 1912, twenty-five teams worked between New Hazelton and the end of steel to bring supplies to the construction camps. The wagon road was in good shape and the bridges were in. Ninety head of horses were shipped up from Vancouver to be put in harness at New Hazelton and used on the Bulkley Valley route. This was a long trip and teams could not be used continuously, but with the arrival of many more head, Foley, Welch & Stewart hoped to carry out their plans as anticipated.

There were labour problems to straighten out during the building of the Skeena Crossing bridge. The first concerned a demand for higher wages, which was granted. A second increase was asked for shortly after, along with improvements in dining and living accommodations. This, too, was acceded to. The last upset was over the release of one of the labourers. A number of his fellows quit work in sympathy. In January 1912, forty new sandhogs were brought in to replace the quitters, with a hundred more on the way. With plenty of help to be had, the contractors were hiring more in order to finish the job sooner.

One more heavy piece of work—twenty-five miles, with an estimated eighty thousand yards of rock to be removed—still remained to be done at Burns Lake. The contracts were let to D. Rankin on the east half and Dan Stewart for the first twelve miles, which were the most difficult. With several hundred men working on it, the company hoped to have it completed by January of 1913. Stewart had for his use two steam shovels and three donkey engines, besides forty teams of horses and all other necessary equipment.

In March it was announced that the indomitable team, Beirnes and

Mulvaney, would run a daily stage between Hazelton and the end of steel. So far there were only three trains per week from Prince Rupert.

Another tunnel, this one about five miles east of New Hazelton on Duncan Ross's contract, was almost finished. This was the longest tunnel on the entire GTP and Mrs. (Reverend) McLean was the first woman to walk through it.

In Prince Rupert there was great activity afoot. The GTP had a busy crew working on their terminals and before too long the entire waterfront would take on a new look. With the company yards using all the property previously occupied by the Prince Rupert Inn, the post office and the city hall, the change would be most evident. (The Prince Rupert Inn was moved to the previous site of P. Burns & Co.'s butcher shop.)

By the end of March 1912, the company was trying for a regular train service from Prince Rupert to Skeena Crossing in answer to an insistent clamour for passenger and freight facilities, the lack of which was driving the officials mad, as without permission, they could accept nothing at all.

Mr. C.E. Dewey, government freight agent, reported the following to the *Vancouver Sun*: "The most wonderful development is taking place along the Skeena. New towns are growing rapidly and the fishing industry along the river shows signs of a big increase. The country along the section where the railroad is in operation is quickly being transformed and Prince Rupert is humming with activity."

In May of 1912 the first pack train of any size left Hazelton for the Babine district—about sixty horses packing seven or eight tons. More would follow in about ten days. The Hudson's Bay Company had sent for the horses—about one hundred of them—and the Indians had brought them in.

While speaking of pack horses it may be well to digress for a moment. F.A. Talbot, in his book *The New Garden of Canada*, has these interesting facts to contribute:

> A pack train is at the same time the easiest and the most difficult vehicle to drive. For the first few days out everything is sixes and sevens. The animals are fresh and restive, darting every few minutes into the bush, causing the packs to get shifted and slackened by constant violent contact with trees and bushes. Delay after delay occurs while the loads are tightened up, and the frisky animals provoke the packer to violence. In the course of a day or so, however, the animals chum up, and take up their positions in the train, and this order they will maintain till their journey's end. Woe betide an animal which attempts to get out of his rotation; his colleagues will bite, kick and worry him until he returns to his settled position. It is curious how a bunch of thirty horses will resolve themselves into small cliques, will keep constantly together, and will act in concert to repel an intruder. One horse will always assume the lead, and will not relinquish the van in any circumstances whatever, not hesitating to defend his post with teeth and heels.

The Skeena Crossing bridge was completed by July of 1912, somewhat ahead of time. Rails were expected in New Hazelton by mid-August, with passenger service hoped for by September 1.

Despite signs on both sides of the new bridge forbidding anyone to cross, a life was claimed almost immediately. Two men, both intoxicated, were seen crossing over at an early hour. One slipped and dropped through to land in the water some forty feet below. He was swept away and might be found at the mouth of the Skeena in the fall or spring, if found he be at all. When the second man was interrogated, he could remember nothing. Had an Indian not reported the accident it might never have been made known.

In August the level of the river was such that steamboating was risky. The GTP announced that all passengers and freight would be cared for as far as the end of steel (now Sealey Gulch). From there to Hazelton would be a simple matter. At this time there was a triweekly service from Prince Rupert to Sealey Gulch.

In September 1912 the last steamer, the *Inlander*, made her farewell voyage down the Skeena, bound for Port Essington. Thus another page in history was turned.

As will be recounted elsewhere, there was quite a struggle getting the rails into New Hazelton, but by October 1912, the feat was accomplished. By November, seven thousand men were being employed on the GTP and it was anticipated that they would be within eighty miles of Fort George by the new year.

January 1913 brought ill fortune, with four men being killed and two seriously injured at Stewart Brothers' camp at Burns Lake. This was caused by a premature explosion of dynamite that had been frozen. In March a train was caught in a landslide at Mile 85, with damage to the rear coach but no casualties.

During March two hundred men were engaged to work on three tunnels—one hundred for the Duncan Ross tunnel and fifty for each of two smaller ones. Twenty men were busily erecting bunkhouses and sleeping quarters. This payroll would bring almost thirty thousand dollars per month in reach of New Hazelton merchants and would do much to boost the economy.

Centre Street, Prince Rupert, June 20, 1908. (4-B)

First locomotive in Prince Rupert. (4-B)

By April 11, 1913, steel was reported laid up to Mile 199 from Prince Rupert east. In May the announcement was made that McAfee's Auto would meet all trains at New Hazelton and make three runs per week to Telkwa. This auto stage would be a great improvement on the horse-drawn vehicles of the past. In May GTP passengers continuing on by ship were advised that their baggage could be checked through and that they, themselves, could procure berths and have their breakfast gratis aboard ship in Prince Rupert after the arrival of the train. This was a real improvement in service.

In August, John Kelly was murdered in cold blood at Burns Lake following a fight he had had the day before. He was a well-known construction man, having worked along the line for several years, and as a sandhog on the Skeena Crossing bridge. There was also a skirmish in the mess house at the Foley, Welch & Stewart headquarters about the same time. Here the Chinese help battled with one another. Results? One scalp wound and one six-month jail sentence.

During late November and early December there were many landslides that created troublesome delays along the Grand Trunk Pacific, but by now an undercurrent of suppressed excitement was creeping in. Both workmen and the public were eagerly looking forward to that fast-approaching day when the last spike would be driven and the line declared completed. As it turns out, 1914 would be THE YEAR!

Townsite Tattle

◆ arranged by Norma Bennett[11]

Hand in hand with railroad construction goes the building of towns. So it was along the Skeena. Many of the names mentioned as townsites in old records are unknown or forgotten today. Some fledglings died where they stood, some were never really born, others were pushed aside or superseded by stronger competitors. Some never fulfilled the dreams of their founding fathers.

In May of 1909 a well-attended auction sale of Prince Rupert town lots began. The bidders vied for possession of the best locations, their brisk offers spiralling the prices. One corner lot, fifty by one hundred feet, sold for $16,500. In two days' time $900,000 had been realized on the sale of 750 lots. We read that the government sale of Prince Rupert lots ended in late August of 1912. Over $1.25 million changed hands and $1,155 per foot was paid for the corner of Second Avenue and Seventh Street. So the prices seem to have held up during those three crucial years.

In January 1910, the *Omineca Herald* stated:

Important announcements may be expected soon regarding townsites in the interior, along the Grand Trunk Pacific. Confidential agents of the townsite company which is an adjunct of the railway company, have been through the country and while it has been generally supposed by those best informed that the sites of the divisional points and the largest towns had been known among railway people for a year or more, it is only recently that an actual transfer of property has taken place.

When the townsites will be platted and sold is a matter of speculation. The railway people will probably take their own time in the matter. The advancement of railway construction will force the whole matter forward, however, and next summer should see something done.

On April 2, 1910, the same source rhapsodized:

The part of British Columbia traversed by the line of the Grand Trunk Pacific railway is truly today the "Land of Opportunity." For wide diversity and wealth of natural resources, no other spot on earth can offer equal advantages to the man who is not settled in life.

A few short years ago a number of white men made a living out of placer mining and trading with the Indians. Today the foundations have been laid for the great industries that support large populations and create natural wealth; it can be pointed out to the stranger what the country is producing, what will grow on our lands, what ores have been found, what

GTP Railway along the Skeena River. (17-A)

Eastbound GTP passenger train. (17-A)

Freight train crossing trestle. (22-B)

coal measures have been uncovered. It is no longer a case of prophesying what will happen when the railroad is done. Crops are being produced each year that are an absolute guarantee of the fertility of the soil and the adaptability of the climate for mixed farming.

Along the Skeena is a fruit district where some of the pioneers are growing apples, plums and other fruits of first quality. Large amounts of money are being spent for fruit lands and in establishing the industry, and its success is assured. How far this fruit country will prove to extend into the interior can only be determined by experiment and no limit is as yet fixed. For all small fruits and berries the whole district is pre-eminently adapted. The yield is enormous and the quality superb. With markets on the coast and east to Edmonton and beyond, coupled with the fact that berries and small fruits ripen two or three weeks later here than at the boundary line, this district will have an unlimited demand for all that can be produced in that line.

As to farming in general it may be said that everything can be raised here that can be produced in the northern tier of States. Winter wheat, oats and barley are all successfully grown and all roots and vegetables give prodigious returns.

Dairying, it is claimed, will become the greatest industry with the farmers and it is certain there is plenty of room for expansion in that line. Conditions are almost ideal for dairying. Enough rain falls to keep the grass growing all summer and the slopes of the mountains bordering the valleys will always be available for summer grazing as they can never be used for anything else.

There is placer and lode mining as well, with unlimited opportunities.

All this district needs is more people and money.

We continue with the *Omineca Herald*:

First house built in Prince Rupert after the sale of lots, June 5, 1909. (4-B)

House construction, Prince Rupert. (4-B)

June 4, 1910: THE ELLISON TOWNSITE

F.R. Mitchell, of Vancouver, one of the syndicate owning the new townsite of Ellison, about three miles down the Skeena from Hazelton, arrived on the steamer *Hazelton* Thursday afternoon in connection with business relating to the new townsite.

Surveyors are now at work and expect to have finished platting in six weeks, and shortly after that lots will be placed on the market. The name, Ellison, was given in honour of the chief commissioner of lands, Price Ellison.

A deal has been completed whereby the GTP have taken a half interest in the townsite and in return agree to make the station for this vicinity on the townsite.

From the amount of interest already shown and the applications already received for lots in the new town, Mr. Mitchell considers there is no question but that Ellison will be the largest town on the GTP between Prince Rupert and Edmonton.

On September 24, 1910, the *Herald* wrote:

They are now engaged in clearing streets and some of the lots have been sold. There is a sawmill on the townsite but Mr. Mitchell does not think any building will be done this year as it is too late to get supplies up the river.

Note: The name "Ellison" was later changed to "Sealy," for a Hazelton hotel proprietor. Despite all the hullabaloo this town never really amounted to anything. When South Hazelton was started, Sealy was allowed to die. Those who had already invested in lots in the now defunct town were allowed to take property in South Hazelton in exchange.

New buildings, Prince Rupert. (4-B)

July 30, 1910
On the Grand Trunk Pacific westward from Winnipeg, a distance of 960 miles, a new town is to be located during the next year-and-a-half at a distance of every eight miles, or 120 towns for the total distance. Most of these towns have already been marked on the construction maps and the majority of them are named. On the mountain division of the same road, which is to terminate at Prince Rupert on the Pacific, 35 new towns are to be platted.

The history of these towns is to be unlike that of any other in existence. They are not to be merely platted and named, and then left to vegetate. They are to be forced into life. That is the remarkable thing about them. And this is neither a guess nor a hope. It is the result of a "game of town building," which has been played out by the government as carefully as one might play a game of chess.

May 9, 1911
The Prince Rupert *Daily News* reported that a party of surveyors under Mr. F.C. Green left for upriver points to plan the town of New Hazelton. The townsite was the property of Mr. Robert Kelly and lots should soon be on the market.

On January 5, 1912, the *Omineca Herald* reported:

The lots in New Hazelton are selling fast. Every day a large number are reserved, both here and in the south. The results from the outside advertising are just now beginning to come in and from now on there will be a constant flow . . . The public have faith in the new town and they will continue to invest their money in the coming city of the interior.

On April 26, 1912, it was stated that "the greatest wave of progress and prosperity on earth today . . . centres around New Hazelton."

August 16, 1911: Prince Rupert *Daily News*
RUSH FOR LOTS IN NEW TOWN OF TERRACE
Key to the Fertile Kitsumkalum and Lakelse Valleys—Littleton Station on the GTP is Close to Little Canyon Bridge
The new townsite of Terrace is now on the market. Even before the announcement of sale had been out for an hour or two, numbers of leading Prince Rupert citizens had planked their money confidently into Terrace lots.

March 7, 1913: The *Omineca Herald*
The following is part of an advertisement: "Fort Fraser, BC, is positively the finest townsite on the entire line of the GTP Railway between Edmonton and Prince Rupert, and we state it will be the largest city between these two points etc., etc."

March 13, 1913: The *Daily News-Advertiser*, Vancouver
OFFICIAL ANNOUNCEMENT
The Board of Railway Commissioners at Ottawa has approved of the station site at "Smithers," the second divisional point east of Prince Rupert, Mile 226.5, Lot 5289, Range 5, Coast District, on the GTP Railway about 9 miles west of Telkwa and Aldermere. The townsite will be for sale in August

The rush to buy lots, June 1909. (4-B)

1913, and Messrs. Aldous and Murray, Hazelton, have been appointed agents for the sale of lots.

It is expected that the plan of the townsite and the prices of the lots will be ready for distribution about the first of July.

(Signed) G.U. Ryley,
Land Commissioner.

This announcement went on to say, "with all these advantages Smithers will undoubtedly be the largest city between Prince Rupert and Fort George."

Note: Smithers was named in honour of the chairman of the Board of Directors of the Grand Trunk Railway. With the choice of Smithers as the divisional point, the towns of Aldermere and Hubert disappeared. (Pacific was the first divisional point but no town was ever built there. It is not far from Kitselas.)

The old newspaper giving the above information on Smithers was found under a piece of linoleum in Lillooet, and was given by Mrs. Russell Mills of Telkwa to Mr. Robert Phillips of the same town.

Town Promotion ... 1913 Style

♦ Stan Rough (from the Terrace *Omineca Herald*)[12]

I have before me a sixty-four-page illustrated booklet entitled "GTP South Hazelton Northern Interior Metropolis." The front cover depicts a large town with imposing buildings and no less than seven large factories belching smoke. A large number of people are gathered on the platform of a GTP station to welcome an incoming train. The back cover is also intriguing for would-be investors. In the lush hills behind the townsite are four huge smelters with a total of fourteen large chimneys pouring forth white smoke (the front cover's chimneys have black smoke). In the foreground is a large powerhouse and in the background is the Rocher de Boule Mountain set against a wonderful sunset.

The booklet was compiled by the Fraser Advertising Agency, printed by Evans & Hastings Ltd., and issued by W.J. Saunders, sole authorized agent for the Official Grand Trunk Pacific Railway, the Provincial Government of British Columbia, the Board of Trade of the old town of Hazelton, the inhabitants of Hazelton and district and the Board of Railway Commissioners for Canada. It was issued in 1913.

The introductory page states the following:

> The Grand Trunk Pacific Railway has, through its various departments during the past two or three years, received thousands of letters from

intending settlers and investors in all parts of this continent asking WHEN and WHERE it would establish an important townsite on its main line east of Prince Rupert, and particularly in the famous Hazelton district.

This widespread interest is due to the fact that the Hazelton district contains immense areas of agricultural lands; vast mineral wealth, including the only anthracite coal in Canada; and almost unlimited supply of water power, considerable timber and other forms of natural wealth, and a healthful climate. Even though the country has so far been without transportation, its riches have become widely known and hundreds of far-seeing people, for these reasons, have wanted to know when and where an important new GTP city would be established in this district.

NOW is when.

SOUTH HAZELTON is where.

The New North and the Last West.

The Grand Trunk Pacific has thousands of men working on both ends of its transcontinental line in Central British Columbia. The toot of its engines is already heard between Prince Rupert, the western terminus, and South Hazelton, the coming metropolis of the Hazelton district.

On the day the last spike is driven a new era for more than half the great province of British Columbia will begin. Farmers will come in, miners will realize the boom of transportation, for which they have waited so long; all industries will be stimulated; cities and towns will grow up as if by magic.

Smithers in 1915. Note the Grand Canal left of Main Street. (22-B)

First stores in Smithers. (22-B)

  This booklet tells the story of the most important of these coming cities—South Hazelton. It has taken time to prepare; information has been taken from the latest government pamphlets where possible, unembellished by the writer's art, and is conservative. This is an age of rapid change and perhaps before this reaches you, there will be more to tell. If there are any details we have left out, we invite correspondence from those interested.

  We will only mention the following headlines without quotes: "Our Greatest Province," "Keenest Minds of America Make Strong Statements Regarding Future of Northern and Central British Columbia," "What Hill Thinks," "Sees Two Million Settlers in Province."

  Rarely in the history of North America has a city started under such favourable conditions as South Hazelton—the heart of the Northwestern interior of BC. It has an ideal site as could be imagined at the confluence of the Skeena and Bulkley Rivers and the GTP Railway. South Hazelton will start in point of population and commence where many other townsites finish.

  Forty years ago the Hudson's Bay Company recognized its strategic location and opened a trading post at Hazelton. The same prophetic insight which located the "posts" as the nucleus of the big western cities of today—Winnipeg, Edmonton, Calgary, Victoria—will soon be again justified in the rich northern interior of British Columbia by the new modern city of South Hazelton.

Editor's Note (1962): South Hazelton hasn't made it yet. The 1961 census of the area between Mud and Chicago Creeks, which takes in South and New Hazelton, totals 671. South Hazelton has a hotel, gas station, general store, post office, lumber mill, a community hall and plenty of civic spirit and pride.

Driving the Golden Spike

Excitement mounted as railway construction entered the year 1914. The Fort George *Herald* reported:

November 15, 1913
Collingwood Schreiber, government engineer for the GTP en route from Edmonton to Prince Rupert, said, "At present work is proceeding more rapidly than at any time since construction commenced. Over 6,500 men are employed. The gap between the two ends of steel, less than 300 miles, is rapidly being closed and the rough grading has been done nearly all the way. Trains are running from Edmonton to McBride and east from Prince Rupert to Rose Lake."

Mr. Schreiber predicted that the Golden Spike could be driven in June or July.

March 14, 1914
Only 48 miles separate the two ends of steel. It is not likely that the occasion will be officially celebrated until some time in summer, when it is expected that Prime Minister Borden will drive the golden spike.

The "backbone" of the GTP—April 2, 1914. Stewart Bros. steam shovels taking out the last cut on the GTP, allowing steel to be connected up. (32-A)/BCARS 80821

First hotel at Fort Fraser, BC, 1914. The last spike on the GTP was driven at Fort Fraser that year. (42-C)

March 21, 1914
Steel will meet in 10 days. Both gangs are laying at the rate of 3 miles per day. The Western gang have about 12 miles still to complete while the Eastern gang have about 23 miles more to lay, making about 35 miles in all. The gangs will meet somewhere in the region of Fort Fraser.

March 28, 1914
ENDS OF STEEL WILL BE JOINED APRIL 6.
The latest news from the ends of steel in the vicinity of Fraser Lake is to the effect that the national transcontinental will be complete from coast to coast on April 6.

News from Winnipeg is to the effect that a large party of officials is preparing to make the trip and will arrive here in private cars at the end of next week. The party will include Pres. E.J. Chamberlin, Vice-Pres. Donaldson, G. Ryley and a number of British stockholders.

The report current today that the Prince of Wales would drive the last spike has not been confirmed.

April 4, 1914
DATE NOT YET DECIDED FOR DRIVING GOLDEN SPIKE
H.H. Brewer, general superintendent of the GTP passed through here this week on his way to the head of steel near Fraser Lake for the purpose, it is reported, of making final arrangements for the linking up of the steel. The general belief is, however, that the formal ceremony of

Track layer arriving from the east, making the last connection, April 7, 1914. (32-A)/BCARS 80820

Engineer Harlow, in charge of painting on rail: "Point of Completion—April 7th, 1914." (22-B)

Crowd of visitors and officials at the joining of the steel (east and west). (22-B)

Where the two tracklayers met, April 7, 1914. (45-C)

Grand Trunk Pacific Railway sign at Fort Fraser, BC. (30-C)

♦ Pioneer Legacy ♦ Volume II ♦

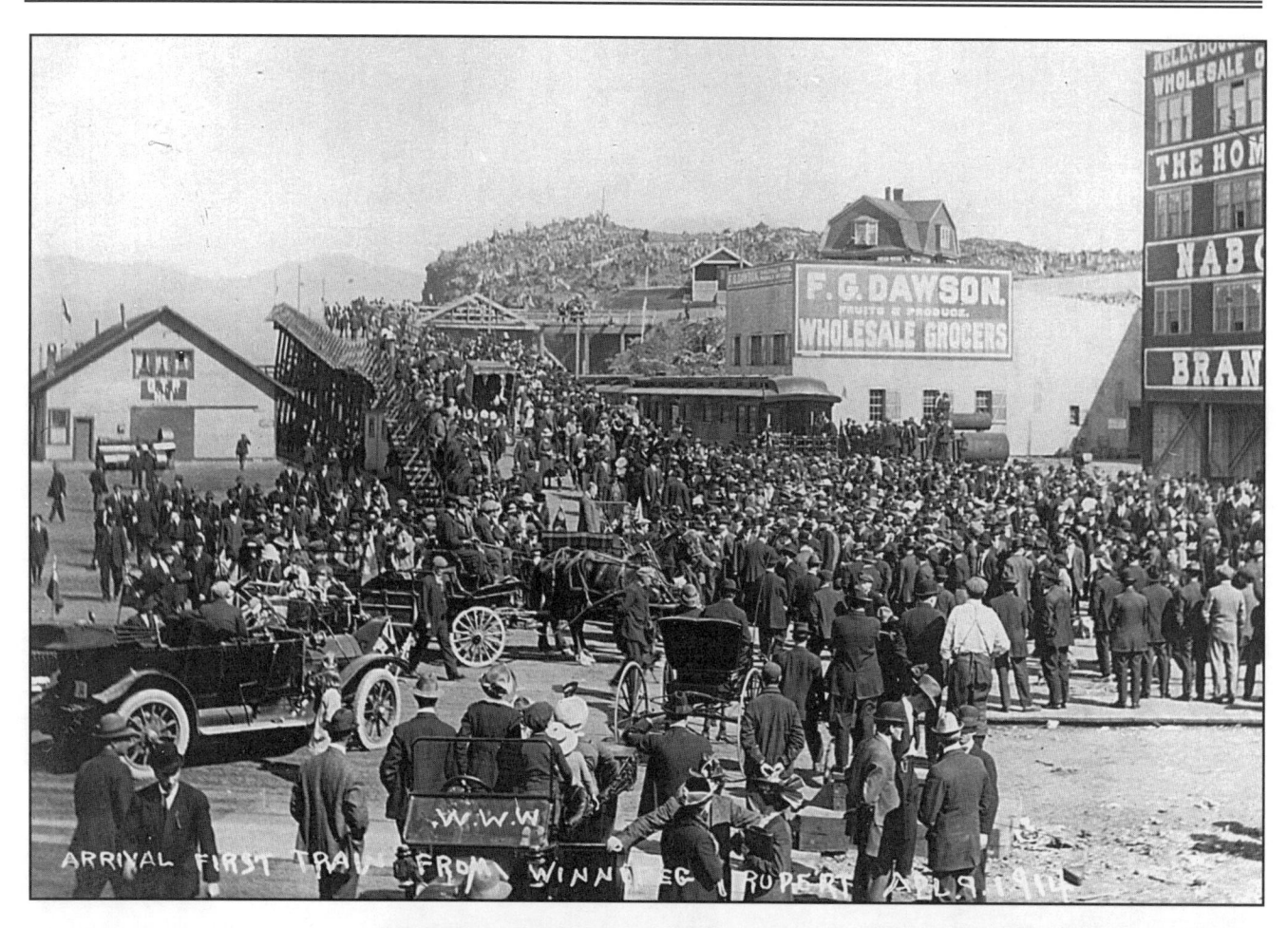

The first train arrives in Prince Rupert from Winnipeg, April 8, 1914. (32-A)/BCARS 80801

Arrival of first through train, Prince Rupert, April 9, 1914. (4-B)

driving the golden spike will not take place until May or possibly, June. The reason is said to be that the line has been rushed to completion so rapidly that portions of it are not ready for heavy traffic. In order to facilitate construction, light steel was laid in some places ahead of the grade and many temporary bridges have yet to be replaced by permanent structures.

April 11, 1914
LAST SPIKE IS DRIVEN ON GTP
The informal linking up of steel on Canada's greatest transcontinental railway took place at a point near Mile 373, about 2 miles east of Fort Fraser on Monday, April 6, at 12:30. About 20 railway officials from Winnipeg arrived on the scene early in the day by special train, and although no public announcement had been made and no invitations issued, there were over 1,500 persons present at the history-making ceremony.

The track-laying gangs had previously arranged to have a mile of grade left open for a speed contest between the gangs from East and West. Both teams started off together but it was soon evident that the men from the East had more order and system in their work and were easy winners with 14 minutes to spare. A large flagpole was erected at the centre post where the large crowd gathered, and the official photographer and the moving picture man got into position. The eastern crew was headed by Foreman Dempsey. When they came together there was a scene of great enthusiasm and the Union Jack was hoisted to the top of the pole. There remained still about half a length of rail to connect and this was cut and set by Mr. Egan in about 3 minutes. The last spikes, about nine on each rail, were driven by the several officials attending. The Special, containing the GTP officials, left immediately after the ceremony on its way to Prince Rupert.

Personnel of the party were:

V. Pres. & Gen. Mgr.—Morley Donaldson
Asst. to Vice-Pres.—George W. Caye
Solicitor—H.H. Hansard
Local Treas.—W. Ross
Auditor—J. Rosevear and many others.

A LINK OF EMPIRE

♦ from the *London Times*

London, April 10, 1914: The *Times* this morning pays Canada the compliment of devoting an editorial to the important event of the linking up of the prairie and mountain sections of the Grand Trunk Pacific Railway, under the title, "A Link of Empire."

The completion of the GTP must appeal to the least imaginative. The characteristically Canadian modest climax of a task which has filled years of labour and demanded enormous sums of money should not obscure the magnitude of the achievement. The undertaking has been a battleground for the political parties; political influences have considerably affected its prosperity. Nevertheless, there is no doubt whatever that Canadians regard the new system as an asset of almost untold national value, though they may be justified in thinking that it should have been secured far cheaper. The GTP is the result of the magnificent faith of Canadians in their country's future. It is the triumph of human determination over formidable obstacles and another proof of the resolution and fellowship of the British peoples.

*General superintendent's car.
(25-A)/BCARS 69696*

Notes

1. Based on "Northern Christmas" by Corday MacKay Atkinson, published in *BC Outdoors*, November–December 1974.

2. From *BC Public Works, 1937–July 1940*, Vancouver Public Library; further permission granted by the author's son, R.S. Cunliffe.

3. From the *Shoulder Strap*, No. 10, p. 62.

4. Further credits: BC Provincial Archives; John B. Daniell, "Collins Overland Telegraph," published in *Northwest Digest*, Vol. 16, February 1960; R.S. Cunliffe; Art Downs.

5. Report of Hon. H.L. Langevin, C.B., minister of public works, Ottawa, March 1872, Vancouver Public Library.

6. Further Credits: Guy Lawrence, "Yukon Telegraph Service," published in *The Alaska Sportsman*, Vol. 24—1958, Vol. 25—1959; *The Beaver*, September 1943; the Victoria *Daily Colonist*, September 1966.

7. Canada Post; BC Provincial Archives.

8. Canadian National Railways.

9. Public Relations, Canadian National Railways, Vancouver, BC.

10. BC Provincial Archives.

11. Further credits: *Omineca Herald*; Prince Rupert *Daily News*; Vancouver *Daily News-Advertiser*; Robert Phillips, Telkwa.

12. Further credit: GTP "South Hazelton Northern Interior Metropolis."

Note: Unsigned portions of this book are the work of Norma Bennett.

Photo sources

Our pictures were obtained from many sources, all of which deserve recognition. The same applies to the way in which these pictures were reproduced. Therefore, we employed a simple code whereby full details may be obtained.

At the bottom left-hand corner of each picture there appears, in brackets, a number followed by a letter, thus: (14-A). The number refers to the donor of the photograph, the letter to whoever reproduced the picture.

In some cases, right next to this credit there is a further and longer number. Thus a full credit may read, for example, (3-A)/BCARS 24567). This is the identification number of the BC provincial archives (the British Columbia Archives and Records Service—BCARS) and it must be used whenever requesting a copy of that certain picture from the archives.

Photo sources:

1. Mattie Frank Collection
4. Phylis Bowman
10. Gordon Sparkes
12. Clarence Michiel
17. Annie Noonan
18. Katie O'Neill
20. Rutter Collection--Margaret Bartlett
22. Ernest Hann
23. Canadian National Railways
25. Provincial Archives of British Columbia
26. Murray Hamer
27. Terrace Museum Collection
30. W. Mohr
32. R.J. Phillips
38. Don Cooper
41. Elsie M. Whitlow
42. Norma Bennett
45. Mr. Thomson
47. Edith Essex
48. Judy Degerness
51. Bruce Wilson
61. Bill McRae
63. Kitty Nelson
65. O. Lindstrom
66. S. Felber
67. D. Steele
68. H. Hamilton
69. B. Larson
70. Prince Rupert City Regional Archives
71. Prince Rupert City Regional Archives and Museum of Northern BC
72. Kitimat Museum
73. Smithers Museum

Photo finishing:
A. BC Provincial Archives
B. Ken's Photo
C. Gifted by donor

Index

A
Abbot, Andy, 173
accidents, 63–64; boating, 210–11; railway, 190, 206–7, 210, 214, 215
Adam, Charlie, 26
Adams, Jimmy, 39
Aiyansh, 109–10, 112, 120, 123
Alaska Highway, 83
Aldermere, 225
Alexander, J.M.L., 134
Alice Arm, 70
Alling, Lillian, walk to Russia, 93–9
Anakwawa, 60
Ankitlas, 54
Atlantic & Pacific Transit & Telegraph Company, 81
Atlin, 87
auto stage, 218

B
"B" girls, 180
Bacon, J.H., 136
Baird, T.M., 49
Balrymple, J.E., 206
Bartlett, Margaret, 114
Bateman, Beatrice, 23, 28
Bateman, James E., 23, 30
Bateman, Mrs. James E., 23–24
Bateman's Landing, 23, 25, 28, 29. See also Remo
"B&B": see Grand Trunk Pacific Bridge and Buildings
BC Digest, 178
BC Mining Record, 78
Beaton, Angus, 209
Beirnes, George, 131, 133, 134, 136, 139, 140
Beirnes and Mulvaney, 131, 132, 138–39, 204, 215–216
Belway, Joe, 122, 140
Bennett, Norma, 8, 188, 214
Big Canyon Weekly, 191
Birch, H.B. "Hughie," 89, 91
Bodwell, E.V., 157
Bonser, J.H., 57, 58
bootlegging, 181
Boscowitz, 135
Boss, H.N. "Hank," 136
Bostrom, Fred, 173
Bostrum, John, 193
Bowman, Phylis, 166
Boyd, Blain, 178
Boyd, Pat, 178, 179
Breakenbury, George, 32
Breakenbury, Violet, 32
Breakenbury, William C., 32
Breckenridge, Harry, 29, 30
Breckenridge, Harry Jr., 29, 30
Breckenridge, Mrs. Harry, 29, 30
Breckenridge's Landing, 23, 30
Brewer, H.H., 229
Brewer, Thomas, 140
Bright, Mrs. Samuel, 54
Bright, Samuel, 54, 55, 71, 135
Brown, William, 130
Bruce, Billy, 33
Bulkley, Charles, 81
Bulkley River, 84
Bulkley Valley, 23, 197
Burgess, M.F., 210, 214
Burns, P., 195
Burns, Patsy, 136
Burns & Company, 197, 200, 216
Burns Lake, 84
Burrage, W., 78
Butler, W.F., 82
Byng, Julian Hedworth George, 189

C
cabins, telegraph, 83, 90, 92, 96, 97, 98, 107, 108, 112
Callaghan, Patsy, 134
Camosum, 111
Camosun II, 199
Campbell, Ulysses, 195
camps: railway 37, 171, 182-3, 194, 208; telegraph 116
Canadian National Railway (CNR), 89, 150, 165, 176
Canadian Northern Railway, 154
Canadian Pacific Railway (CPR), 24, 140, 153, 166, 167
Canadian Pacific Telegraph, 87
canneries, 24
canning, home, 60, 61
canoes, dugout 107; mail carriers 129, 135, 138; melanshuks 61
canoes, travel, 31, 50, 58, 60, 61. 63, 71, 72, 110, 111, 129, 197, 199, 205
Cariboo Wagon Road, 78
Carr, Arthur, 32
Carr, Dick, 31
Cataline, Jean, 196
cattle drives, 194–201, 208
Caye, George W., 233
Cedar River, 105–106, 111
Cedar River bridge, 106
Cedarvale, 54, 56, 67, 68, 129. See also Holy City; Meanskinisht
cemeteries: Kitsumkalum 38, 40,42; Terrace 42
Cerci, A., 215
Chamberlin, Edson J., 150, 206, 229
Charleson, E.E., 100
Charleson, J.B., 101, 104
Chesley, E., 211
Chieftan, 131
childbirth, 29, 53, 188–89
Chinese labourers, 79, 81, 83, 218
Christie, Jim, 96, 98, 99
Christmas, on the telegraph line, 122–23

Church Missionary Society, 58, 59
churches: at Cedarvale 55, 56, 66, 69; at Kitsumkalum 41; services 204
Clifford, C.W.D., 134
Cline, Sperry "Dutch" 131, 132, 140; *The Mailman* 143; *The Surveyor* 187
Collati, D., 215
Collins, Perry McDonough, 77, 80, 84–85
Collins Overland Telegraph Company, 75, 80–82, 83–86, 87–89; Date Capsule 77–78
communities, religious. See missions
Conroy, Henry, 47
Conveyor, 156, 168
Cooper, Sid, 173
Cooper, Syd, 203–04
Copper City, 51–52
Copper River, 49, 52, 53
cordwood, 19, 25, 26, 41, 52, 69, 179
Cottage City, 45
Cox, H.R., 100
Creech, Harvey, 53
Creech Hotel, 53
Crosby, Thomas, 57
Cullen, Tom, 151
Cunliffe, S.A., 80, 89
Cunningham, R., 60
Cunningham & Sons, 131
Cunningham Cannery, 49
Curran, Pete, 136

D
Daily News Advertiser, 224
Danube, 135
Daoust, A., 101
Deacon, Rose, 37
Decker Lake, 84
Dewey, C.E., 216
dining cars, 189
Distributor, 168, 193, 194
Dobbie, children, 51
Dobbie, Jemima (Stuart), 50–52
Dobbie, Simeon Wilson, 50–52, 101
Dobbie's Landing, 50
Dockrill, Frank, 132
doctors, 29, 30, 31, 54, 56, 86
dog teams, 27, 31, 53, 91, 98, 127, 129, 130, 131, 133, 134, 135, 140, 180, 204
Dogteam Trail post office, 136
Dominion Fish Hatchery, 136
Dominion Government Telegraph office, 33
Dominion Government Telegraph Service, 100–113
Dominion Iron & Steel Company, 206
Donaldson, Morley, 229, 233
Dover, Elsie, 43

Dover, Jean, 43
Dresser, F., 101
Duncan, William, 54, 56, 58, 70
Duncan Ross tunnel, 217
Durham, Charles "Jigger," 51, 101, 137, 172
Durham, Fred, 145
Durham, George, 25
Durham, Helen (Adams), 137
Durham, Irene, 52
Durham, Nellie, 52
Durham, Paddy, 52

E
E. Eby & Company, store, 36, 43
Earlandson, Jens, 32
Eby, Edward A. "Ed," 33, 34, 36, 40–41, 128
Eby, Sam, 34
Eby, Vernon, 33, 39
Eby, Vina, 34, 35
Eby, Vina (daughter), 35
Eby's Landing, 27, 28, 33, 34, 36, 40, 41, 43, 48, 131
Eby's Landing Hotel, 34, 45
Echo Lake, 97
elections, 25
Ellison, Price, 164, 222
Ellison townsite, 164, 222
Elwyn, T., 78
engineers, 184–85
epidemic, black diptheria, 44
Ericson, Charles, 214
Essex, Edith M., *Stolen,* 72, 73

F
Fairbairn, A., 95
farmimg, 55, 64, 65, 221
Felber, Joe, 43
firemen, sternwheeler, 179
fires: forest 52, 107, 112; house 52, 62-63
First Nations, 26, 27, 57, 59, 60, 61, 64, 65, 66, 70, 89, 108, 178
First Nations labourers, 81, 83
First Nations protest document, 118
fish warden patrol, Skeena River, 40
Flewin, Walter, 50
Floyd, Ivan, 42
Foley, Welch & Stewart Company, 134, 156, 164, 167, 194, 202, 205, 209, 210, 212, 213, 214, 215, 218
Fort Fraser, 81, 224, 229
Fort Stager, 78, 79, 81–82
Frank, Belle, 39, 42
Frank, Ella, 39
Frank, Floyd, 38, 39, 42
Frank, Harry, 40
Frank, Henry L., 33, 38–40, 127
Frank, Ivan, 39
Frank, Jack, 39
Frank, Luella, 42

♦ 238 ♦

Index

Frank, Mattie, 38, 39, 42
Fraser Advertising Agency, 225
freight teams, 180
freighting, 33, 35, 45, 215

G
Gainor Lake, 107
Galacian labourers, 184
Gaynor, Cecil, 108
Georgetown Sawmill Company, 202
Gibson, Pete, 173
Giggey, Clair, 40, 47
Gitlacdamix, 119
Gitlakdamiks, 109, 113
Glacier Creek, 110
Gobeil, A., 101
Goodwin, Billy, 40
Government Ranch, 197
Government Telegraph Service, employees, 102–3
Graham, Mrs. J.W., 128
Grand Trunk Pacific Bridge and Buildings gang, 203
Grand Trunk Pacific Coast Steamship Company, 156, 165
Grand Trunk Pacific Railway (GTP), 50, 72, 132, 134, 200, 201, 220, 222
Grand Trunk Railway; accidents 209, 210, 217; advertisements 177, 225-27; bill 154
Grand Trunk Railway; construction 149, 152-165, 166-177, 180-81, 183, 215, *230-231*
Grand Trunk Railway; Date Capsule 151; financing 155, 158, 176; history 147-50
Grand Trunk Railway; labour problems 207, 215; last spike 150, 228-33; mail service 132
Grand Trunk Railway; map 148; receivership 150;
Grand Trunk Railway; service 150, 164, 165, 170, 177, 211, 213, 220, 232,
Grand Trunk Railway; snow slides 201, 203-4, 209; surveys 147, 149, 152, 158, 159, 166
Grand Trunk Railway; ticket price 170, wages 184
Grant, Bob, 198
Grant, William, 95, 210–211
graves, Native, 37, 51
Graveyard Point, 25, 50
Gray, J.H., 137
Great Eastern, 81
Green, F.C., 223
Green's Camp, 160
Greig, Velma, 43
Grieg, Mrs. M., 142

H
Hagwilget, 82
Hall Creek. See Rosswood
Hankin, Herb, 137, 138
Hansard, H.H., 233
Hansen, Henry, 214–15
Hart, Joe, 47

Hatfield, Jim, 203
Hays, Charles Melville, 147, 149, 153, 157, 165, 166, 176, 206, 208
Hays, David H., 224
Hazelton, 23, 86, 100, 127, 128, 129, 139, 180, 193, 199, 226
Hazelton, 20, 57, 115, 222
Hazelton Hospital farm, 71
Hep, Moses, 54
Hep, Mrs. Moses, 54
Hep, Peter, 54
Hipp, George, 43
Holy City, 54, 57, 67. *See also* Cedarvale; Meanskinisht
homestead law, 184
horse logging, 45
hospitals, 63, 185–86, 190
hot springs, 136
Houlden, Alex, 38
Houston, 172
Houston, John, 172
HRH Duke of Connaught Special, crew, 145
Hubert Times and Bulkey Valley Advertiser, 190
Hudson's Bay Company, 134, 139, 140, 164, 216
Hulbert, H.L., 32
Hull, Don, 140

I
immigration, 207, 208
Inlander, 17, 50, 128, 139, 217
Inverness Cannery, 49
Ireland, Willard F., 83
Irish labourers, 184
Italian labourers, 184, 202

J
jail, 68
Janze, Charlie, 96
Jasper, Wes, 195—201
Jensen, John, 96
Johnson, Kathleen (Tomlinson), 70
Johnson, Kathy, 58
Johnson, S.B., 193
Johnston, A.E. "Ted," 33, 49, 101
Johnstone, J. Bruce, 136
Jopp, Emil, 32

K
Kaien Island, 149, 157, 167, 168
Kaien Island Investigation, 157
Kalum Lake, 33, 34, 43, 45
Kalum Lake Hotel, 43
Kalum Riffle, 28
Kalum school, 41
Kalum Store and Hotel, 34
Kelliher, H.B., 164
Kelly, John, 218
Kelly, Robert, 223
Kendall, Charles, 134
Kenney, Ed, 213
Kenney Real Estate, 39
Kennicott Mountain, 84
Kirkaldy, Onnalee (Grieg), 140, 142
Kirkaldy, Sam, 140–42
Kispiox, 89
Kispiox River, 84
Kispiox Valley, 148

Kitenmax, 89
Kitimat, Hazelton & Omenica Railway, 132, 134
Kitimat Trail, 36
Kitsclas, 24, 51, 130
Kitselas Canyon, 50, 115, 128, 193
Kitsumkalum, 28, 29, 37, 40, 41, 42, 105, 117, 170
Kitsumkalum, 48
Kitsumkalum Lake, 46, 117, 140
Kitwanga, 54, 56, 57
Klatter, Dan, 32
Klondike, gold rush, 87
Kova, E.H., 210, 214

L
Laborne, E.K., 81
labourers, immigrant, 83, 169, 184, 202, 218
Laird, Bob, 32
Laird, Tom, 32
Lakelse Lake, 136
Langevin's Report, 86
Lapley, Joe, 32
Large, Evelyn, 35
last spike, Grand Trunk Pacific Railway, 228-33
Laurier, Wilfred, 154, 166, 168
Lava Lake, 107–8, 121
Lawcett, Roy, 151
Leech, P.J., 78
library, 213
Lillesberg cabins, 45
Lindstrom, Bill, 29, 30
Lindstrom, Charles Jr., 29
Lindstrom, Charlie, 26, 27, 29
Lindstrom, Claire, 23, 29
Lindstrom, Emma (Bateman), 23, 27, 29
Lindstrom, Helen, 29
Lindstrom, Marie, 29
Lindstrom, Otto, 29
Lindstrom homestead, 28
Lineman's Prayer, 122
linemen, telegraph, 89, 90–91, 112
liquor, 180–81, 197, 198
Little, Arthur C., 41, 45, 128, 132, 139, 170, 204
Little, George, 41, 45, 128, 132, 170, 204
Little's General Store, 142
Littleton. *See Kitsumkalum*
logging, 23–24
London Times, 234
Lost Lake, 35
Lower, J.W., 152

M
MaAfee's Auto, 218
MacDonald, Eleanor, 157
MacDonald, J.B.L., 49
MacGregor, Dan, 142
MacNicholl, G.A., 49
mail service, 27, 31, 32, 57, 69, 108, 127–43; auto, 142; boat, 140; carriers, 130, 131, 133; Date Capsule, 127; express, 133; run, 130; sorting, 131
marine transportation, 156
Marsh, Alberta Jane, 36–38, 41, 48

Marsh, Etonda, 38, 41
Marsh, Henry, 38
Marsh, Thomas Brown, 36, 38, 41, 204
Marsh, Thomas Jabez, 28, 30, 36–38, 41, 48
Marsh, Thomas Reid, 38
Maughlin, Ed, 108
McBride, Richard, 158, 167
McClure, J., 79
McDougal, Archie, 202
McDougal's tunnel, 202
McGibbon, Duncan, 109, 133
McGinnis, Bill, 173
McHugh, Tony, 193
McInnes, Archie, 101
McInnes, Mrs. Archie, 189
McInnes, Neil, 101
McIntosh, J.E., 101
McIntosh, Mrs. R.L., 136
McIntosh, R.L., 37, 40, 41, 42, 136
McLeod, Norman, 193, 210
Meanskinisht 52, 54-69, 193. *See also* Cedarvale, Holy City
medical care, 37, 186
melanshuks, 61
Mill Bay Cannery, 120
Mills, J. Wellsford, 93
Mills, Mrs. Russell, 225
Milton Badger, 81
missionaries, 36, 54, 57, 58, 135
missions, 54, 58, 135
Mitchell, F.R., 222
Moberly, Annie (Tomlinson), 56, 58, 68, 69, 70
Monroe, Charlie, 140
Moore, John W., 191–92
Morgan, Stephen, 68, 130
Morris' Landing, 23
Morrison, Charles, 83
Morrison, Lindsay, 45
Morrison, W.H., 28, 212, 213, 214
Morse, F.W., 157–58
Mount Royal, 23, 65
mule trains, 79
Mulvaney, Lyster "Barney," 133, 136, 140
Mulwain, J., 130
Mumford, 78

N
Naas River, 79–80, 109, 110–111, 119–120
Nehring, E., 211
Neidhart, John, 24, 30, 31
Neidhart's Landing, 23
New Garden of Canada, 92, 182, 185
New Hazelton, 164, 224
New Metlakatla, 56
Nicholson, Angus, 193
Nightwine, Frank, 43
Noble, Walter, 39
Noonan, Annie, 35
Northern Cross, 70
Northern Interior Land Company, 164
Northwest, 26, 31, 158, 193

O
Ogilvie, Drysdale "Scotty," 97, 98, 99

Ogrezobich, Eli, 210, 214
Old Town, 109, 110
Olson, Elof, 25, 26, 27, 32
Omenica Herald, 37, 42, 50, 53, 122, 132, 137, 187, 195, 203, 204, 212, 214, 219, 223, 225
Omineca, 168
O'Neill, Katie, 65, 66, 68, 71
O'Neill, W.J. "Wiggs," 101, 131, 132, 136, 190, 201–202
O'Neill's boat service, 132
Open-Air Express, 175
Operator, 156–168
Oriental labourers, 208
Osterhout, S.S., 58
Otisovich, John, 210, 214

P
Pacific, 173
Pacific construction camp, 171
pack horses, 90, 91, 195
pack trains, 44, 90, 215, 216
Patterson, J.W., 127
Peterson, C., 101
Phillips, Robert, 225
Phillipson, Barney, 52
Pillsbury, J.H., 167
Pioneer, 174
Pioneer Telegraph Survey of British Columbia, 78—80
Pioneers of the Area, 49
Pleasant Valley 172. *See also* Houston
polling station, 72
Pope, F.L., 75
Port Essington, 24, 26
Port Simpson, 128, 211
Post, Mary (Stuart), 51
Post, Paul, 51
Post children, 51
post offices, 45, 72, 73, 127, 128, 142. *See also* mail service
potlatch, 109
Prince Albert, 165
Prince George, 201
Prince George, 156, 165
Prince George Herald, 228
Prince John, 165
Prince Rupert, 27, 106, 111, 114, 149, 156, 157, 167, 178, 213, 214, 217, 218, 219, 221, 222, 223
Prince Rupert, 156, 165, 200
Prince Rupert Daily News, 210, 211, 223
Prince Rupert Empire, 158, 204
prison, 67

Q
Quesnel, 78, 81
Quornstrom, Charles, 210, 214

R
railway camps, 184
railway conductors, 189
railway tie contract, 27
Rankin, D.A., 193, 215
Raymond, George, 151, 173, 188–89
Regan, Tom, 30
Remo, 23, 24, 30, 31. *See also* Bateman's Landing; Neidhart's Landing

riverboats, 31, 90. *See also* sternwheelers
RMS dog team, 134
roads, 33
Robinson, George, 130
Roby, M.A., 49
Rogerson, Rita, 50
Ron, Pete, 173
Roosevelt, Theodore, 166
Rosevear, J., 233
Ross, Annie, 43, 44, 47, 140
Ross, Duncan, 193, 216
Ross, Frank, 45
Ross, Inez, 45, 47
Ross, Robert, Jr, 44–7, 105–13, 114
Ross, Tom, 45
Ross, W., 233
Ross Camp, 159
Ross homestead, 47
Rosswood, 45
Rough, Stan, 57, 71, 129, 225
Rushbrook, Walter, 70
Russian labourers, 171
Rutter, Henry Percival, 118
Ryley, G., 229

S
Salvation Army, 56
Salvus, Peter, 193, 206
Salvus, William, 206–207
Sand Lake, 107, 117
Sargeant, R.S., 135, 137
Saunders, W.J., 225
sawmill: at Cedarvale 54-55, 59, 60, 63; at Aiyansh 112
Scandinavian labourers, 184
school: at Cedarvale 55, 62, 66, 67; at Kalum 41
schoolhouse, 61–62
Schooling, Bert, 140
Schreiber, Collingwood, 228
Scottish labourers, 169
Sealey, J.C.K., 89, 100
Sealey Gulch, 171
Sealy, 163, 164, 222–23
Service, W.J., 93, 94
Sheady, Michael, 193
shipwreck, 65
Shoulder Strap, 82, 93
Skeena, 15, 36
Skeena, 37, 168, 210
Skeena Crossing, 209, 210, 213, 215, 217
Skeena River, 17, 19, 23, 30, 57, 77, 81, 100, 129, 133, 141, 161, 167, 191–94, 203–204, 212, 216
Skeena River, map, 18
Skinner, Leslie G., 53
Skinner, Mildred S. (Sparkes), 53
Skinner, Murray, 53
Skinner, Percy R., 53
Skinner, Ralph, 53
Skinner Brothers General Store, 53
Skinner's Landing, 53, 136. *See also* Copper River
Smithers, 171, 224–25, 226, *227*
Smithers, A.W., 150, 171
snow slides, 201–202, 203–204
snowplow train, 203
South Hazelton, 226, 227

Sparkes, Bill, 34
Sparkes, Jack, 141–42
Sparkes, Mrs. Will, 53
speculators, land, 179–80
Split Mountain, legend of, 32
Spokeshoot, 49
St. Matthew's Anglican Church, 38
Star, Walter, 173
Starr, Grandma, 29, 30
station men, 169, 183, 184
steamboats. *See* sternwheelers
sternwheelers, 17, 18, 19, 57–58, 69, 77, 81, 128, 135, 162, 167, 179, 193, 194, 217
Sterrett, Charles, 137
Stewart, Dan, 45, 215
Stewart, Edward, 54, 59
Stewart, Esther, 54
Stewart, F.W., 156
Stewart, Jack, 158
Stewart, Mrs. Edward, 54
Stewart Brothers, 228
Stikine, 80
Stolen, 73
Strongheart, 136, 202
Stuart, David, 49, 50
Stuart, Jane (Smith), 49, 50, 54
Stuart, Janet, 49, 51
Stuart, Jemima, 49
Stuart, Mary, 49
Stuart, Pricilla, 49
Stuart's Landing, 49
survey party, 117, 119
surveyors, Grand Trunk Pacific Railway, 205
Sutton, Mrs. Philip, 56, 71, 135
Sutton, Philip, 71, 129–30
Sutton, Robert, 71
Swan, G.M., 100
Swanson, Charles, 31
Swanson's Landing, 23

T
Talbot, F.A., 92, 185, 216
Tees, 24, 135
telegraph camp, 116
Telegraph Creek, 82
telegraph line: construction 33, 78-80, 82; crew 79, history 77-8;
Telegraph Point, 26
Telegraph Trail, 82–83, 199
Templeman, William, 139
Terrace, 34, 139, 170, 224. *See also* Kitsumkalum
The Mailman, 143
The Surveyor, 187
Thompson, William, 55
Thornhill, Thomas, 38
Thornton, Henry Worth, 176
Tomlinson, Agnes (Parr), 70
Tomlinson, Alice Mary, 54, 55, 56, 68, 71
Tomlinson, Alice Mary (Woods), 54, 55, 56, 64, 70
Tomlinson, Annie, 54, 56
Tomlinson, E., 101
Tomlinson, Lily, 54, 55, 56, 62
Tomlinson, Nellie, 54, 62
Tomlinson, R., 101
Tomlinson, Richard, 54, 56, 66, 135, 137

Tomlinson, Robert Jr., 54, 55, 56, 57, 62, 70, 72, 129, 130, 135, 137
Tomlinson, Robert Sr., 54, 55, 56, 58, 59, 66, 68, 71, 72, 129–30, 193
Tomlinson, Roxana, 71
Tomlinson Co-Operative sawmilll, 71
Tomlinson home, *62*
Tooley, Cyril, 97, 98
totem poles, 109, 110, 111, 113, 121
track laying, 172, 174, 175, 230
trapping, 26
Tsinkut Lake, 92
Tully, W.H., 210
tunnels, 168–169, 170, 193, 202, 214, 216, 217

U
Union, 77, 78
United Church, 56
Usk, 176

V
Van Arsdol, C.C., 49, 164
Victoria Daily Colonist, 100

W
wages, 100–101, 184, 185, 206, 215
Walkland, B.J., 151
Warner, Walter, 43, 122
Warren, Frank, 188
Watt, Belle (Frank), 48
Weeks, Samuel Charles "Dad," 36, 37, 40, 41, 42
Wells, J.D., 101
West, A.J., 101
Western Union Telegraph Company, 78, 82, 86
Western Union Telegraph Expedition, 83
White Pass & Yukon Railway, 87
Whitlow, Elizabeth (Durham), 19
Whitlow, E.M., 54
Whymper, F., 81
Williams, Amos, 68
Wilson, Edward, 55
wolf attacks, 32
Wrathall, Jack, 92
Wrathall, William W., 92

Y
Yellowhead Pass, 149, 181–82
Young, Tom, 142
Young Men's Christian Association (YMCA), 41, 212–214
Yukon Telegraph Line, 87–9, 92–3, 98; employees and wages 100–103

Z
Zanardi Rapids, 162, 168
Zenardi-Landi, Carlos, 168